Key Variables
in Social Investigation

Key Variables
in Social Investigation

Edited by Robert G. Burgess

Routledge & Kegan Paul
London, Boston and Henley

First published in 1986
by Routledge & Kegan Paul plc

14 Leicester Square, London WC2H 7PH, England

9 Park Street, Boston, Mass. 02108, USA and

Broadway House, Newtown Road,
Henley on Thames, Oxon RG9 1EN, England

Set in 10 on 12 pt Baskerville
by Inforum Ltd, Portsmouth
and printed in Great Britain
by St Edmundsbury Press Ltd,
Bury St Edmunds, Suffolk

Library of Congress Cataloging in Publication Data
Main entry under title:

Key variables in social investigation.

Includes indexes.
1. Sociology—Research—Addresses, essays, lectures.
2. Social sciences—Research—Addresses, essays, lectures.
I. Burgess, Robert G.
HM48.K46   1986   301'.072   85–2302

British Library CIP data available

ISBN 0–7100–9901–0
ISBN 0–7102–0621–6 (pbk.)

Contents

Notes on contributors   vii

Preface   x

1   Introduction   *Robert G. Burgess*   1

2   Age   *Janet Finch*   12

3   Gender   *D.H.J. Morgan*   31

4   Race and ethnicity   *Martin Bulmer*   54

5   Health and illness   *Sally Macintyre*   76

6   Education   *Robert G. Burgess*   99

7   Social class and occupation   *Catherine Marsh*   123

8   Work, employment and unemployment
    Kate Purcell   153

9   Leisure   *Stanley Parker*   178

10   Politics   *David Jary*   200

11   Voluntary associations   *C.G. Pickvance*   223

12   Do concepts, variables and indicators interrelate?
     Martin Bulmer and Robert G. Burgess   246

Name index   266

Subject Index   275

Notes on contributors

Martin Bulmer is Senior Lecturer in Social Administration at the London School of Economics & Political Science. For a period in the mid-1970s he was a statistician in the Population Statistics Division of OPCS, and he has edited *Censuses, Surveys and Privacy* (1979). His most recent publications are *The Uses of Social Research* (1982), (editor) *Social Research Ethics* (1982), (editor, with D. P. Warwick), *Social Research in Developing Countries* (1983), (editor) *Sociological Research Methods* (2nd edition, 1984), and *The Chicago School of Sociology* (1984). He also edited with Robert Burgess a special issue of *Sociology* (Vol.15(4), November 1981)on 'The Teaching of Research Methodology'.

Robert Burgess is a Senior Lecturer in Sociology at the University of Warwick. He has conducted research on aspects of social research methodology and in the field of education. His main publications include: *Experiencing Comprehensive Education* (1983), *In the Field: An Introduction to Field Research* (1984) and *Education, Schools and Schooling* (1985). He has also edited: *Teaching Research Methodology to Postgraduates: A Survey of Courses in the UK* (1979), *Field Research: A Sourcebook and Field Manual* (1982), *Exploring Society* (1982), *The Research Process in Educational Settings: Ten Case Studies* (1984), *Field Methods in the Study of Education* (1985) and *Strategies of Educational Research: Qualitative Methods* (1985). He is especially interested in the development of research methodology in the study of educational settings. He was Honorary General Secretary of the British Sociological Association between 1982 and 1984.

Janet Finch is a Senior Lecturer in the Department of Social Administration at Lancaster University. Her background is in sociology and she is active in the British Sociological Association, serving as its chairperson in 1983–4. Her research interests are in sexual divisions, the family and education. Publications include: *Married To the Job*

(1983); *Education As Social Policy* (1984); and with Dulcie Groves, *A Labour of Love* (1983).

David Jary is Head of the Department of Sociology at North Staffs Polytechnic and was previously senior lecturer in sociology at the University of Salford. He was educated at LSE and the University of Leicester. His publications include: *The Middle Class in Politics* (joint editor), *The Development of Sociology in the Polytechnics, Leisure and Society in Britain* (contributor), and articles on political sociology and sociological theory. He is the current chairman of the Combined Social Sciences Board of the CNAA and a member of the editorial board of *The Sociological Review.*

Sally Macintyre has been Director of the Medical Research Council's Medical Sociology Unit since 1983. She has worked in that Unit since 1971, her research being mainly in the field of the sociology of human reproduction, but with interest also in the topics of perceptions of illness and of doctor/patient interaction. Her publications include: *Single and Pregnant* (1977) and articles on the management of childbirth, antenatal care, migraine and old age.

Catherine Marsh spent two years in the Social Science Research Council's Survey Unit in the mid-1970s. Since 1976, she has been a lecturer at the Social and Political Sciences Committee at the University of Cambridge, and Fellow of Newnham College. Her main research interests have been in validity issues in social surveys, and she is author of *The Survey Method: the Contribution of Surveys to Sociological Explanation* (Allen & Unwin 1982).

David H. J. Morgan has lectured in the Sociology Department at Manchester University since 1964. His main publications that discuss sex and gender are *Social Theory and the Family* (1975) and 'Men, Masculinity and the Process of Sociological Enquiry' that was published in Helen Roberts' *Doing Feminist Research* (1981). He was one of the organizers of the 1982 British Sociological Association's Conference on 'Gender and Society' and has been a member of the B.S.A. Executive Committee and the Equality of the Sexes Committee since 1981.

Stanley Parker gained his Ph.D. at London University in 1968 for a study of work–leisure relationships. He has written many articles and several books on the sociology of industry, work, leisure and retirement, including *The Sociology of Industry* (4th edition, 1981, with others), *The Sociology of Leisure* (1976), *Work and Retirement* (1982) and

Leisure and Work (1983). He was a researcher with the Office of Population Censuses and Surveys 1964–83 and is now a freelance researcher, writer and consultant. He has lectured widely in Britain, Europe, North America and Australia.

C. G. Pickvance is Reader in Urban Studies at the University of Kent at Canterbury. He was previously at the University of Manchester and has held visiting positions at the University of Amsterdam, Australian National University, Bogazici University, Istanbul, Concordia University, Montreal and the University of Toronto. His interest in voluntary associations goes back to research done in 1971–3 but his main interest is now in urban and regional studies, with particular emphasis on the state and political processes. He edited *Urban Sociology: Critical Essays* (1976) and is author of *The State and Collective Consumption* (1982) and of a large number of journal articles and contributions to books. He is Review Editor of the *International Journal of Urban and Regional Research.*

Kate Purcell studied sociology at Bedford College, London University, where she gained the Nina Boyle Memorial Award in 1974, and at Manchester University. She has carried out research and taught Sociology and Women's Studies at Manchester Polytechnic, Manchester University and for the WEA and currently teaches part-time, tutoring Oxford University and Open University students. She edited the British Sociological Association's newsletter *Network* from the end of 1980 until January 1984. Her main research interest, on which she has given papers widely in this country and abroad, is the significance of gender in interaction, particularly in work organizations and the general sexual division of labour.

Preface

Although there have been many major advances in the development of empirical social research in the last decade there are still many gaps where both those who conduct research and those who use its results demand some guidance. One such area concerns the relationship between theory and research: the specification of concepts and their translation into variables so that a series of indicators may be developed. The intention of the papers in this volume is to provide students, teachers and researchers with some help in addressing these basic issues. Students and teachers need some assistance with questions of comparability in substantive fields of sociology, while researchers need some assistance concerning the relationship between conceptual and technical problems and the presentation of empirical data. The papers therefore examine key variables in social investigation with these issues in mind.

While 'key variables' are the focus of all the chapters, each author has been given the freedom to focus to a greater or lesser degree on concepts, variables, indicators and measurement. As a consequence the papers may be used for three purposes. First, as brief methodological reviews of substantive findings in an area of study which highlights current preoccupations, and summarizes empirical relationships. Second, as guides to the ways in which concepts, variables and indicators have been used in specific studies and areas of social research. Third, as discussions of the problems involved in comparing and presenting empirical material in a substantive sub-field. It is to be hoped that this collection of essays will encourage sociologists and other social scientists to think about the conceptual and empirical problems in using and evaluating key variables in social research. In this respect, the volume complements earlier collections of essays that were edited by Margaret Stacey in *Comparability in Social Research* (Heinemann, 1969) and by Elizabeth Gittus in *Key Variables in Social*

Research (Heinemann, 1972).

I am indebted to a number of people who have helped in the production of this volume. First, to Elizabeth Gittus who suggested that this set of essays should be commissioned and published with the support of the British Sociological Association. Second, to the Association who supported this venture. Third, to a number of people who have given advice, support, encouragement and help throughout the project: Martin Bulmer, Hilary Burgess, Anne Dix, Mike Milotte and the authors of the individual chapters who have spent much time discussing this project with me. Finally, I have had the help of a number of secretaries all of whom have provided first class secretarial assistance and to whom I am very grateful: Hilary Bayliss, Valerie Campling, Sarah Fulton, Frances Jones, Pam Smitham, and Sue Turner.

Robert Burgess
University of Warwick
June 1984

Introduction   1

Robert G. Burgess

In the preface to an earlier discussion on the use of variables in social research T.H. Marshall (1969) remarked that 'one essential condition for the development of sociological theory and of sociology as a scientific discipline is the comparability of data assembled by those engaged in research' (p.viii). Most sociologists and social researchers would be in broad agreement with this statement which highlights the need for sociologists to be aware of the ways in which comparability can be achieved in first hand empirical study, the secondary analysis of existing data sets and the use of published research. In each case researchers are engaged in considering basic questions relating to the definition and use of concepts, the identification of variables and their measurement where this becomes appropriate.

While these aims and objectives can be easily identified their use is much more problematic. Indeed, critiques of social research seem to suggest that many social researchers have yet to come to terms with the main questions and difficulties involved in the use of concepts, variables and indicators in social research for Smith (1975) has identified the main criticisms arising from current research as being characterized by:

1 lack of conceptual clarity and theoretical precision;
2 the failure to clearly identify variables and hypotheses statements;
3 misappropriate selection of indicators used to measure variables;
4 lack of sampling controls;
5 inattention to construction of measures and scales;
6 inattention to problems of reliability and validity;
7 the failure to consider alternative interpretations of data;

8 disproportionate attention to psychological variables at the expense of social structural variables; and

9 problems defined on the basis of untested assumptions and selected for political reasons.

(Smith, 1975, pp.xvii–xviii)

This volume takes up some of these issues as the essays focus on the ways in which researchers who are engaged in empirical research can define and collect data about key social variables. It seeks to bridge the gulf which divides the theoretical and empirical realms, particularly in sociology, by analysing key concepts and discussing how they can be studied empirically. There are still a number of gaps in the social science research literature, as despite developments in substantive sub-fields of sociology, researchers have still not bridged the gap between theory and research, and between theoretical debates and empirical practice. As a consequence, basic questions concerning the place of sociological concepts and the rise of key variables in sociological research still need to be answered as do major problems involved in the relationship between data collection and data analysis.

The objective of this volume is to follow, complement and update the essays in Stacey (1969) and Gittus (1972). However, over ten years have elapsed since the last volume was published and this book therefore seeks to provide some guidance in the light of advances in empirical research during the 1970s and early 1980s; especially in Britain. The rationale for the book lies in the perennial problem of bridging the gap between theory and empirical evidence, in trying to relate the one to the other meaningfully, so that data are not treated merely as a formless mass nor are *a priori* theoretical categories merely imposed on the data.

This book, therefore, contains papers that address three broad themes. First, how to strengthen the links between social science theory and empirical research. Second, how to use general concepts in empirical research. Third, how to encourage comparability between different pieces of empirical research into similar phenomena. While each of the contributors has covered these themes to a greater or lesser degree the whole volume sets out to provide a critical analysis of key variables in social investigation by:

1 reviewing key basic concepts and indicators used in social and sociological research;

2 examining the relationships between data collection and data analysis bringing out their crucial interdependence;

    3 providing some guidance on the kinds of questions that can be posed in a field of study with a view to generating comparable data.

There is no list of variables that all sociologists would agree constitutes the best descriptive schema. However, a fairly well standardized list has been identified by Zetterberg (1965) as the schema that pollsters used in describing a person. Many of these items are referred to as face sheet variables and classificatory variables that are selected from the following list:

   I Past Contextual Variables
      1 Place of birth (native or foreign); sometimes also parents' place of birth
      2 Type and size of community in which most of childhood was spent (rural, small town, city, metropolis)

  II Present Contextual Variables
      1 Type and size of community in which the respondent lives
      2 Geographical region of country

 III Contemporary Statuses: Ascribed
      1 Sex
      2 Age
      3 Ethnic background
      4 Religious affiliation

 IV Contemporary Statuses: Achieved
      1 Occupation; sometimes also husband's or wife's occupation
        A classified according to occupation rank (upper, middle, lower)
        B classified according to work situation (salaried, self-employed)
        C classified according to institutional realm (business or industry, civil service or politics, education or science, religion, art, welfare, institutions, private household)
      2 Family Statuses
        A Marital (single, married, widowed, divorced)
        B Parental (no children, children living at home, children living away from home)
      3 Memberships in voluntary associations (including business associations and unions); political party affiliation or preference

V Past Statuses
  1 Father's occupation
  2 Type of schools attended
  3 Military Service
  4 Past full-time occupations

VI Stratification
  1 Riches
    A Family income
    B Family property
      a Residence (owns, rents, boards)
      b Consumer goods (e.g. auto, TV)
  2 Knowledge or competence
    A Years of schooling; sometimes also husband's or wife's
      years of schooling and children's education
  3 Power
    A Executive position
    B Political office
    C Office in voluntary associations

(Zetterberg, 1965, pp. 58–60)

In addition a British Sociological Association working party convened by Margaret Stacey in the mid 1960s found that the most common variables used in social research included: age, sex, marital status, occupation, family and household size and composition, education, income, place of birth, housing, leisure activities, social class, religion and politics. It was these lists of variables from Zetterberg and from Stacey's group that helped in the identification of variables that were to be reviewed here. In particular, attention has been given to variables that had not been examined in the earlier volumes (Stacey, 1969; Gittus, 1972) and those such as education that needed updating, given the administrative changes that have occurred in the intervening period.

Common to all the chapters is a language of concepts, variables, and indicators all of which are treated in a colloquial way within the social sciences. Accordingly some brief definitions are required here as a general guide to the reader (cf. O'Muircheartaigh and Francis, 1981; Mann, 1983). The main terms (which are also discussed in the final chapter in this volume by Bulmer and Burgess)are as follows:

Variable: The representation of a social characteristic or social factor in empirical research. Variables are constructed by defining a concept and developing an indicator or indicators for a concept.

Indicators: A means of representing or measuring sociological concepts using items for which empirical data may be collected.

The key issue involves the way in which concepts can be operationalized and the gap bridged between concepts and indicators in order that theory and research can be linked. Among sociologists, it is Paul Lazarsfeld who has suggested that the main questions to be addressed are: How are broad conceptual ideas converted into instruments of empirical research to provide evidence on a topic of enquiry? How can the 'variables' so developed be manipulated to lead to broader generalizations? Lazarsfeld (1958) suggests that the typical process involved in establishing 'variables' for measuring complex social objects involves four steps:

1 Breaking the concept down into dimensions that are essential to translate it into any kind of operation or measurement.
2 Specifying the dimensions of the concepts.
3 Selecting observable indicators.
4 Combining indicators into indices.

As subsequent contributions to this volume indicate this is an *ideal* sequence that provides a framework within which the researcher can operate.

Although the following chapters cover a range of different areas there are a number of *issues* which are common to several variables:

1 Variables involved in the research process

Recent discussions of research methodology (Hammersley and Atkinson, 1983; Burgess, 1984) have indicated how certain variables: age, sex and gender, race and ethnicity and social class are not only variables in the substantive area of investigation but also how these characteristics of the researcher may influence the relationship with the researched. In this volume, the essay by Morgan on gender draws specific attention to the ways in which this variable influences the research process. Clearly, age, race and ethnicity, social class and educational background are also social characteristics that can have some bearing on the relationship between researcher and researched.

Although not all the authors have considered this element it is as well for readers to recall that background variables assist both the researcher and the researched to place each other within the social structure.

2 The interaction of variables

While each of the contributors has been invited to review a particular field of study several have indicated the importance of interconnections between variables. For example, Macintyre highlights the importance of the relationship between social class and health, while Burgess reviews some of the ways in which social class and education relate to each other. Meanwhile, both Parker and Pickvance consider from different perspectives the interconnections between work and leisure. Further discussions of the relationship between different variables are contained in many of the chapters; a situation that leaves the reader to consider *how* variables may be used alongside each other.

3 Variables in quantitative and qualitative research

It has become commonly assumed that there is a sharp dividing line between quantitative and qualitative research (cf. Filstead, 1970; Halfpenny, 1979) with the result that some commentators have assumed that the language of variables and indicators has no part to play in qualitative styles of investigation (cf. Bogdan and Biklen, 1982). Nevertheless, recent studies (Silverman, 1984) have indicated that this is too sharp a division and that there are distinct advantages to be gained from the juxtaposition and integration of these two styles of research. Accordingly the chapters on age, gender, work and education discuss the way in which variables are involved in both kinds of data collection and analysis. In turn, readers might consider the extent to which other variables have relevance for qualitative *as well as* quantitative studies.

4 Establishing definitions

Throughout this volume an attempt has been made to contribute to theoretical developments as well as reviewing empirical work. In these terms, the contributors pay special attention to the way in which sociologists have devoted space to the careful specification of concepts. Of all the contributions, it is Pickvance's discussion of the criteria that can be used to establish a definition of a voluntary association that highlights a way in which conceptual specification can occur. Some of the other contributors also indicate some of the difficulties involved in conceptual specification. In particular, Macintyre illustrates how concepts relating to the field of health and illness are problematic given that health may be defined using a medical as well as a sociological model. The result is that while the former fails to take into account positive health or psychiatric health or objective disease and subjective perception the latter may only allow a definition of health that is *post hoc* or a definition that is too relativistic. Examples such as these indicate that readers need to consider on what basis conceptual specification takes place in each of the areas under review.

5 Conceptual equivalence

Among social researchers it has become commonplace to assume a degree of conceptual equivalence. However as Bulmer (1983) and Mitchell (1983) point out in the context of discussing social research in developing countries the degree of variation that occurs within and between countries together with linguistic differences renders the whole situation problematic. As Bulmer (1983) indicates it is not simply an operational matter or a technical matter involving the problem of exact translation. For example, if a question is translated from one language to another there is a problem of meaning that is dependent on the context in which the concepts might be used. Accordingly, researchers have to pay attention to the extent to which they have used the same concept in a series of studies. Many of the contributors to this volume have highlighted this issue. For example in the field of health, Macintyre highlights the problem of comparative analysis, while in education Burgess indicates how the differences between educational systems (even within the United Kingdom) have to be taken into account. Homogeneity cannot be assumed and therefore readers need to consider the extent to which conceptual equivalence can be achieved to ensure that the same concept is being examined.

6 Time

As well as changes occurring across countries changes also occur through time with the result that the same event – 'death in childhood' or 'being educated' has a different meaning depending on the time factor involved. For example, Macintyre's discussion of health and illness indicates how childbirth, mortality and life expectation have a set of different meanings in England in the nineteenth and twentieth centuries. In a similar way, Burgess indicates how changes that have taken place in English education over the last twenty years renders direct comparability problematic. In a review of studies in the field of race and ethnicity Bulmer's chapter illustrates how shifts have occurred in the concepts that are used in just over thirty years. Meanwhile Morgan's contribution highlights how it is only in recent years that 'gender' has been problematized within sociological investigations. Together these contributions indicate that researchers and readers need to be aware of the ways in which time is itself a key variable in social investigation and needs to be taken into account in the conduct and evaluation of social research.

7 Comparability

As indicated earlier in this introduction comparability has been considered to be one of the main problems involved in the use of key variables. Finch, for example, points out the problems involved in making comparisons when different age categories are used. Similarly, Marsh indicates, in relation to her discussion of social class and occupation, the problems involved in making comparisons; especially when the researcher is dealing with a new system of occupational classification. Her examples, together with illustrations that are provided in several other chapters might lead the reader to consider the extent to which a standard set of official categories would be advantageous and desirable in the conduct of social research.

8 Formulating questions

A theme which is very much related to bridging the gap between concepts and indicators concerns the formulation of questions. Several of the chapters provide illustrations of the ways in which questions have been posed in a variety of surveys. For example, Bulmer draws questions from different surveys on race and ethnicity, while Burgess examines some of the education questions that have been used in the General Household Survey. Similarly, Jary illustrates the use of concepts and questions in the study of politics, while Pickvance indicates the ways in which questions have been formulated to tap different dimensions of voluntary associations. Accordingly, these examples will hopefully provide readers with illustrations of good practice in question wording and at the same time attune them to some of the major problems involved in translating a concept into a set of questions.

9 Measurement and indicators

Among the major issues involved in the use of concepts and variables in social investigation is the way in which concepts are translated into variables so that a series of empirical indicators, measuring instruments or scales can be developed. Some chapters give greater attention to the formation of indicators and issues of measurement than others. In particular, the chapters by Bulmer and Marsh deal with measurement, while Macintyre on health and Parker on leisure are concerned with the use of indicators. It is examples such as these that generate such questions as: What are indicators? How are they formulated? How are they used? Fundamentally such questions should lead the reader to consider: do the measurements really measure what they claim to measure? A question that is central to the use of variables in social investigation.

Finally, throughout all the chapters, reviews are provided of research that is drawn from a number of different sources. While some chapters such as Purcell's on 'work' and Parker's on 'leisure' provide a detailed review of sources in their respective areas, others are content to highlight sources that are useful in a particular sub-field within the area under review. In examining the chapters it will be found that there are a number of sources which are common to several areas. The most comprehensive review of source material for social researchers involved in secondary analysis is provided by Hakim (1982) who discusses the material that is available and which includes: the population census; continuous and regular surveys such as the General Household Survey; *ad hoc* surveys conducted by a variety of investigators; cohort studies; data sets obtained from administrative or public records and multi source data sets from a number of different sources.

In the course of using survey data and evaluating the use of measurement in social investigation a number of questions need to be addressed. These include:

> How are conceptual ideas converted into research instruments?
> How can research instruments be used in relation to other techniques of investigation?
> Can the measurements employed be used in natural settings?
> Does the measurement procedure reflect the properties and relations of the object or event it claims to reflect?
> Will the measurement procedure yield similar readings on repeated applications?
> Do the mesurements and observations permit theoretical analysis?

Such a range of questions strike at the heart of social investigation as they involve validity and reliability as well as issues concerning the relationship between theory and research and comparability.

It is to be hoped that the issues reviewed in this volume will help to promote research and to close the gap between the concepts developed by theorists and the variables and indicators developed by researchers. In turn, it is also hoped that they will go some way towards fulfilling Zetterberg's wish that

> theorists should be encouraged to show how their terms can be used in descriptive schemas, and . . . researchers should be encouraged to contemplate how the descriptive schemas they employ are related to the terms developed by the theorists. (Zetterberg, 1965, p.62)

References

Bogdan, R. and **Biklen, S.K.** (1982) *Qualitative Research for Education: An Introduction to Theory and Methods*, Boston, Allyn and Bacon.
Bulmer, M. (1983) 'General introduction' in M. Bulmer and D.P. Warwick (eds) *Social Research in Developing Countries: Surveys and Censuses in the Third World*, Chichester, Wiley, pp.3–24.
Burgess, R.G. (1984) *In the Field: An Introduction to Field Research*, London, Allen & Unwin.

Filstead, W.J. (1970) (ed.) *Qualitative Methodology: Firsthand Involvement with the Social World*, Chicago, Markham.

Gittus, E. (1972) (ed.) *Key Variables in Social Research*, London, Heinemann.

Hakim, C. (1982) *Secondary Analysis in Social Research: A guide to data sources and methods with examples*, London, Allen & Unwin.

Halfpenny, P. (1979) 'The analysis of qualitative data', *Sociological Review*, vol.27, no.4, pp.799–825.

Hammersley, M. and **Atkinson, P.** (1983) *Ethnography: Principles into Practice*, London, Tavistock.

Lazarsfeld,'P. (1958) 'Evidence and inference in social research', *Daedalus* (Fall) reprinted in M. Bulmer (1977) (ed.) *Sociological Research Methods*, London, Macmillan, pp.78–90.

Mann, M. (1983) (ed.) *The Macmillan Student Encyclopedia of Sociology*, London, Macmillan.

Marshall, T.H. (1969) 'Preface' in M. Stacey (ed.) *Comparability in Social Research*, London, Heinemann, pp.viii-x.

Mitchell, R.E. (1983) 'Survey materials collected in the developing countries: sampling, measurement and interviewing obstacles to intranational and international comparisons' in M. Bulmer and D.P. Warwick (eds) *Social Research in Developing Countries: Surveys and Censuses in the Third World*, Chichester, Wiley, pp.219–39.

O'Muircheartaigh, C. and **Francis, D.P.** (1981) *Statistics: A Dictionary of Terms and Ideas*, London, Arrow Books.

Silverman, D. (1984) 'Going private: ceremonial forms in a private oncology clinic', *Sociology*, vol.18, no.2, pp.191–204.

Smith, H.W. (1975) *Strategies of Social Research: The Methodological Imagination*, Englewood Cliffs, New Jersey, Prentice Hall.

Stacey, M. (1969) (ed.) *Comparability in Social Research*, London, Heinemann.

Zetterberg, H.L. (1965) *On Theory and Verification in Sociology*, (3rd edn. enlarged) Totowa, New Jersey, Bedminster Press.

Age   2

Janet Finch

Introduction

Age is an elusive variable in social research. It is almost always collected but very often not used – or at least, not used to any real effect, beyond noting that participation in CND, frequency of sexual activity, use of the telephone, or whatever, varies with age. Sometimes one is tempted to wonder whether data on age are collected simply because they are easy to collect: age has the appearance of being a nice, safe 'fact', one of the few questions to which a 'true' answer actually exists, even if one cannot guarantee that an accurate answer will be given. It is, in other words, a good warm-up question in an interview. When findings are reported, they are dutifully presented – as the well-worn demographer's joke would have it – with the research population 'broken down by age and sex'. But then what? In the case of age, moving beyond simple correlations to the use of age in ways which are theoretically informed as well as empirically rigorous is relatively uncharted territory. Still less has age been developed as an important topic for research in its own right. Successive academic commentators in both America and Britain have noted that – apart from early papers by Linton (1942), Parsons (1942) and Mannheim (1952) – the sociology of age has remained a relatively under-developed area (for example: Neugarten, Moore and Lowe, 1965, Riley, Johnson and Foner, 1972, Allen, 1973); and social researchers who have wanted to focus age have routinely noted the lack of comparable studies in their own specialist fields (for example: Wuthnow, 1976; Musgrove and Middleton, 1981).

This chapter examines some ways in which age is commonly used in social research, considering both its problems and its potential as a variable.

1 Age and descriptive documentation of a research population

Age is used very commonly as a descriptive category in a wide range of social research, including demographic: that is, the age of the total population or a given group within it is simply documented, but not necessarily used in the process of constructing explanatory accounts. This kind of descriptive documentation, whilst perhaps of itself appearing not specially interesting, is important for social scientists for several reasons.

First, documentation of the age structure of a population (along with other features) is important for understanding social and cultural contexts of a given society at a specific point in time. Much important material of this sort is produced by government departments and agencies. For example, documentation of mortality rates in Britain – and especially age at time of death – shows that in the years 1838–44, 47 per cent of all deaths were of children under the age of fourteen years; whereas the comparative figure for 1975 was 2 per cent (OPCS, 1978, p.5). This simple documentation of the very high level of childhood deaths in the nineteenth century should alert the researcher into Victorian literature or social policy to the quite different context of childhood by comparison with contemporary experience, where the death of the child is a rare tragedy, not a commonplace (if unwelcome) event.

Second, descriptive demography is important in helping social scientists to generate research questions which require further investigation. In contemporary Britain, for example, it has shown a significantly 'ageing' population in the late twentieth century. Results of the 1981 census confirm the steady rise in the numbers of persons of pensionable age over the past twenty years (OPCS, 1983). This obviously raises important research questions, such as: what will be the impact of an ageing population on the organization of welfare services over the next two decades? (Finch and Groves, 1982.)

The usefulness of descriptive accounts in both these respects may be limited or enhanced by the ways in which data are presented. As a statistical variable, age has the important characteristic that it is continuous and therefore it can be presented in a number of different ways (Stacey, 1969; pp. 77–8). Most commonly, the age of interviewees is recorded in years (usually age at last birthday), but there are some instances where it is collected more exactly. An example of this would be the OPCS study of infant feeding in which, for example, the prevalence of breast or bottle feeding in the first year of life is presented in tables which give the child's age in weeks up to two months, then in months thereafter (Martin, 1978; Table 3.11). Decisions about the way material is to be both collected and presented always have to be related to the particular research context in which it is to be used: clearly a study of breast-feeding young babies has to present age data in weeks or months; in a study of voting patterns at a general election, such detail would almost certainly be unhelpful.

The fact that age is a continuous variable also makes possible certain kinds of statistical manipulation such as the calculation of averages. Again the way in which material is presented has to be related carefully to the research context, because different types of averages can produce quite different accounts. For example, in the official statistics of marriage and divorce, the mean age at marriage for women in 1980 was 26.72 years, while the median age was 23.18. This quite considerable disparity is accounted for by different methods of calculation and occurs because the age distribution is not symmetrical: marriage may take place from any age between 16 and 100 (or more), but the majority take place nearer to 16 than 100. This produces a mean age which is greater than the median (OPCS, 1980).[1] If one wanted to know, for example, at what age the majority of a given group of young women were most likely to marry, averages calculated by the method of either mean or median would give rather different kinds of answer, and both would probably be less appropriate than the modal age (not given in the OPCS statistics) – that, is, the age at which marriages are most numerous.

Frequently age data are presented by means of grouped categories, not in exact age; often data are actually collected in that form. Obviously the designation of categories has to be appropriate for a specific research problem, and researchers may decide on their age categories using notions of age 'groups' (see next section). So far as the more technical aspects of using age categories are concerned, textbooks on survey research often use age as an example of how to avoid pitfalls in classification. Precisely because it is a continuous variable, a wide variety of groupings is possible. The most basic technical point is that there must be no ambiguity about the beginning or end point of the range in each category and that all categories must be mutually exclusive (Hoinville and Jowell, 1978; p.165). An example is given in Table 1, which is taken from an article about the age structure of occupations in the United States: the categories are 18–21, 22–7, and so on rather than 18–21, 21–7. This latter

Table 1 Illustrative Age Distributions: Young, Middle-Age and Old-Age Profiles

Occupation No.	Mean Age	Age Group							
		18–21	22–27	28–33	34–39	40–45	46–51	52–57	58–64	Over 65

Source: Kaufman and Spilerman (1982) *American Journal of Sociology*

(incorrect) way of categorizing would make it impossible to place some-one whose age falls on the border between categories – in this case, 21.

Although there are considerable gains in being able to decide on the numerical designation of age categories most appropriate for each research project, that very flexibility creates problems of comparabil-ity between different research findings. There are, however, certain conventions about where boundaries between age categories are drawn and the most important of these is in government statistics. Researchers ought to be in a position to relate their data to relevant demographic data on the particular population which they are studying. Therefore it is a good idea to collect age data in such a way that they can be categorized in the form used in official statistics for purposes of comparison, even if other categories are also used. If an analysis using the categories of official statistics is done but not used in published work, it should be retained in a form to which other researchers can have access should it be relevant to their own project, perhaps through the use of a data archive.

2 Age 'groups'

Much social research utilizes the notion of age groups, identified either by numerical boundaries based on calendar age, or by less clearly designated terms such as childhood, youth, middle age, and so on (see e.g. Foner, 1980). The issues raised by this go well beyond the purely technical.

Whilst numerical boundaries may have the attraction of methodo-logical tidiness, the fundamental problem is to relate the boundaries drawn to any social significance which age groupings may have in the real world (Bengtson, Furlong and Laufer, 1974, pp. 15–16; Elder, 1975, p. 173). This is always an issue unless age 'groups' are to be nothing more than convenient numerical categories with no social meaning – in which case their usefulness in most social research is not entirely apparent. Even where the researchers have not explicitly analysed their age categories as meaningful groups, assumptions may be made by them or by their readers about the characteristic life style, cultural practices or economic circumstances to be found within each 'group'. On the other hand, if explicit attempts *are* made to ensure that numerically defined categories also represent meaningful social 'groups', there may well be considerable difficulties about where to draw the boundaries.

An example of the confusions which are possible can be found in the work of Kaufman and Spilerman (Table 1). Although (as has already been noted) the authors are technically correct in their numerical categorizations, they give their table very confusing headings. The main heading indicates that they are examining 'young, middle-age and old-age profiles', and the sub-heading 'age groups' is given; the data then follow in a table divided into nine numerical age categories. The problem here is that there is no indication of how the reader is to relate the notion of three age 'groups' to the nine numerical age categories. In the absence of alternative guidance, most readers would probably assume that three age categories should be assigned to each age 'group': but how are we to know if this is anything other than totally arbitrary, or whether the groupings thus produced bear any relationship to social life?

This kind of confusion is easy to replicate, because it is not simply a technical matter but partly a consequence of the ambiguities of age categories as they are used in social life, and as they define personal identity (Fogarty, 1973, pp. 13–14). Fundamentally, age 'groups' are socially constructed categories, formulated in the context of particular economic, social and political circumstances, and therefore subject to change and modification over time. For example, age sixty-five now marks a highly significant social boundary in both Britain and the United States. But, as Neugarten and Moore have shown in relation to the United States, it was chosen as the age of retirement in the mid-1930s because of the economic and demographic conditions which prevailed at the time (Neugarten and Moore, 1968, pp. 18–19). As social conditions change, significant age boundaries are likely to be modified. Muriel Nissel has shown how this has operated in Britain, in an article about changes in family patterns since the second world war. In comparing the experience of mixed-age cohorts in 1952 and 1977, she finds it necessary to treat the boundaries between age 'groups' as having shifted in terms of their social meaning during that period. Thus in 1952, 'childhood' could be designated as 0–21 but by 1977, principally because of changes in the law of majority (see below) and in the greater economic independence possible for many young people, 'childhood' had to be considered as finished by the age of eighteen. Similarly, in Nissel's view, 'old' age began at sixty in 1952, but at sixty-five in 1977, because of the improved health and life expectancy of old people, and because of their increasing numbers in the population (Nissel, 1982). It is possible, of course, to dispute both the nature of these assumptions and the use to which they are put; but the virtue of writers like Nissel is that they make their assumptions explicit, thus enabling readers to make a proper assessment of their arguments.

The vagueness of boundaries between age 'groups' may be inconvenient for researchers, but that very vagueness makes it possible for them to be used in social life as powerful mechanisms for inclusion and exclusion, precisely because the boundaries between groups can change in different contexts. This process can be seen very clearly in relation to the youth-adult boundary. The question 'when does a young person become an adult?' has quite different answers in different social contexts. Thus, in Britain for example, the answer in respect of marriage is age 16: in respect of the right to vote it is 18: and so on.

The significance of these categories in social life can be seen very clearly in the deliberations of the Latey Committee on the age of majority (Report of the Committee on the Age of Majority, 1967). The report also offers an apt illustration of the interplay of biological, social and economic dimensions in construction of the youth-adult boundary. At the time the committee was set up, the legal age of majority in Britain was twenty-one, and the committee recommended that this should be lowered to eighteen. In reviewing the historical development of age twenty-one as the age of majority, the committee concluded that its significance dated essentially from the middle ages when this was the age at which most men eligible for knight service were capable of wearing a heavy suit of armour and of lifting a lance or sword at the same time. It seems, observed the committee, rather grotesque that this should govern the age at which a couple may get a mortgage, or marry without parental consent, in the mid-twentieth century (ibid. para. 46). But just as in the middle ages the beginning of adulthood was defined by a mixture of physical/biological and social (in that instance, military) considerations, so too the Latey committee itself tried to reconcile a range of disparate considerations into one single recommendation. These ranged from the purely biological matters, in particular the issue of whether it can be demonstrated that young people now reach physical sexual maturity at an earlier age (para. 142); through a competing range of moral positions, for example, about whether family life – and especially parental authority – would be eroded by allowing marriage without consent at an earlier age; to frankly economic considerations, such as the unanimous desire of 'the business world' to extend transactions to younger people (especially those involving debts, which cannot legally be contracted before the age of majority) (para. 82). The complexity of the issue of where the youth-adult boundary should fall, and the pattern of competing interests who wish to define it at one point or another – all of which is admirably reflected in the Latey report – should make us wary of any piece of research which treats such boundaries as unproblematic.

Several points can be taken from this discussion of age groups and applied to the use of age as a key variable. First, age groups, however constituted, should not be treated as if they have some autonomous and lasting significance outside the particular social and economic contexts which give them meaning. Second, researchers should always make explicit their own assumptions about the age categories which they utilize and be clear about whether they are intended simply as numerical categories, or whether they are meant to reflect meaningful age groupings in the social world. Third, where age groupings are intended to be socially meaningful, their meaning should be demonstrated rather than assumed, and related to the specific social, economic and political contexts from which that meaning derives.

3 Age as an explanatory variable

(a) *Theoretical issues*

As an explanatory variable, age can be used (either explicitly or implicitly) as a factor which is said to explain a particular social grouping, social process, or piece of individual or collective behaviour. It can be used in this way in a whole range of methodologies, both quantitative and qualitative. The emphasis in this section will be two-fold: on problems associated with the use of age as an explanatory variable; and on exploiting and developing its potential.

Put at its simplest, the problem about age as an explanatory variable is this: can age ever be said to *explain* social actions? Take, for example, evidence about participation in formal political processes, as measured by proportions of people voting in elections (cf. Jary, in this volume). The evidence of Riley and Foner for the United States shows that proportions of age groups exercising their vote rises substantially for older groups, being at a peak for those aged 45–54 (Riley and Foner, 1968, p. 464). Should it be concluded therefore that large numbers of people have gone out to vote *because* they have reached the age of forty-five? Probably not. But researchers can and do try to construct explanations based on the ageing process more generally, or upon the comparative position of age 'groups' in a given society – for example, Agnello has argued that age variations in voter participation can be explained by the relative political powerlessness of different age groups (Agnello, 1973).

When trying to construct explanations of this sort which do ultimately rest on notions that age or ageing *explains* social actions, three important questions need to be borne in mind, all of which essentially are about causality. First: is there a danger of sliding into the logical fallacy that correlation equals explanation? This of course is a very general point about the use of research findings, but age is especially vulnerable because it is a variable which lends itself to presentation in tables, histograms and so on. Second, one needs to ask: does age *per se* explain the phenomenon in question or is its apparent explanatory power a consequence of its acting as a summarizing variable, an umbrella term for a number of changes which tend to occur as people get older? As Riley puts it, age and date of birth are 'blunt instruments' for precise measurement and analysis and often act as surrogates for other variables (Riley, 1973, p. 47). In the example about changing patterns of voting behaviour, this would entail looking beyond the age-related patterns to questions about precisely what differences there are in the social and economic circumstances of people after the age of forty-five which could be meaningfully related to enthusiasm for voting – as Agnello does in his argument about perceptions of power and powerlessness. Third: is there a potential confusion between biological age and its social significance? As was noted in the discussion of age groups, the significance of reaching the age of twenty-one or sixty-five derives from the social meaning assigned to those ages, and the material and personal consequences which follow from that. On the other hand, age is a phenomenon which does have a biological basis as well as socially-defined meaning. The point is simply noted here, because it is discussed more fully in relation to conceptualizations of age (see below).

Another way of looking at the same issue is to put it in this form: Can age be seen as an unproblematic 'independent' variable?[2] Clearly age *is* an independent variable in the sense that it operates asymmetrically with other 'variables': age may perhaps alter one's propensity to drink alcohol or form close friendships, but not the other way round. On the other hand, whether one's friendships or one's alcohol consumption really are affected by one's age clearly is a matter for empirical investigation, and cannot be assumed just because statistics appear to show variations by age. It has to be *demonstrated* that these are contingent upon age, not *assumed* that they are.

(b) *Issues of method*

All these theoretical issues have implications when considering what methods are most appropriate for age-related social research. The most important of these is the distinction between age used as a cross-sectional variable and its use within various longitudinal strategies. Cross-sectional measures record a particular pattern of social behaviour or social experience at one point in time, and there are important limitations when analyses related to age are based on this technique of the cross-sectional 'snapshot'. To take again the example of the proportions of different age groups who exercise their right to vote: a sample taken at one specific time (say, the British 1983 general election) and then divided into age categories would not tell us anything generally about the relationship of age to voting. As Riley argues, the unwary researcher may be tempted to interpret such data as showing how voting behaviour *changes* as people get older – but of course it shows nothing of the sort. It is equally possible that different age cohorts have developed different levels of political activity which do not change over the life-time of individuals; therefore cross-sectional data taken twenty years later – or fifty years before – could produce a quite different pattern (Riley, 1973). The use of comparative sets of data can overcome this problem in part, but as Birren puts it, 'cross-sectional research on aging is a compromise or substitute for the ideal longitudinal study' (Birren, 1968, p. 549).

What kind of longitudinal strategies are available for research on ageing, and how can they be used? In survey research, longitudinal strategies are available in the form of panel or age-cohort studies. These entail setting up a specific sample of individuals upon whom a bank of data is accumulated by collecting information at regular intervals, usually but not necessarily through interviewing (see Zeisel, 1970 for discussion). A cohort can be composed in different ways: it can, for example, be made up of people marrying in the same year, or of people securing their first full-time job in the same year, and so on; but its potential in relation to age is obviously greatest where a cohort is composed of people born in the same year and ageing together. Several important British cohort studies have been of this type. A study funded by the Medical Research Council and directed by J.W.B. Douglas was based on a sample of more than 5,000 children born in a single week in March 1946, and the National Children's Bureau study similarly took a cohort of 17,000 born in one week in 1958 (Butler, Kellmer-Pringle and Davie, 1966). Both studies have resulted in influential publications especially in the field of education, as the respective cohorts passed through the schooling system (Douglas, 1964; Douglas, Ross and Simpson, 1968; Davie, Butler and Goldstein, 1972; cf. Burgess, in this volume). A rather smaller cohort, but one which has also produced important data has been undertaken by Elizabeth and John Newson, based on 709 children in Nottingham (Newson and Newson, 1963; 1968; 1976a). Both Douglas and the Newsons have provided interesting and thoughtful accounts of how they came to undertake their own studies and how they assess the value of longitudinal study on the basis of this experience (Douglas, 1976; Newson and Newson, 1976b).

A rather different kind of longitudinal strategy, which utilizes principally qualitative techniques, is the life history. Although a method used for at least half a century within sociology it has remained relatively under-developed and comparatively little used as a central technique in social research until recently, when it has enjoyed something of a revival in popularity (Faraday and Plummer, 1979; Bertaux, 1981a; Plummer, 1983). As Denzin puts it, the basic theme of the life history is the presentation of experience from the perspective of the focal subject or subjects. Its particular value as a method is that it represents intensively analysed cases, which enable subjective experiences to be compared to objective events. Thus they offer a way of documenting subjective experiences which is not available in most other methods, and can offer important interpretations of more quantitative findings expressed in statistical or correlational form (Denzin, 1970; introduction). Becker, in his defence of the method, goes somewhat further arguing that it can be superior to other methods, in that life histories help to build up a mosaic picture, placing objects and people in relation to each other. Thus it can give meaning to the overworked notion of 'process' which most methods, in his view, prevent us from seeing (Becker, 1970). Bertaux makes a related point in his strongly argued case for the centrality of life histories as a way of developing a distinctive kind of sociology, superior to what he regards as the sterile inheritance of positivism. He argues that this kind of 'qualitative' method can be equally rigorous in the matter of representativeness, data analysis and issues of proof, but it also yields 'direct access to the level of *social relations* which constitute, after all, the very substance of sociological knowledge' (Bertaux, 1981b, p. 31). It enables us to explore not only social structures but their historical movement.

As far as age-related studies are concerned, the potential of life histories is that, like cohort studies, they enable us to study processes over time and within particular historical contexts. Their special strength is their emphasis on subjective meaning, which makes them particularly appropriate for studies of a certain kind and especially, as Faraday and Plummer argue, for those which utilize an interactionist theoretical framework (Faraday and Plummer, 1979).

One important difference between life histories and cohort studies is that life histories collect data retrospectively. This means that one's data consists of what an individual has remembered, plus the way in which they have made sense of it (that is, their present interpretation of past events). By contrast a cohort study follows through events as they occur, and offers more possibility for the researcher to make direct observation of changes. On the other hand, one very real problem with longitudinal cohort studies is that the study is initially set up with a set of research questions in mind, but as it progresses the results of other research will become available and theoretical developments will occur (West, 1973, pp.236–7; Douglas, 1976, p.18).

Does the longitudinal strategies completely overcome the problems associated with cross-sectional analysis of age? The study of cohorts born in the same year can certainly enable us to test empirically questions about social change over time as well as specific questions about the effects of growing older upon individuals, if this is related carefully to the historical circumstances of the period through which the cohort is passing. But the logical fallacy of interpretation in cross-sectional studies can be paralleled in longitudinal studies if one assumes that, by demonstrating that certain changes have occurred over the life of one cohort, similar changes will occur for successive cohorts (Riley, 1973). As Foner puts it, 'because each cohort cuts off a unique segment of historical time as its members age, the life course patterns of successive cohorts differ' (Foner, 1980, p. 776). In terms of constructing explanations based on age, the central problem is: how do we know which aspects of change observed in a given cohort are a consequence of ageing, and which are a consequence of changing historical circumstances? One way of overcoming this is to compare data from successive cohorts growing up and ageing at different times, although this also has to be handled carefully (Mason, Mason, Winsborough and Poole, 1973). Ryder has put forward the very useful suggestion that age cohort studies should be constructed as far as possible in ways which are comparable with each other, that is by using the same methods of identifying the cohort to be studied. This would mean that research results could be compared with each other in a much more systematic fashion than hitherto has been possible and would facilitate the building up of 'composite cohort biographies' which would be very useful in the study of social change (Ryder, 1977; pp. 144–5).

The implication of this discussion of methods is that longitudinal strategies – including cohort studies – should be used much more extensively in social research related to age. This exhortation may well be greeted with scepticism because of many of the practical difficulties involved in mounting and sustaining such studies. Chief among these at the present time is the question of cost, particularly if a large-scale, national sample is to be studied, say over a period of twenty years. Douglas, arguing from the basis of his own experience of running a cohort study, has suggested that the cost issue may not be as formidable as others have suggested: comparable data collected through a series of cross-sectional studies would be just as expensive, in his view (Douglas, 1976, pp. 16–17). They would of course also suffer from the methodological and theoretical defects of cross-sectional studies. The question of cost is related closely to sample size, and it may well be that a small-scale longitudinal study will yield more appropriate data to questions related to age than a single large-scale cross-sectional one. Life histories of course are far less costly, unless very large numbers are to be collected.

4 Conclusion: contextualizing age as a variable

A number of important theoretical issues are raised by the concept of age which cannot be explored fully here, since the emphasis in this chapter is upon the use of age as a variable in social research. However, in this concluding section two themes will be considered briefly because they serve to indicate how the concept of age needs to be contextualized in wider theoretical debates if its potential is to be fully realized.

First, age is a variable – like gender and race – which raises questions about the relationship of biology to social life (see chapters by Morgan and Bulmer, in this volume). Clearly age is a social category with a biological basis, but biology tells us little about its social meaning and significance. The importance of distinguishing between the biological basis of age and its social meaning can be seen in relation to both the young and the old. For example, adolescence as a 'phase' of life has a biological basis in changes associated with puberty, but the experience of these changes and the significance accorded to them is subject to major cross-cultural variations, as has long been recognized (Wood, 1976). Therefore we cannot simply 'read off' changes in social actions and social experiences from age-related biological changes.

The distinction between biological and social adolescence can be paralleled by biological and social old age. Cowgill and Holmes' cross-cultural study of ageing indicates that, whilst all societies seem to have some category of people called 'old', the use of calendar age to assign individuals to this category is a feature only of what they refer to as 'modern' societies which have sophisticated ways of measuring time and recording its passage (Cowgill and Holmes, 1972). The use of the chronological measure of age to denote entry into the category 'old' indicates that it is a social not a biological category, since the relationship between calendar age and the physical changes associated with ageing is by no means straightforward (see also: Featherstone and Hepworth, 1982). There can, however, be confusion on this point, since people who are assigned to the category 'old' by means of a socially-defined measure may well be assumed to display the characteristics associated with biological ageing. Thus in social research the indicator of retirement age is often used as a measure for assigning people to the category 'old', but it is not always clear whether this is being used only as a social category or also implicitly as a biological one. The fact that, in Britain, women reach retirement five years before men (sixty and sixty-five respectively) makes nonsense of any piece of research which treats people past retirement age as 'old' in the biological sense, since there is no basis for assuming that women experience the physical effects of ageing five years earlier than men.

As well as being accurate in these matters of definition, social research needs to be able to capture the subtleties of the ways in which age is used in social life to encompass both biological and social dimensions. The concept of the 'right age' to marry is one illustration of this (Leonard, 1980, pp.72–4).

These examples also point to the second issue of context raised here: that age should be seen as one important social division in a complex pattern of social divisions which intersect with each other (Riley, Johnson and Foner, 1972, ch. 10; Bengston, Furlong and Laufer, 1974, pp. 22–3). Questions can be posed both empirically and theoretically about how social divisions based on age intersect with those based on gender, race or class. For example, in contemporary American society, there is evidence that men's perception of their passage through age divisions varies with class (Elder, 1975, p.173), but relatively little is known about this cross-culturally.

A rather different example can be found in writing about young people, where the issue of whether it makes sense to treat 'youth' as a single category can have practical as well as theoretical consequences.

In an article which focuses on youth work, Mica Nava (1981) demonstrates the very practical consequences of treating 'youth' as a unitary category; since 'youth' in practice has meant 'boys' almost exclusively, girls and the needs of girls have got lost in the development of youth services. By contrast, other writers go on treating 'youth' as if it were an undifferentiated category. Marsland (1982), for example, in his discussion of the need to re-establish a 'sociology of youth', implies an entirely unidimensional analysis of the experience of young people. His programme for what would constitute a sociology of youth contains no mention of divisions based on gender, race or class.

In terms of developing principles for application in social research, the intersection of social divisions has to be taken into account in ways appropriate to the particular project. But at the minimum, the guiding criterion should be that any age-related social category such as 'youth' or 'elderly' should never be treated as a unitary category without first establishing whether other social divisions do cross-cut it in significant ways.

In a variety of ways, therefore, the use of age as a variable highlights issues which are central to our understanding of social relations and social processes: the interplay of the biological and the social in human experience; the relationship between personal and social change; and – to put it in Mills' (1970) terms – the intersection between biography and history. Age needs to be developed not merely as a face-sheet variable, but as a topic for study in its own right.

Notes

1   Mean, median and mode are different methods of calculating and expressing averages. The mean is the simple arithmetic calculation (i.e. in the case of age, adding together the ages of all respondents and dividing by the total number of respondents). The median is the middle of the range, when the ages of all respondents are arranged (either grouped or ungrouped) in ascending order. The mode is the age which occurs most frequently.

2   The phrase 'independent variable' refers to a presumed relationship between two personal or social characteristics (eg. age and the consumption of alcohol). In survey research, if two such variables are linked at a statistically significant level, a researcher will ask whether the one (the dependent variable) is explained by the other (the independent variable). Of course, it may be that no such

causal relationship exists. In this example, age could be the independent variable, but not the dependent one – since varying levels of alcohol consumption cannot change a person's age.

References

Agnello, T. (1973), 'Aging and the sense of political powerlessness', *Public Opinion Quarterly*, Vol.37, No.2, pp.251–9

Allen, S. (1968), 'Some theoretical problems in the study of youth', *Sociological Review*, Vol.16, pp.319–31

Becker, H. (1970), 'The relevance of life histories'. In N. Denzin (ed.), *Sociological Methods: a Sourcebook* (Chicago: Aldine)

Bengtson, V., Furlong, M. and **Laufer, R.** (1974), 'Time, aging and the continuity of social structure: themes and issues in generational analysis', *Journal of Social Issues*, Vol.30, No.2, pp.1–30

Bertaux, D. (ed.) (1981a), *Biography and Society: the Life History Approach in the Social Sciences* (Beverly Hills: Sage)

Bertaux, D. (1981b) 'From the life history approach to the transformation of sociological practice', in D. Bertaux (ed.), *Biography and Society* (Beverly Hills: Sage)

Birren, J. (1968), 'Principles of research on aging', in B. Neugarten (ed.), *Middle Age and Aging: A Reader in Social Psychology* (Chicago: University of Chicago Press)

Butler, N., Kellmer-Pringle, M. and **Davie, R.** (1966), *11,000 Seven Year Olds* (London: Longmans)

Cowgill, D. and **Holmes, L.** (1972), *Aging and Modernisation* (New York: Appleton Century)

Davie, R., Butler, N. and **Goldstein, H.** (1972), *From Birth to Seven* (London: Longmans)

Denzin, N. (ed.) (1970), *Sociological Methods: a Sourcebook* (Chicago: Aldine)

Department of Education and Science (1977), *Education in Schools*, Cmnd.6869 (London: HMSO)

Douglas, J. (1964), *The Home and the School* (London: MacGibbon and Kee)

Douglas, J. W. B. (1976), 'The use and abuse of national cohorts', in M. Shipman (ed.), *The Organization and Impact of Social Research* (London: Routledge & Kegan Paul)

Douglas, J. W. B., Ross, J. and **Simpson, H.** (1968), *All Our Future* (London: P Davies)

Elder, G. (1975), 'Age differentiation and the life course', *Annual Review of Sociology*, Vol.1, pp.165–90

Faraday, A. and **Plummer, K.** (1979), 'Doing life histories', *Sociological Review*, Vol.27, No.4, pp.773–98

Featherstone, M. and **Hepworth, M.** (1982), 'Aging and inequality: consumer culture and the new middle age', in D. Robbins (ed.), *Rethinking Social Inequality* (London: Gower)

Finch, J. and **Groves, D.** (1982), 'By women, for women: caring for the frail elderly', *Women's Studies International Forum*, Vol.5, No.5, pp.427–38

Fogarty, M. (1973), *Forty to Sixty: How we waste the middle age* (London: Centre for Studies on Social Policy/Bedford Square Press)

Foner, A. (1980), 'The sociology of age stratification: a review of some recent publications', *Contemporary Sociology*, Vol.9, No.1, pp.771–9

Hoinville, G. and **Jowell, R.** (1978), *Survey Research Practice* (London: Heinemann)

Kaufman, R. and **Spilerman, S.** (1982), 'The age structures of occupations and jobs', *American Journal of Sociology*, Vol.87, No.4, pp.827–51

Leonard, D. (1980), *Sex and Generation: a Study of Courtship and Weddings* (London: Tavistock)

Linton, R. (1942), 'Age and sex categories', *American Sociological Review*, Vol.7, pp.589–603

Mannheim, K. (1952), 'The problem of generations', in P. Kecskemeti (ed.), *Essays on the Sociology of Knowledge by Karl Mannheim* (London: Routledge & Kegan Paul)

Marsland, D. (1982), 'The sociology of adolescence and youth', in A. Hartnett (ed.), *The Social Sciences in Educational Studies*, (London: Heinemann)

Martin, J. (1978) *Infant feeding 1975: Attitudes and Practice in England & Wales* (London: HMSO)

Mason, K., Mason, W., Winsborough, H. and **Poole, W. K.** (1973), 'Some methodological issues in cohort analysis of archival data', *American Sociological Review*, Vol.38, pp.242–58

Mills, C. Wright. (1970), *The Sociological Imagination* (Harmondsworth: Penguin)

Musgrove, F. and **Middleton, R.** (1981), 'Rites of passage and the meaning of age in three contrasted social groups: professional footballers, teachers and Methodist ministers', *British Journal of Sociology*, Vol.31, No.1, pp.39–55

Nava, M. (1981), ' "Girls aren't really a problem . . . " So if "youth" is not a unitary category, what are the implications for youth work?', *Schooling and Culture*, No.9, pp.5–10

Neugarten, B., Moore, J. and **Lowe, J.** (1965), 'Age norms, age constraints and adult socialisation', *American Journal of Sociology*, Vol.70, pp.710–17

Newson, J. and **Newson, E.** (1963), *Infant Care in an Urban Community* (London: Allen & Unwin)

Newson, J. and **Newson, E.** (1968), *Four Years Old in an Urban Community* (London: Allen & Unwin)

Newson, J. and **Newson, E.** (1976a), *Seven Years Old in the Home Environment* (London: Allen & Unwin)

Newson, J. and **Newson, E.** (1976b), 'Parental roles and social contexts'. In M. Shipman (ed.), *The Organisation and Impact of Social Research* (London: Routledge & Kegan Paul)

Nissel, M. (1982), 'Families and social change since the second world war', in R. N. Rapoport, M. P. Fogarty and R. Rapoport (eds), *Families in Britain* (London: Routledge & Kegan Paul)

Office of Population, Censuses and Surveys (1978), *Trends in Mortality 1951—1975*, Series DHI, No.3 (London: HMSO)

Office of Population, Censuses and Surveys (1980), *Marriage and Divorce Statistics* (London: HMSO)

Office of Population, Censuses and Surveys (1982), 'The 1981 Census and population trends in 1981', *Population Trends*, No.30, Winter, pp.1–8 (London: HMSO)

Office of Population, Censuses and Surveys (1983), *Census 1981: Persons of Pensionable Age* (London: HMSO)

Parsons, T. (1954), 'Age and sex in the social structure of the United States', in T. Parsons, *Essays in Sociological Theory*, 2nd edn (New York: Free Press), first published 1942

Plummer, K. (1983), *Documents of Life*, (London: Allen & Unwin)

Report of the Committee on the Age of Majority, The Latey Report, Cmnd.3342, 1967

Riley, M. (1973), 'Aging and cohort succession: interpretations and misinterpretations', *Public Opinion Quarterly*, Vol.37, No.1, pp.35–49

Riley, M. W. and **Foner, A.** (1968), *Aging and Society, Vol.1: An Inventory of Research Findings* (New York: Russell Sage Foundation)

Riley, M. W., Johnson, M. and **Foner, A.** (1972), *Aging and Society,*

Vol.3: A Sociology of Age Stratification (New York: Russell Sage Foundation)

Ryder, N. B. (1977), 'The cohort as a concept in the study of social change', in M. Bulmer (ed.), *Sociological Research Methods* (London: Macmillan)

Stacey, M. (1969), *Methods of Social Research* (Oxford: Pergamon)

West, D. (1973), *Who Becomes Delinquent?* (London: Heinemann)

Wood, M. E. (1976), 'Changing social attitudes to childhood', in R. Chester and J. Peel (eds), *Equalities and Inequalities in Family Life* (London: Academic Press)

Wuthnow, R. (1976), 'Recent pattern of secularisation: a problem of generations?' *American Sociological Review*, Vol.41, October, pp. 850–67

Zeisel, H. (1970), 'The panel', in N. Denzin (ed.), *Sociological Methods: a Sourcebook* (Chicago: Aldine)

Gender 3

D. H. J. Morgan

Introduction

Gender, as a key variable, is both ubiquitous and hidden. It is ubiquitous in that it is one of the most common 'face-sheet' variables (Stacey, 1969, xiii) and yet hidden in that, despite this commonness, it is often ignored or buried beneath some other more inclusive category such as 'children', 'rate-payers', 'professionals', or 'students'. The higher realms of sociological theory remain, apparently, gender-free; the higher the level of generality the more likely it is that gender differentiation will yield to more abstract categories such as 'role', 'social actor', 'organization', 'class' and 'system'. Feminist theory may, in part, be seen as an insistence that gender belongs up there with the more familiar categories of sociological discourse; that, indeed, it exists at the highest levels of generality. Moreover, gender enters the complete process of research itself, the form and style of the project in its various stages from start to completion as an article or thesis.

It would seem, therefore, that the central question in the treatment of gender as a key variable is one of when it is to be used and it would also appear to be the case that a persuasive case could be made for the response, 'always'. The questions which are raised elsewhere in this volume – questions of identification, operationalization, choice of appropriate indicators, grouping and classification and measurement – would appear to be of little significance in the case of gender. And yet, is there not something in the very simplicity of the operations which enable us to allocate items to columns labelled 'Men' and 'Women' that should make us pause for thought? What kinds of assumptions are being made when a set of data is analysed 'according to sex'? Note, that here I have shifted from use of the term 'gender' to the more familiar face-sheet term, 'sex'. The meanings and implications of this distinction will be considered later.

The purpose of this chapter is not so much to argue the case for gender as a 'key variable'. In the light of the many volumes of theoretical and empirical work that have been written in recent years[1] that much can almost be taken for granted, although the continued omission of gender in sociological studies evidenced later in this chapter should remind us of the need to translate this work into routine sociological practice. Rather, the questions which will be asked here hinge around the various senses in which gender can be understood to be a key variable and the way in which it is used.

Gender as a key variable?

Gender is one of fourteen or so variables which are most likely to be recorded by interviewers or required in questionnaires, along with age, occupation, place of birth, type of dwelling and so on (Gittus, 1972; Stacey, 1969). Nor need its use be confined to quantitative research; ethnographers are likely to record the gender of subjects observed in field situations. At the simplest level, therefore, gender may be a key variable as part of the business of 'descriptive documentation', to use Finch's phrase (Finch, this volume, p. 13). In breaking down the data by age and sex, theorizing is usually implicit and unexamined, a conformity to established practice or to a vague sense that they might be important.

In terms of Finch's second category, the use of gender as an 'explanatory variable', theory plays a more positive and explicit role. Here the assumption is that gender has some kind of casual significance, as for example where gender may be linked to attitudes about welfare, support for a political party or church attendance. In many cases, of course, gender is not treated alone but in combination with other variables as, for example, where Lupton treats gender as part of a 'cluster of variables', explaining the presence or absence of collective norms output and earnings on the shop floor (Lupton, 1963).

In addition to being part of everyday descriptive documentation and to its deployment as an explanatory variable, gender's status is also enhanced by political and ideological considerations. Feminist sociology has reminded us that the inclusion or non-inclusion of gender in a research project is as much a political decision as a theoretically-based choice. In this connection, one central and all pervasive area of research has been into the sexual division of labour (Purcell, this volume). In spite of the fact that many feminist researchers would reject, or at least be suspicious of, the very language which speaks of 'variables' (Graham, 1983), it is the activities of such feminists that have problematized the use of gender as a key variable, taking it out of the realm of the taken-for-granted.

1 *Female/Male; Woman/Man*

The familiar dichotomous approach to gender makes for simplicity in coding, 'don't knows' rarely, if ever constitute a problem, and comparability and reproducibility is assumed and assured. This dichotomous approach to sex and/or gender reflects and is reflected in theoretical orientations, most notably Parsonian functionalism although it is also part of the taken-for-granted world of much Marxist and feminist theory (Matthews, 1982).

This distinction between 'sex' and 'gender' is stated by Oakley in these terms:

> 'Sex' refers to the biological division into female and male; 'genders' to the parallel and socially unequal division into femininity and masculinity.
>
> (Oakley, 1981a, p. 41)

Oakley maintains that this usage is 'well established' and is certainly repeated, with some slight variations, elsewhere in the literature. Matthews, in a critical discussion of the use of gender in sociological research, cites the following distinction by Gould and Kern-Daniels:

> Sex is defined as 'the biological dichotomy between female and male, chromosomally determined and, for the most part, unalterable', while gender is 'that which is recognised as masculine and feminine by a social world'.
>
> (Matthews, 1982, p. 31)

There does, however, seem to be some element of choice as to which biological factors may be selected. Eichler writes:

> Biological sex is determined in different ways: chromosomal sex, gonadal sex, internal accessory organ, external genital appearance. In addition, the assigned sex and gender role may be consistent or inconsistent with the other determinants of sex.
>
> (Eichler, 1980)

Similarly, Kessler and MacKenna list a variety of ways in which biologists make such distinctions (Kessler and MacKenna, 1978, p. 69).

The assumptions behind the sex/gender division would seem therefore, to be as follows:

a)   A distinction between the biological and the social/cultural;
b)   two parallel dichotomies in each sphere: female and male; feminine and masculine;
c)   in the case of Oakley and some others, a recognition of the 'socially unequal' nature of the latter dichotomy.

It is stated that the dichotomies are 'parallel' although the geometrical metaphor is not intended to be taken literally. There are interrelationships between the biological and the cultural (Reid and Wormald, 1982, p. 2), although these are not always clearly stated.

There are, therefore, a variety of difficulties with the sex/gender division and for gender's status as a 'key variable'. In the first place, the distinction, with its proposed parallelism between female/male and feminine/masculine, continues to maintain, to take for granted, a dichotomous view of gender differences. This, Matthews argues (ibid., p. 30), leads to the reification of gender and gender categories and the reproduction of 'sex' (i.e. the biological) in spite of the emphasis on the cultural and social.

Biology, however, itself provides no clear warrant for a dichotomous view. Birdwhistell, for example, distinguishes between primary, secondary and tertiary sexual characteristics, the first referring to 'the clear demarcation between the production of ova and spermatozoa', the second to anatomical features and the third to social and cultural constructions. Secondary sexual characteristics, he argues (including bone structure, distribution of body hair, and so on) are distributed according to two overlapping bell-shaped curves rather than to a single bimodal distribution (in Lee and Stewart, 1976, p. 315).[2] Neitz, noting that sex/gender distinction originated in the study of transexuals, argues for seeing both as continuous variables (Neitz, 1982).

It is, in fact, often in culture where we find the sharper dichotomous differentiations; we have only to think of the ways in which children make very distinct differentiations between men and women on the basis of clothing rather than genitalia (Oakley, 1981a, pp. 82–3). Transexuals and transvestites may often, at some considerable cost, adhere to a highly rigid and stereotyped version of sex and gender differences (Bogdan, 1974; Eichler, 1980, pp. 72–90; Kessler and MacKenna, 1978). Looking at the matter in a cross-cultural perspective raises the challenging perspective that some folk classifications may not necessarily conform to a dichotomous model of sex/gender.[3] Attempts to force 'anomalies' (such as the *'berdache'* of some North American Indian societies) into these dichotomous models may do violence to local understandings (Martin and Voorhies, 1975, pp. 86–100; Kessler and Mackenna, 1978, pp. 24–32).

Whatever distinctions are made between the biological and cultural it would seem to be important to recognize that there is constant interaction between them. Biological facts, as Matthews argues, are themselves socially constructed (Matthews, 1982, p. 31) in terms of which facts are selected as being decisive and according to the degree of significance allocated to these constructed facts. If certain distinctions between men and women came to be seen as crucial, this itself is a cultural fact and has its consequences as such, although this is the outcome of a complex interaction between the biological and the cultural, rather than the primary assertion of the former. Birdwhistell's own analysis of different facial expressions and bodily postures of men and women in contemporary American society provides a neat illustration of the interaction between the cultural and the anatomical (which become socially defined as biological differences), the postures and expressions deriving meaning from interactional situations rather than through any inherent quality as 'sexual signals' (ibid.).

In contemporary society there is not one version of gender differentiation but a range of versions available for use by different persons in different situations. At a time of considerable change in gender definitions and identities, overlaps and similarities become often more important than differences (Lee and Stewart, 1976, p. 29). To adhere to a dichotomous construction of gender differences is to run the risk of reproducing, often unconsciously, stereotypical assumptions about men and women and of failing to do justice to the complex, paradoxical and sometimes contradictory understandings of gender in contemporary society.

2 *Masculine/Feminine*

If the female/male or man/woman distinction tends to be nominal and dichotomous, the feminine/masculine distinction would seem to be more obviously continuous and ordinal. It is part of our common taken-for-granted assumptions about gender that there are some 'feminine men' and some 'masculine women'; that, in other words the two scales do have some degree of independence (Eichler, 1980,

pp. 63–9). In terms of sociological research, however, the distinctions
feminine/masculine are rarely overtly used although assumptions
about these distinctions may be built into sociological analysis. Social
anthropologists have, however, used the terms often treating the
degree and kinds of variation as topics for investigation in cross-
cultural research. Best known is Margaret Mead's classic discussion
of the different constructions of sex and temperament in three primitive societies (Mead, 1935). More recently, Sanday (using a much
more comprehensive range of societies for comparative purposes) has
looked at the degree and nature of sexual differentiation and patterns
of dominance, differing constructions of masculinity and femininity
and the way in which these can be related to types of economy and the
sexual scripts provided by religious symbolism (Sanday, P.R., 1981;
see also Lee and Stewart, 1976, Part 11). One of the difficulties with
much anthropological research is the importing of Western models
into the analysis of other societies. The use of the clause 'differences as
conventionally understood in contemporary/Western society' can
only be a partial solution for it still assumes that the society under
investigation has some understanding as to what it means to make
gender differentiation (albeit different from 'ours') and that, indeed,
the observer has an accurate model of 'our own' models of gender
differentiation. In short, we have a set of traits – aggressiveness,
passivity, etc. – and a polarity, feminine-masculine, the traits being
allocated to the appropriate gender categories. While 'biological'
females and males may not necessarily manifest the expected traits –
indeed may manifest the opposite or may share many of the traits – it
is assumed that the actual labels, feminine-masculine, do have some
wider meaning.

The other areas in which the masculine-feminine distinction is used
is in social psychology which, like social anthropology, may impinge
upon sociology at various points. A variety of measures of masculinity
and femininity have been drawn up and used for a variety of purposes
(Eichler, 1980, pp. 60–72). Brim, for example shows how masculinity
and femininity may vary according to a set of variables associated
with siblings; number of siblings, gender of siblings, birth order in
terms of gender, and so on. The initial measures of femininity and
masculinity are based upon judges' assessments of the gender of
particular traits and whether the traits are valued positively or
negatively (Brim, 1958). In the case of Brim's study, and several
others of this kind, it is made clear that the authors are dealing with (it
is assumed) relatively culture-bound constructions of femininity and
masculinity rather than biological givens and that, to some extent,

these values are not unproblematically mapped on to persons defined as being either men or women. There is often a recognition that feminine and masculine traits could coexist in various mixes within the same individual. Nevertheless, use of measures and models of femininity and masculinity may still tend to reproduce and perpetuate notions of gender differences which tend to the bipolar rather than emphasizing points of similarity and overlap (Lee and Stewart, 1976, 31, p. 361). As Eichler points out, even the concept of androgyny assumes that there exist some standards of femininity/masculinity against which to record these 'deviations' (Eichler, ibid.).

Sociologically, measures of masculinity and femininity are little used, at least not as key variables although it is open to question as to the degree to which the gender labels, female and male, presuppose some taken for granted notions of gender characteristics. Until fairly recently, for example it has been assumed that women are more passive and more conservative and this explains a variety of alleged differences between men and women in terms of industrial and political attitudes and behaviour. Closer analysis more often than not calls these assumptions into question, finding them to be minimal or untrue, dependent upon particular sets of circumstances or a reflection of other differences (Cunnison, 1983; Edgell and Duke, 1983; Purcell, 1979; Randall, 1982; Wormald, 1982). Where these terms have been more systematically investigated it has been to examine their deployment in ideological constructions, in other words the uses and representations of gender traits in everyday life, especially in literature and the media. Thus there have been studies of the presentation of gender stereotypes in school textbooks (Children's Rights Workshop, 1976), in women's magazines (Ferguson, 1982), and in advertising (Millum, 1975). Goffman's study seeks to show how gender advertisments work (Goffman, 1979).

Generally, however, whether we are concerned with anthropological, social psychological or sociological studies, the central dilemma remains: how is it possible to use the labels 'feminine' and 'masculine' without falling into some kind of essentialism? This problem may also confront feminist-inspired work. Thus, for example, if it is argued that science (Easlea, 1981) or social science has some kind of masculinist bias how far is it possible to use this label without in some way perpetuating the very stereotypes that a feminist inspired study seeks to undermine?

38   *D.H.J. Morgan*

3 *Sexuality*

Associated with the question of gender, although not a key variable in the 'face-sheet' sense of the word, is the question of sexuality. It may be viewed, very simplistically, as part of the 'package' of constructed gender identities. Thus part of the social definition of femininity is a construction of female sexuality, that of masculinity a construction of male sexuality. Indeed, in practice it is probably very difficult to distinguish between the more general characterizations of male and female traits and more specific assumptions about their sexualities. The aggressiveness associated with masculinity, for example, is often associated, directly or indirectly, with the assumed role attributed to the male in sexual intercourse and to the role of the phallus.

For a long time, the mapping of characteristics associated with certain forms of sexuality on to men and women was seen as relatively unproblematic in sociological research. Alternatively, a male model of sexuality was held to stand for sexuality in general. Studies of premarital sexual experience, for example, were based upon scales, ranging from kissing and petting to genital penetration, which reflected a highly phallocentric view of the world (Schofield, 1968, Chapter 3). In more recent years, however, studies have concentrated more thoroughly on the ways in which sexuality, male and female, have been socially constructed (Brake, 1982; Edwards, 1981; Foucault, 1979). The emphasis has grown to be more on sexualities, male and female, heterosexual and homosexual. Douglas's study of the nude beach (Douglas *et al.*, 1977), Rasmussen and Kuhn's study of massage parlours (Rasmussen and Kuhn, 1977) and Cloyd's study of the market-place bar (Cloyd, 1977), direct our attention away from essentialist notions of sexuality and sexual signals and focus attention on to the interactional situations in which sexuality is negotiated. Humphreys' rejection of the distinctions masculine/feminine and aggressive/passive in favour of the more objective inserter/insertee distinction in his study of the 'tearoom trade' (Humphreys, 1970, pp. 51–2) shows a willingness to depart from stereotypes of homosexual behaviour as does his classification in terms of 'trade', 'ambisexuals', 'gays' and 'closet queens' (ibid., Chapter 6). Ponse, similarly, writes of 'women-related women' recognizing that they might call themselves lesbians, straights, bisexuals or celibates (Ponse, 1978, p. 3). Perhaps here, more than in other aspects of the study of gender, the variety of human sexual expression, definition and understanding is coming to be recognized, and the inadequacy of bipolar or bimodal models has been underlined. This understanding, however, has yet to feed back into more general assumptions about gender or uses of gender labels in sociological analysis.

4 *The sexual division of labour*

As Purcell argues (this volume), the sexual division of labour is a key feature of this and almost all other societies. The labour market, for example, is significantly differentiated in terms of gender. This is true whether we are considering the differential distribution of men and women as between particular jobs or as between different hierarchically ordered statuses (Murgatroyd, 1982; Purcell, this volume; Webb, 1982).

The sexual division of labour, however, also addresses itself to the distinction between home and work (and to associated distinctions such as that between the public and the private) and to distinctions within the home, as well as to distinctions within the labour market. As such it should be seen as a crucial variable in the understanding of a contemporary society. It is a matter of gender rather than sex (to return to the conventional distinction) in that it is socially and politically constructed although the construction often makes use of biological notions to justify the maintenance of any particular gender order. The use and understanding of sexuality also may be a crucial feature in the maintenance of the gender order in a particular context, whether it be at home, at work (Purcell, 1982) or in the interstitial areas of the street (Hanmer and Saunders, 1983). The sexual division of labour may be seen as a crucial element in the understanding of the class structure of a capitalist society. Wright and his associates, for example, conclude that: 'a sizable majority of the U.S. working class is composed of women and minorities' (Wright *et al.*, 1982; also Wright and Perrone, 1977).

Gender is an important variable when considering such questions as unemployment (Walby, 1983) or social mobility (Rosenfeld, 1978; Payne *et al.*, 1983). To fail to consider the sexual division of labour and its part in the class structure has been characterized as a form of intellectual or official sexism (Acker, 1973; E.O.C., 1980; Oakley and Oakley, 1979).

Issues in the use of gender

1 *Recognizing gender*

Thus, one important issue in the use of gender as a key variable is the extent to which its use is based upon and thereby serves to perpetuate gender stereotypes. But there are several other issues that deserve attention. In the first place, there is the apparently obvious question of recognizing gender. To develop the issue let us consider one common way of assigning an individual to a social class category:

(1) *An Individual* has (2) *An Occupation* which is (3) *Coded as* Working Class
                                                        Middle Class

                                                        Skilled
                                                        Unskilled, etc.

This highly simplified scheme states that an individual is expected to provide some kind of occupational title which is then, following standardized, laid down procedures, coded in more general class or occupational group terms. Similarly, in the case of age, an individual's date of birth is the basis for the assignment of that individual to some more generalized age categories (Finch, this volume).

What happens in the case of gender? Here:

(1) *An Individual* has (2) (*?*) which are (3) *Coded* as Female
                                                      Male

In this case, Stage (2) appears as a kind of black box but where, it is assumed, the common-sense assumptions of investigators are accorded some degree of licence. Gender is either self-assigned or assigned by the investigator, presumably on the basis of a variety of non-verbal signals (Frieze *et al.*, 1981, pp. 321–34). The fact that this operation is so often smooth and untroubled should not blind us to the fact that this business of gender assignment is a remarkable cultural achievement (Kessler and McKenna, 1978). The very stability and untroubled nature of gender assignment is itself a valuable clue to our understanding of the character of gender itself, namely that an individual has a gender which is unproblematically recognized and not liable to change. It is clear that this is still a relatively under-researched area; studies of transexuals and transvestites (Bogdan, 1974; Eichler, 1980; Garfinkel, 1967; Kessler and McKenna, 1978) need to be complemented by studies of the rules and procedures by which social investigators and lay persons make gender categorizations.

2 When to use?

' . . . the value of feminist critiques to the discipline of sociology lies in the accumulating evidence that gender is not a good index to understand the social world.'

(Matthews, 1982, p. 29)

The case for not treating gender as a key variable might in some ways seem to be as strong as the case for so treating it. Much of the argument would seem to hinge around the meaning of words like 'importance' and 'use'. Matthews is presumably referring to the cumulative traditions of social psychological and sociological research that have gradually whittled down supposed gender differences to two or three dealing with spatial and reading ability and with aggressiveness (Lee and Stewart, 1976; Frieze *et al.*, 1981, pp. 45–68). There may further be a bias towards the publication of significant differences thus condemning to obscurity the greater number of non-significant differences (Frieze *et al.*, 1981, pp. 51–3). To put the matter crudely, search for differences and you can find differences; test for similarities and you find similarities. Thus Matthews would seem to be concerned with those areas of gender research where the investigator is either attempting to establish some essential gender differences or is using an implicit understanding of these supposed gender differences for subsequent analysis.

Another kind of research which would presumably come under Matthews' strictures is the kind of study where gender characteristics are 'read off' from the fact that a set of people in a particular situation are observed to be either men or women. This may be said to be a feature of some studies of work and workshop behaviour where, for example, the presupposition may be that gender 'makes a difference' and that observed behaviour will be interpreted in terms of the characteristics that the workers are supposed to bring into the workplace as wives, mothers, daughters etc. (Morgan, 1981). Researchers may, therefore, endorse a managerial perspective that women at work somehow present some kind of problematic status. Men's workshop behaviour will be understood as having something to do with class, women's workshop behaviour is something to do with gender (Feldberg and Glenn, 1979). What is perhaps interesting in a large number of studies of work situations is not so much that assumed gender characteristics are uncritically taken as having some kind of casual significance but that gender in this case tends to mean 'women'. The male gender at the workplace is not seen as providing a subject for analysis; or, men at work are taken as providing the standard of normal workshop behaviour, against which women are seen as deviating.

Yet, against Matthews' argument, it can be said that a large number of studies are concerned not with gender characteristics (assumed or otherwise) but with the gender inequalities of the sexual division of labour. The danger, therefore, is not so much one of ignoring gender in some highly abstract sense but in subsuming gender inequalities under some wider, non-gender label such as class, professional group, children and so on. Sociologists, it will be argued, ought to be concerned to continue to monitor these gender inequalities in particular where they are masked by conventional labels and classifications. Clearly any straightforward way out of this dilemma is difficult; the guidelines at the end of this chapter may provide some suggestions.

3 *Gender and the research process*

Gender is not something which exists simply as an object of study or as a variable in sociological analysis. It enters into the research process itself, into the selection of the problem and methodology, the conduct of the research and the assumptions guiding the analysis. Here, I focus on one aspect of this; the fact that the observer or investigator has a gender identity (Hammersley and Atkinson, 1983, pp. 84–7; Wax, 1979). In particular I focus on the interviewing situation, according to the following matrix:

		Interviewed	
		Men	*Women*
Interviewers	*Men*	1	2
	Women	3	4

1 There has been little directly written about men interviewing men although it is undoubtedly a common situation. There seems to be some evidence that men are more likely to have a negative attitude towards disclosure (Brannen and Collard, 1982) and it is possible to argue that men in our culture are more likely to prefer the more structured questionnaire to the

open-ended interview. Clearly some more work needs to be done here.

2 This is the case which is most congruent with the power situation in everyday life. Attention is usually focused on the difficulties around possibly embarrassing questions to do with sexual or personal life. The actual dynamics of men interviewing women still have, however, to be explored in some detail.

3 Women often constitute the underclass of sociological research and are, therefore, more likely to be found among the ranks of interviewers (Wakeford, 1981, p. 507). It is often assumed that women, in common with stereotypical notions of femininity, are better able to put their subjects at ease, to establish rapport (Douglas, 1976, p. 211). The double-edged character of these assumptions is well explored by McKee and O'Brien (McKee and O'Brien, 1983; also Easterday, 1977).

4 The question of women interviewing women has developed following the growing interest in feminist research methodology. Here it is argued that the conventional positivist, fixed-choice questionnaire is based upon a masculine version of sociological enquiry and that a more open-ended 'conversation', with few of the hierarchical assumptions of men interviewing women is more appropriate (Graham, 1983; Oakley, 1981b). However, certain ethical and political problems are raised in the consideration of this kind of methodology (Finch, 1984; Oakley, 1981b).

This matrix does not, of course, include what may be the most common research situation: one of both genders on both 'sides' (Stenhouse, 1984). Questions of the gender of the interviewer and interviewee have been given some attention in the literature but the emphasis has been either upon possible difficulties to overcome or possible advantages in terms of the interview itself. The deeper questions, however, have been raised by the growing interest in the development of a feminist methodology (Stanley and Wise, 1983). Clearly, also, more attention must be paid to the whole process of research and to the whole range of methodologies. It has been suggested, for example, that the sexism of official statistics may have something to do with the gender structure of such agencies (EOC, 1980).

Cases

Space does not permit a detailed examination of the use or non-use of gender in recent years.[4] An examination of the journals *Sociology* and the *American Sociological Review* (ASR) over roughly the past ten years revealed the following patterns:

i) Gender is more often assumed than either stated or used. This was particularly true in the British journals.

ii) 'Men only' studies continue to be numerous in both journals (e.g. studies of mobility and stratification) but here gender is not treated as a topic or variable in its own right.

iii) Women are only infrequently the subject of analysis and where they do form the research subjects they are more likely than men to be problematized.

iv) Studies which are based upon samples of men and women are more numerous in the American journal; moreover, direct comparisons and the use of gender as a variable are more likely to be discovered in the ASR.

v) Contrary to what might be expected there do not appear to be any clear trends towards an increasing recognition of gender as a key variable over this period.

Matthews' fears about the possible over use or abuse of gender are hardly supported by this examination of two key journals.

De-constructing gender

If it is important to retain, perhaps even increase, the use of gender as a key variable and yet also to avoid reification or importing taken-for-granted stereotypes, what is the solution? What is proposed here is a variety of ways of de-constructing gender, maintaining gender as a key variable while remaining alert to its complex and composite nature and to the sources of overlaps between genders. This may allow for more flexibility than simple dichotomies.

1 In the first place it may be argued that gender consists of a set of various kinship or family identities. These would include, in our society, daughter/son, mother/father, wife/husband, sister/brother, aunt/uncle. In other cultures more distant identities such as mother's brother, father's sister may be important. Also included here would be quasi and fictive

kinship designations such as 'going for brothers' (Liebow, 1967) and co-parent, *compadre* relationships in Latin American cultures (Mintz and Wolf, 1967).

To be labelled 'man' or 'woman' is, among many other things, to be attributed with at least one of these particular gender-anchored identities. If it be correct to argue that the potentially reificatory uses of terms such as 'marriage' and 'family' should be constructed in order to reveal the gender fault-lines that run through them (Bernard, 1973; Thorne and Yallom, 1982) so it may be equally important to avoid the potentially reificatory use of gender identities by locating them in family and kinship structures. Bernard's own argument could indeed be reworked to suggest that it is not enough to use the terms 'men' and 'women' in order to compare different incidences of reported symptoms but to break these down according to marital status and employment status (ibid.). Bernard was, of course, following lines of investigation suggested by Durkheim when he argued that gross comparisons of men and women were not enough in the study of suicide; marital and parental status were also of key importance (Durkheim, 1952). More recently, Reiss has argued that sexual permissiveness (in terms of attitudes) varies not simply in terms of factors such as gender but also in the family life cycle, with parents being less permissive than young children or unmarried adults (Reiss, 1967).

2 Cross-cutting variables. Another way of decomposing gender is to see how it interacts with the other kinds of variables such as age, generation and social class. It is well known for example, that gender differentiation is less marked among infants than among childen in many societies (Barry, Bacon and Child in Lee and Stewart, 1976, pp. 219–20). Apart from some of the more obvious distinctions in terms of age and social class (and perhaps religion, ethnicity, etc.) there are some less obvious variables such as social network. Recently, for example, Brannen and Collard have suggested that social network is an important intervening variable, interacting with gender in such questions as deciding to seek help for marital problems, attitudes to disclosure and so on (Brannen and Collard, 1982). There are many recorded examples of apparent gender differences that almost disappear when other variables, especially age, are taken into account. Political conservatism (voting labour or conservative) may lose

any slight association with gender when age (or is it generation?) is taken into account. Edgell and Duke, examining
attitudes of men and women to cuts in social services, found
that factors such as employment status, sector of employment and union membership were more important factors
than simple gender and consequently, they called into question, once again, the myth of the passive female workers
(Edgell and Duke, 1983).

The examination of the interaction between gender and
other variables could have a variety of possible outcomes.
The de-construction of gender through cross-cutting variables may help to suggest the circumstances under which
gender becomes crucial and may serve as a corrective against
a catch-all use of gender as a source of analysis. In most
cases, however, the situation will not be so clear cut, and
gender and (say class) will interact to form a new status that
has elements of both but which is not reducible to either.
Ethnographic studies of the workplace provide several good
accounts of the strictly interactive character of class and gender (Gamarnikow et al., 1983a; Pollert, 1981; Purcell, 1982).

3 Interactive variables. The tendency has been to treat gender
as an independent variable. More detailed sociological work,
particularly of an ethnographic kind, may suggest that gender (in common with some of the other characteristics) is a
latent variable, exaggerated in some cases and relatively
muted in others. Kanter, for example, has shown the importance of numbers in influencing gender relations within organizations (Kanter, 1977). How men relate to women in
organizations will, to some extent, be dependent upon the
proportion of women at various levels within these organizations. 'Tokens' are more likely to be defined in terms of a
relatively limited range of stereotypical female roles. Within
a wide range of occupational and organizational settings,
gender image and gender presentation may be shaped by the
particular mix of elements within these contexts, mixes of
hierarchical positions, age and proportions of men and
women at various levels and in various age categories. One
kind of mix may give rise to sexual banter and harassment,
another kind of mix may give rise to female solidarity while
yet another may give rise to relatively easy and amicable
relations between the genders with sexual antagonism relatively muted.

4 Wider generalizations. One further way in which gender might be constructed is to place it in a more general context of relationships between dominants and subordinates (Oakley, 1981a, pp. 89–90). This would have the beneficial effect of maintaining the issue of gender inequality (which Oakley, among others, would wish to see as part of a definition of gender) while avoiding the reificatory tendencies in the use of gender alone. Goode, for example, has examined 'Why Men Resist'? placing his analysis in a wider framework of studies of domination, and seeking to examine the conditions under which dominants resistance might be expected (in Thorne and Yallom, 1982, pp. 131–50).

One possible objection to the line of argument so far would be that it has served to blunt the critical edge which the study of gender, inspired by the feminist movement, has brought to sociological enquiry. To treat gender as yet another variable – which may be modified or decomposed at will – is to run the risk of neutralizing it, of incorporating it into mainstream sociology. Clearly there are a variety of issues and dilemmas here. One is the extent to which gender is not simply a variable but, in a sense *the* variable, i.e. the major cleavage within society. The theoretical debates around the nature of patriarchy focus precisely on this question and have come up with a variety of solutions. The dilemma which relates to this is whether the emphasis on gender leads to the adoption of an essentialist position, one which posits an absolute opposition between men and women, masculine and feminine and which is rooted in differences which are outside any particular social formation or historical epoch (Coward, 1983). A paper in this context and of this length cannot help to resolve these issues. What clearly needs to be done is the recognition of the continuing and often overriding importance of gender inequalities while not obscuring the patterns of variation and overlap and, indeed, some of the sources of, and potential for, change.

I finish with some suggestions for researchers:

1 While it may, in some cases, not be possible to have other than the simple female/male dichotomy, the possibilities of using more subtle differentiations in terms of gender identification should at least be considered. We should begin to take seriously the recognition that we are dealing with

continua rather than dichotomies. Where the simple dichotomy is used, state clearly the process by which subjects are
assigned to each class.

2 Avoid using men, male and masculine as some kind of
yardstick against which they measure female 'deviations';
seek, where possible, to problematize men as well as women.

3 In surveys, experiments, etc. always state gender of subject.
Where one gender only is used, do not assume any wider
applicability.

4 In data analysis, where gender is used as an independent or
test variable, always note non-significant findings as well as
those deemed to be significant.

5 Do not assume gender to be a key variable in the analysis of
data and field material. Where possible, test against other
variables, seek to explore which aspect of gender is deemed to
be important and be alert, in the case of field-studies, to
interactional sources of variation.

6 Remember that the researcher has a gender as well; make
this explicit and attempt to assess how gender differences
and similarities may have influenced the research situation.

Notes

1 It would be difficult, and inappropriate here, to provide detailed
bibliographic support for this contention but for a very comprehensive discussion see Oakley (1981a) and for some recent discussions of specific issues see Gamarnikow et al. (1983a; 1983b).

2 Birdwhistell's threefold division in place of the simple sex/gender
difference would seem to maintain some of the difficulties associated with the latter, although he also argues that he does not imply
any functional priority in his terminology and that there is probably interaction between the 'levels'.

3 Illich's distinction between sex and gender owes little or nothing to
more established formulations; to take account of his contrast
between the regime of vernacular gender and the regime of economic sex would require a complete reformulation of this chapter.
The book, at the very least, is however an extremely valuable guide
to much of the relevant literature (Illich, 1983).

4 A more detailed analysis is available from the author: Department
of Sociology, University of Manchester, Manchester, England,
M13 9PL.

References

Acker, J. (1973), 'Women and social stratification: a case of intellectual sexism'. *American Journal of Sociology*, 78(4).

Bechofer, F. (1981), 'Substantive dogs and methodological tails: a question of fit'. *Sociology*, 15(1), 495–504.

Bernard, J. (1973), *The Future of Marriage*. (London, Souvenir Press).

Birdwhistell, R.L. (1976), 'Masculinity and femininity as display' in Lee & Stewart (eds), *Sex Differences: Cultural and Development Dimensions* (New York, Urizen Books).

Bogdan, R. (1974), *Being Different: The Autobiography of Jane Fry*. (New York, John Wiley).

Brake, M. (ed.) (1982), *Human Sexual Relations*. (Harmondsworth, Penguin).

Brannen, J. & **Collard, J.** (1982), *Marriages in Trouble*. (London, Tavistock).

Brim, O.G., Jnr. (1958), 'Family structure and sex-role learning by children'. *Sociometry*, XXI, 1–16. Reprinted in Bell, N.W. & Vogel, E.F. (eds) (1968), *A Modern Introduction to the Family*, Rev. Ed. (New York, The Free Press).

Children's Rights Workshop (1976), *Sexism in Children's Books*. (London, Writers & Readers).

Cloyd, J.W. (1977), 'The market-place bar: the inter-relationships between sex, situations and strategies in the pairing rituals of *Homo Ludens*'. In Warren (ed.), *Sexuality: Encounters, Identities and Relationships* (Beverly Hills, Sage).

Coward, R. (1983), *Patriarchal Precedents*. (London, Routledge & Kegan Paul).

Cunnison, S. (1983), 'Participation in local union organisation. School meals staff: a case study'. In Gamarnikow *et al.* (eds.) *Gender, Class and Work*. (London, Heinemann).

Douglas, J.D. (1976), *Investigative Social Research*. (Beverly Hills, Sage).

Douglas, J.D. *et al.* (1977), *The Nude Beach*. (Beverly Hills, Sage).

Durkheim, E. (1952, Eng. Ed.), *Suicide*. (London, Routledge & Kegan Paul).

Easlea, B. (1981), *Science & Sexual Oppression*. (London, Weidenfeld & Nicolson).

Easterday, L. *et al.* (1977), 'The making of a female researcher: role problems in fieldwork'. *Urban Life*, 6(3), 33–48. Reprinted in

Burgess, R.G. (ed.) (1982), *Field Research: A Sourcebook & Field Manual*. (London, Allen & Unwin), 62–7.

Edgell, S. & **Duke, V.** (1983), 'Gender and social policy: the impact of the public expenditure cuts and reactions to them'. *Journal of Social Policy*, 12(3), 357–78.

Edwards, S.M. (1981), *Female Sexuality and the Law*. (Oxford, Martin Robertson).

Eichler, M. (1980), *The Double Standard: A Feminist Critique of Feminist Social Science*. (New York, St. Martins Press).

Equal Opportunities Commission (1980), 'Women and government statistics'. *EOC Research Bulletin*, No. 4.

Feldberg, R.L. & **Glenn, E.N.** (1979), 'Male & female: job versus gender models in the sociology of work'. *Social Problems*, 26(5), 524–38.

Ferguson, M. (1982), *Forever Feminine: The Sociology of Women's Magazines*. (London, Heinemann).

Finch, J. (1984), ' "It's good to have someone to talk to": the ethics and politics of interviewing women' in Bell, C. & Roberts, H. (eds.), *Social Researching*. (London, Routledge & Kegan Paul).

Foucault, M. (1979), *History of Sexuality: Part 1*. (Harmondsworth, Penguin).

Frieze, I.H. *et. al.* (1981), *Women and Sex Roles*. (New York, Norton).

Gamarnikow, E. *et al.* (eds.) (1983 a), *Gender, Class and Work*. (London, Heinemann).

Gamarnikow, E. *et al* (eds.) (1983 b), *The Public and the Private*. (London, Heinemann).

Garfinkel, H. (1967), *Studies in Ethnomethodology*. (Englewood Cliffs, Prentice-Hall).

Garnsey, E. (1978), 'Women's work and theories of class stratification'. *Sociology*, 12(2), 223–45.

Gittus, E. (ed.) (1972), *Key Variables in Social Research*. (London, Heinemann).

Goffman, E. (1979), *Gender Advertisements*. (London, Macmillan).

Goldthorpe, J.H. & **Llewellyn, C.** (1977), 'Class mobility in modern Britain: three theses examined'. *Sociology*, 12(3), 257–88.

Goldthorpe, J.H. *et. al.* (1978), 'Trends in class mobility'. *Sociology*, 12(3), 441–68.

Graham, H. (1983), 'Do her answers fit his questions? Women and the survey method'. In Gamarnikow *et al.* (1983 b).

Hammersley, M. & **Atkinson, P.** (1983), *Ethnography: Principles in Practice*. (London, Tavistock).

Hanmer, J. & **Saunders, S.** (1983), 'Blowing the cover of the protective male: A community study of violence to women'. In Gamarnikow, E. *et al.* (eds) (1983 b), 28–46.
Humphreys, L. (1970), *Tearoom Trade.* (London, Duckworth).
Illich, I. (1983), *Gender,* (London, Boyars).
Kanter, R.M. (1977), *Men and Women of the Corporation.* (New York, Basic Books).
Kessler, S.J. & **McKenna, W.** (1978), *Gender: An Ethnomethodological Approach.* (New York, John Wiley).
Lee, P.C. & **Stewart, R.S.** (eds) (1976), *Sex Differences: Cultural and Development Dimensions.* (New York, Urizen Books).
Liebow, E. (1967), *Tally's Corner,* (Boston, Little, Brown).
Lupton, T. (1963), *On the Shop Floor.* (Oxford, Pergamon).
McKee, L. & **O'Brien, M.** (1983), 'Interviewing men: Taking gender seriously'. In Gamarnikow, E. *et al.* (eds.) (1983 b), 147–61
Martin, M.K. & **Voorhies, B.** (1975), *Female of the Species.* (Columbia University Press).
Matthews, S.W. (1982) 'Rethinking sociology through a feminist perspective. *American Sociologist,* 17, pp. 29–35.
Mead, M. (1935), *Sex & Temperament in Three Primitive Societies.* (New York, William Morrow).
Millum, T. (1975), *Images of Women: Advertising in Women's Magazines.* (London, Chatto & Windus).
Mintz, S.W. & **Wolf, E.R.** (1967), 'An analysis of ritual co-parenthood). In Potter, J.M. *et al.* (eds), *Peasant Society.* (Boston, Little, Brown).
Morgan, D. (1981), 'Men, masculinity and the process of sociological enquiry'. In Roberts, H. (ed.), *Doing Feminist Research.* (London, Routledge & Kegan Paul).
Murgatroyd, L. (1982), 'Gender and occupational stratification'. *Sociological Review,* 30(4), 574–602.
Neitz, M.J. (1982), 'Comment' (On Matthews). *American Sociologist,* 17, 37–8.
Oakley, A. (1981 a), *Subject Women.* (Oxford, Martin Robertson).
Oakley, A. (1981 b), 'Interviewing women: a contradiction in terms' in Roberts (ed.), 30–61.
Oakley, A. & **Oakley, R.** (1979), 'Sexism in official statistics'. In Irvine, J. *et al.* (eds.), *Demystifying Official Statistics.* (London, Pluto Press).
Payne, G. *et al.* (1977), 'A reappraisal of social mobility in Britain'. *Sociology,* 11(2), 289–310.

Payne, G. *et al.* (1983), 'Trends in female social mobility'. In Gamarnikow *et al.* (eds.) *Gender, Class and Work.* (London, Heinemann).

Platt, J. (1981), 'The social construction of positivism & its significance in British sociology'. In Abrams, P. *et al.* (eds), *Practice and Progress.* (London, Allen & Unwin), 73–87.

Pollert, A. (1981), *Girls, Wives, Factory Lives.* (London, Macmillan).

Ponse, B. (1978), *Identities in the Lesbian World.* (Westport, Connecticut, Greenwood Press).

Purcell, K. (1979), 'Militancy & acquiescence amongst women workers'. In Burman, S. (ed.), *Fit Work for Women.* (London, Croom Helm).

Purcell, K. (1982), 'Female manual workers, fatalism & the reinforcement of inequalities'. In Robbins, D. *et al.*, *Rethinking Social Inequality.* (Aldershot, Gower).

Randall, V. (1982), *Women and Politics.* (London, Macmillan).

Rasmussen, P.K. & **Kuhn, L.L.** (1977), 'The new masseuse: play for pay'. In Warren (ed.), *Sexuality: Encounters, Identities and Relationships.* (Beverly Hills, Sage).

Reid, I. and **Wormald, E.** (eds) (1982), *Sex Differences in Britain.* (London, Grant McIntyre).

Reiss, I.L. (1967), *The Social Context of Pre-Marital Permissiveness.* (New York, Holt, Rinehart & Winston).

Roberts, H. (ed.) (1981), *Doing Feminist Research.* (London, Routledge & Kegan Paul).

Rosenfield, R.A. (1978), 'Women's intergenerational occupational mobility'. *American Sociological Review*, 43, 36–46.

Sanday, P.R. (1981), *Female Power and Male Dominance.* Cambridge, Cambridge University Press).

Schofield, M. (1968), *The Sexual Behaviour of Young People.* (Harmondsworth, Penguin).

Stacey, M. (ed.) (1969), *Comparability in Social Research.* (London, Heinemann).

Stanley, L. & **Wise, S.** (1983), *Breaking Out: Feminist Consciousness and Feminist Research.* (London, Routledge & Kegan Paul).

Stenhouse, L. (1984), 'Library access, library use and user education in academic sixth forms: An autobiographical account'. In Burgess, R.G. (ed.), *The Research Process in Educational Settings; Ten Case Studies.* (Lewes, Falmer Press).

Stoll, C.S. (1974), *Female and Male.* (Dubuque, Iowa, William C. Brown Co.).

Thorne, C. & **Yallom, M.** (1982), *Rethinking the Family*. (London, Longmans).

Wakeford, J. (1981), 'From methods to practice: a critical note on the teaching of research practice to undergraduates'. *Sociology*, 15(4), 505–12.

Walby, S. (1983), 'Patriarchal structures: the case of unemployment'. In Gamarnikow, E. *et al.*, *Gender, Class and Work*. (London, Heinemann).

Warren C. (ed.) (1977), *Sexuality: Encounters, Identities and Relationships*. (Beverly Hills, Sage).

Wax, R.H. (1979), 'Gender and age in fieldwork and fieldwork education: No good thing is done by any man alone'. *Social Problems*, 26(5), 509–22.

Webb, M. (1982), 'The labour market'. In Reid and Wormald (eds), *Sex Differences in Britain*. (London, Grant McIntyre).

Wormald, E. (1982), 'Political participation'. In Reid and Wormald (eds), *Sex Differences in Britain* (London, Grant McIntyre).

Wright, E.O. *et al.* (1982), 'The American class structure'. *American Sociological Review* 47, 709–26.

Wright, E.O. & **Perrone, L.** (1977), 'Marxist class categories and income inequality'. *American Sociological Review*, 42, 32–55.

Race and ethnicity*   4

Martin Bulmer

'Race' and 'ethnicity' are among the most elusive terms to define clearly in social science research. Their use as key variables is correspondingly different. This chapter will focus upon the way in which these variables have been defined and measured in empirical social research, with briefer attention to the complex conceptual issues which involve not only sociology but social and physical anthropology, human biology, and the history of ideas.

'Ethnicity' is a more inclusive concept than race. An 'ethnic group' is a collectivity within a larger society having real or putative common ancestry, memories of a shared past, and a cultural focus on one or more symbolic elements which define the group's identity, such as kinship, religion, language, shared territory, nationality or physical appearance. Members of an ethnic group are conscious of belonging to the group (Petersen 1969a: 92–140; Schermerhorn 1978:12).

'Race' is a more narrowly defined concept referring to a distinct sub-system, membership of which is defined in biological terms. The general use of the term in English has ranged from a family line at one extreme to the entire species on the other ('the human race'). Physical anthropologists have used the term to denote a subpopulation that differs significantly from others in the frequency of one or more genes, with 'significantly' depending on the purpose of the investigator. The idea that an objective classification of mankind's major biological groupings into 'races' is possible or useful has, however, been progressively discredited. Though there are discernible differences in, for

* For comments on all or part of an earlier version, the author is indebted to Robert Burgess, to Sheila Patterson, Colin Brown and David Smith in London, to Mark Johnson and Malcolm Cross in Coventry, and to William Kruskal and Tom W. Smith in Chicago.

example, skin colour, head form or type of hair among members of the human race, no satisfactory general classification exists to which individuals may be assigned.

The use of the term 'race' in the context of social research refers to the way in which members of a society perceive differences between groups in that society and define the boundaries of such groups, taking into account physical characteristics such as skin colour. Such groups are not identified merely in terms of physical attributes but in terms of their situation in a particular society which makes them socially distinct groups in their own eyes and in the eyes of others. Robert Park's classic definition is an excellent summary:

> Race relations are the relations existing between peoples distinguished by marks of racial descent, particularly when these racial differences enter into the consciousness of the individuals and groups so distinguished, and by doing so determine in each case the individual's conception of himself as well as his status in the community. Thus, anything that intensifies race consciousness; anything, particularly if it is a permanent physical trait, that increases an individual's visibility and by doing so makes more obvious his identity with a particular ethnic unit or genetic group, tends to create or maintain the conditions under which race relations, as here defined, may be said to exist (Park 1950:81).

Both 'ethnicity' and 'race' are variables defined with reference to their subjectively meaningful properties within a particular society. In contrast to social class, where objective definition in terms of occupation or income, and subjective class identification, are separable dimensions, 'ethnicity' and 'race' are socially defined in terms of their meaning for actors. One consequence of this is that the classification used varies from society to society. The socially meaningful distinctions used to differentiate between ethnic groups in Canada or the United States, and between racial groups in the West Indies, South Africa and Britain are all different from each other; and are a social product of the society in which they are used. This is most obvious in the case of racial classification in South Africa (notably in the notorious Population Registration Act) and of French and English ethnic identification in Canada, but is true of all such classifications.

The difficulties of evolving a consistent classification in Britain in part reflect changing historical circumstances and in part the problems of devising consistent classificatory variables defined in terms of subjective meaning. The discussion in the rest of this chapter is concerned primarily with race. There are good discussions of the measurement of ethnicity by Smith (1980a) and Cohen (1981), and a number of significant studies. The definitional and research problems in using race as a variable are, however, more acute.

Concept and indicator

The context in which race has been used as a variable in empirical research has changed over the last generation. Early studies of race relations in Britain were carried out within an anthropological tradition which focused on the small scale. Such theory as was used tended to be of a functionalist variety. As large-scale migration from the Caribbean and the Indian sub-continent gathered pace in the 1950s and 1960s, the focus shifted to the processes of immigration and the adaptation to the host society. Patterson's (1963) model of accommodation, pluralistic integration and assimilation, for example, drew on American and Israeli studies of immigrant and ethnic minority groups and adaptation. An analysis of these processes from a conflict perspective was provided by Rex and Moore's (1967) theory of 'housing classes' within an ecological analysis of the inner city. In the 1970s three strands were particularly apparent in the theories underpinning empirical research on race, a continuing concern with the consequences of immigration and settlement (e.g. Richmond 1973), an attempt to analyse British race relations within the wider framework of imperialism and class relations (Allen *et al.* 1977; Rex and Tomlinson 1979) and a growing interest in the situation of the second generation, black people who were born in Britain. By 1980, 'immigrant' was no longer a correct description of the black and Asian population of the UK

Some of the most sophisticated attempts to measure race as a variable have taken place in large-scale surveys for policy, and in these a change in focus is also apparent, from a preoccupation with the scale of black immigration and with the extent of racial discrimination, to a broader interest in racial disadvantage and the condition of black minority groups compared to the population at large. Politically, race and the measurement of race remains a contentious issue which arouses strong passions. In Britain, the value-laden penumbra is far stronger than in the case of, for example, social class or voluntary associations or religion (with the exception of Northern Ireland). The most extreme cases of conflict centring on race, ethnicity, religion and allied social cleavages affecting social research are to be found in the Third World. For example, in the Lebanon, no census has been possible at all in modern times (Bulmer and Warwick 1983:286). In India, Hindu-Muslim conflicts have been reflected in statistical and research controversy (Wright 1983).

Race as a variable in empirical research

The easiest way to appreciate some of the changes in conceptualization and measurement which have taken place is to examine major empirical studies. The discussion which follows considers seventeen such studies between 1948 and 1983, showing the diversity of approaches used and changes over time. The studies selected range from small scale qualitative to large scale quantitative inquiries, and two concern the Census, which is a special case but highly relevant nevertheless to the variable of race and ethnicity.

(a) Kenneth Little, *Negroes in Britain* (1948) was a study of 'the coloured population of a large Welsh seaport city (Cardiff), mainly made up of the families of African, West Indian and Arab seamen' (p.47). The majority of 'coloured folk' in the area were born there or came from the Commonwealth. Nationality data were therefore of little use.

(b) Michael Banton, *The Coloured Quarter* (1955) was a study of a dockland area of east London. Banton was concerned with 'West Indian and West African Negroes', whom he also refers to as 'coloured people' or 'immigrants' (pp.13–15). No precise definition of the variable is given, nor are census data used.

(c) Ruth Glass, *Newcomers* (1960) was a study of 'coloured migrants who have come from the British West Indies' (p.3). Glass, unusually among these early studies, was sensitive to the considerable terminological difficulties.

> Many of the words which have to be used because no others are available are highly ambiguous, emotionally loaded or simply wrong. They tend to have a dichotomous 'we' and 'they' connotation. The word 'colour' is an obvious example. The term 'British' has to be used when we mean 'local' people, though of course the West Indians are British, too. 'Migrant' is a defective substitute for the even less suitable

word 'immigrant'. The terms 'race', 'racial', or 'race relations' are worst of all: 'race' is not a scientifically valid category (Glass 1960:xiii).

Some of these difficulties were a product of history and of the recent abuse by the Nazis of anti-semitic racist doctrines. With the passage of time, these objections have lessened and it has proved possible to talk of the sociology of race relations, defined in the Parkian manner described earlier.

(d) Sheila Patterson, *Dark Strangers* (1963) was a study of West Indians in Brixton variously referred to as 'coloured people', 'immigrants' and 'West Indians' in the book. Data from the 1961 Census on country of birth were used as a reference point. The study stressed that the variables of recent immigration and 'strangeness' were more important for West Indians in Britain than that of 'race' (pp. 66, 385). 'Race' was seen in terms of 'colour', as a factor likely to intensify the 'strangeness' and to complicate and slow the process of accommodation. The changing character of nomenclature is exemplified by the author's retrospective comment:

> My terminology was that widely used in the majority society (including official sources) by most English informants, and by West Indian contacts. At this period 'coloured' generally meant West Indian. . . . 'Black' used by a white was usually hostile and none of my West Indian informants used it about themselves or liked it. . . . (Patterson 1983).

(e) John Rex and Robert Moore, *Race, Community and Conflict* (1967) was a study of West Indian, Pakistani and Irish immigrants in the Sparkbrook area of Birmingham. The focus of the study was the immigrant communities, whose members were defined in the sample survey in terms of nationality – whether Irish, Pakistani, Indian or West Indian (pp.287–92). Baseline data from the 1961 Census are quoted in terms of nationality (p.47) but appear to be based upon country of birth data. The theoretical sections of the study discuss race in sociological theory, but in the empirical material the term 'immigrant' is used.

(f) W.W. Daniel, *Racial Discrimination in England* (1968) was the first large-scale sociological study using sample survey methods. The study referred to 'coloured people, i.e. people with non-white skins and with their origins in the Caribbean, Africa, Asia and the Middle East' (p.9), and to 'the Commonwealth coloured immigrant population' (p.9). The survey sought to establish the extent of racial discrimination in Britain, and as part of it talked 'to members of minority groups who are the potential victims of any such discrimination and asking them about their experiences' (p.19). In this survey about 'Problems of Immigrants in Britain', respondents were asked in what country they were born (precoded Jamaica/other West Indies/ India/East Pakistan/West Pakistan/Cyprus/Other (state)) and the month and year they came to Britain. Instructions to interviewers made clear that the survey was concerned with certain *countries of origin*.

(g) Anthony Richmond, *Migration and Race Relations in an English City* (1973) was a study carried out in the St. Paul-Montpelier area of Bristol. A comparison was made between native-born residents, white (mainly Irish) immigrants and 'coloured immigrants'. Baseline data was drawn from the 1951, 1961 and 1966 Census country of birth tables, though the author noted that such data tended to be a misleading criterion where racial or cultural attributes were concerned (p.35). A local enumeration carried out in 1965 used country of birth, coupled with parents' country of birth for schoolchildren, as an indicator of race.

(h) Daniel Lawrence, *Black Migrants, White Natives* (1974) was based on a sample survey of two areas of high immigrant concentration in Nottingham. An enumeration of 2,436 male voters in 150 streets yielded 291 'coloured immigrants', half of whom were selected for interview. The study was concerned with 'coloured Commonwealth immigrants', with equal weight given to each of the three elements. All the respondents were adults born in the West Indies, India or Pakistan.

(i) David Smith, *The Facts of Racial Disadvantage* (1976) was a national survey intended to follow the earlier one by W.W. Daniel, but considerably larger and more extensive in coverage. A complex two-phase sample design resulted in a sample representative of areas including three quarters of the population of West Indian, Indian and Pakistani origin. (The sample excluded areas of low concentration.) West Indians were defined as people born in the West Indies or Guyana, or (if born in Britain) people whose families originally came from there. African Asians were defined as people who were racially Asian and either were born in Africa or were living there immediately before coming to Britain, or belonged to families who were originally

African Asians. Indians and Pakistanis were defined as people who were not African Asians and were born in India or Pakistan or who belonged to families which originally came from India or Pakistan. 'Asian' was used to refer only to people originating from the Indian sub-continent. Other Asian groups such as Chinese or Japanese were not included in the sample. People of mixed race were included. 'The criterion used is whether people regard themselves as being black or brown, or whether they look black or brown to others' (p.3). Asian respondents were also classified by their religion. The text of the report refers mainly to 'Asians' and 'West Indians', with occasional uses of the term 'immigrant' where respondents were born abroad and more frequent use of 'racial minority'.

(j) Patricia Jefferey, *Migrants and Refugees* (1976) was a study of Muslim and Christian Pakistani families in Bristol by a social anthropologist using participant observation methods. Data on country of birth in the 1971 Census were used.

(k) Sheila Allen, Stuart Bentley and Joanna Bornat, *Work, Race and Immigration* (1977). This study of race and employment in Bradford included as part of the study a structured interview with Indian, Pakistani and West Indian workers, who were identified in terms of their origin. One question asked: 'Where are you from: (Precodes: India/Pakistan East/Pakistan West/West Indies/Other (specify))'. The authors were unusually explicit about the terminological problems. During the survey, the research team referred to 'Commonwealth citizens' or 'Commonwealth immigrants' or 'Indians, Pakistanis and West Indians'.

> In come cases, however, it is necessary to use a collective term when discussing them in relation to white groups. All three terms in most common use – immigrants, coloured people and black people – present difficulties. Changes have taken place in the *consciousness* of the relationship between the different ethnic groups which is reflected in the terms used by and about them. . . . The term 'black' or 'black people' has not gained a dominant position. . . . We have in general retained the term 'coloured' though we see this as a temporary expedient which in the future may no longer seem applicable, much less acceptable, to the people whom it purports to describe. . . . The term 'immigrant' has come to have a pejorative meaning applied indiscriminately to natives of Britain other than whites (Allen *et al.* 1977:vi).

(1) *The National Dwelling and Housing Survey* (1978) was an extremely large national sample survey of 375,000 households carried out in 1976 following the cancellation of the 1976 Census of Population as an economy measure. The interview was conducted with one respondent per household (normally the head) who was asked the following question about themselves and all other members of the household (the question was copied from the OPCS work described in the next section):

> To which of the groups listed on this card do you consider that . . . belongs? (handing respondent a card, which read:) 01 White/02 West Indian/03 Indian/04 Pakistani/05 Bangladeshi/06 Chinese/07 Turkish/08 Other Asian/09 African/10 Arab/11 Other (give details).

In the published report, housing conditions were analysed by the ethnic group of the head of household, grouped into White/West Indian/African/Indian, Pakistani or Bangladeshi/Other.

(m) *The 1979 Haringey Test Census.* In anticipation of the 1981 British Census of Population, OPCS Social Survey Division undertook methodological development work to try to devise an acceptable census question on race and ethnicity. This began in 1975 and culminated in the 1979 Test Census, a voluntary enumeration covering the entire London Borough of Haringey. (For a full account see Sillitoe 1978; OPCS 1978a,b,c; 1981.) The Haringey Test Census incorporated a split-half design. Half of all schedules included questions asked in the 1971 Census of Poplation about country of birth and country of birth of father and of mother. The other half included a modification of the direct question on race and ethnicity which read:

> 11 Racial or ethnic group. Please tick the appropriate box to show the racial or ethnic group to which the person belongs. If the person was born in the United Kingdom of West Indian, African, Asian, Chinese or 'Other European' descent, please tick one of the boxes numbered 2 to 10 to show the group from which the person was descended.
> The boxes read: 1 English, Welsh, Scottish or Irish/2 Other European/3 West Indian or Guyanese/4 African/5 Indian/6 Pakistani/7 Bangladeshi/8 Arab/9 Chinese/10 Any *other* racial or ethnic group, or if of mixed racial or ethnic descent (please describe below).

In the event, neither the direct question nor a question on parents' country of birth was included in the 1981 Census of Population, which only asked each person's country of birth. There were several reasons for this decision. The simplest explanation is that reductions in government expenditure dictated a shorter schedule and fewer questions. The stormy experience of the Haringey Test showed how public opinion could be inflamed on the issue, potentially increasing non-cooperation and jeopardizing the whole operation. It was argued that existing sources, mainly sample surveys, were an adequate alternative. And professional opinion was quite divided on the merits of the inclusion of a race question, several leading sociologists arguing publicly against its inclusion (House of Commons Home Affairs Committee 1983a:v; Bulmer 1980:16; Thompson and Lewis 1983).

(n) Ken Pryce, *Endless Pressure* (1979) was a study of West Indian life-styles in Bristol, concerned with working class people of Jamaican origin, a high proportion of them coming from the parish of St. Thomas in Jamaica. The research subjects are referred to throughout as 'West Indians' or 'Jamaicans', whether born in the West Indies or in Britain.

(o) John Rex and Sally Tomlinson, *Colonial Immigrants in a British City* (1979) and Peter Ratcliffe, *Racism and Reaction* (1981) both report the same study of the Handsworth area of Birmingham. In the monographs, the terms 'West Indian' and 'Asian' are generally used, with occasional use of 'immigrant' or 'immigrant groups' where this is a correct description, and of 'blacks'. As a general term in comparisons of Asians, West Indians and British, 'ethnic group' is used. The main survey component of the study identified respondents in terms of the country of birth of the head of household, which was classified by the interviewer, using a precode into one of: West Indies/Indian sub-continent/Other 'Asian'/Great Britain/Elsewhere.

(p) Colin Brown, *1981 National PSI Sample Survey of Racial Minorities* (see Brown 1984). This study was carried out to follow those of Daniel (f) and Smith (i) using two-phase sampling procedure to identify members of racial minorities. Unlike the 1974 survey, low concentration areas were included to make the sample nationally representative. Door-to-door enumeration was used in high concentration areas, a new method of 'focussed enumeration' in medium and low concentration areas (cf. Brown and Ritchie 1981). The questions used at the first phase were almost identical to those used by Smith in 1974. At the first phase the interviewer called at an address and asked if there was anyone in the household who was of West Indian or Asian origin. If there was a positive answer, or if a household member looked to the interviewer to be Asian or West Indian, eleven more detailed questions were asked about each member of the household, including:

7(a)   In which country was he/she born (precoded: GB or UK/ West Indies or Guyana/India/Pakistan or Bangladesh/ Africa/Other/DK or NA).

(There was a further question about the family's country of origin if the answer was GB or UK/Africa/Other.) Asian respondents were then asked two further questions:

8   What language does he/she speak most often at home?
9   What other languages does he/she speak fluently? each with the precodes: English/Urdu/Punjabi/Gujerati/Hindi/Other /DK or NA.

At the second, later, phase of the survey, when 5,000 individuals from 3,000 households were interviewed by racially-matched interviewers, speaking if necessary the appropriate Indian language, respondents were asked:

1(a)   In what country were you born, and (if born in the UK)
1(b)   In what country were your parents born, precoded for respondent, and for mother and father: West Indies or Guyana/India/(West) Pakistan/Bangladesh and E.Pakistan /Kenya/Uganda/Tanzania/Zambia/Malawi/Other African/ UK/other country.

All respondents not born in the UK were then asked:

2(a)   In the three months before *you* came to Britain, in which country did you live? Interviewers were instructed to obtain and write in an exact description of country and district and in addition ring one of the following precodes if appropriate:
Caribbean Barbados/Guyana or Belize/Jamaica/Trinidad-Tobago/other Caribbean
(West) Pakistan New Frontier/Mirpur and other Kashmir/ Punjab/Karachi/other (W) Pakistan
Bangladesh/E. Pakistan Border with Assam or Sylhet/Maritime Assam/other Bangladesh
India Punjab/Gujerat/other India

> *Africa*   Kenya/Uganda/Tanzania/Zambia/Malawi/other Africa.
> *Other country*

2(b)   In what month and year did you move to Britain (precoded separately for month and year).

The definitions of 'West Indian', 'Indian', 'Pakistani' or 'African Asian' were the same as those used by Smith in (i) (Brown 1984).

(q) Malcolm Cross and Mark Johnson, *S.S.R.C. Ethnic Relations Unit Urban Institutions Survey* (1983/4). This regional sample survey covered 8,000 addresses selected from the electoral register (for detail, see Johnson and Cross, 1984, pp. 26–30). During the short contact interview, the chief wage earner or head of household was asked for various information about themselves and all other members of the household. In the course of these questions, they were handed a card which read:

> Please say from which of the following groups each member of the household is *descended*
> English/Scottish/Welsh
> Indian/Pakistani/Bangladeshi/Sri Lankan (Asian)
> Irish
> West Indian/African (Afro-Caribbean)
> Other European
> Other (Please state)

The interviewer recorded the responses as one of six precodes on the interview schedule.

If the chief wage earner or head of household was Asian, these further questions were asked:

> 6a What language is spoken most often in your home? (one code only)
> 6b What other languages (does the main wage earner/do you) speak fluently? (more than one code may be ringed)
> 6c And what other languages (does the housewife/do you) speak fluently? (more than one code may be ringed).

For each the same precodes were used, English/Urdu/Punjabi/Gujerati/Hindi/Bengali/Other (state)/No others.

(r) House of Commons Immigration and Race Relations Sub-

Committee, *Ethnic and Racial Questions in the Census* (1983a,b,c). Continuing public discussion of the merits of ethnic and racial questions in the census led a select committee of MPs to consider the matter in 1982/83. After taking evidence from government, members of the black community and academic social scientists, they concluded that census questions on the subject should be asked, and suggested the form which such a question should take. It was the following:

> *Racial Discrimination and Disadvantage.* The answers to these questions will help Government, local authorities, employers and other organisations to identify racial discrimination and disadvantage, to develop more effective policies against them, and to monitor the progress of these policies.

a. Are you white?   Yes/no
b. Are you black?   Yes/no
   If you *are* black, are you   British/West Indian/African/Other (tick as many boxes as apply)
c. Are you of Asian origin?   Yes/no
   If *yes*, are you British/Indian/Pakistani/Bangladeshi/West Indian/Chinese/Vietnamese/Other (tick as many boxes as apply)
d. Other groups.
   Are you   Mixed race/Arab/Greek Cypriot/Turkish Cypriot/ None of these (tick *one* box)

In addition, the inclusion of a question on religion for Southern Asian groups only was recommended, distinguishing between Hindi (sic), Sikh and Muslim. A question on language should also be included, encompassing not only languages other than English (which should include Hindi, Gujerati, Urdu, Bengali, and Punjabi) but *also* English-speaking ability. Experience of US, Canadian and Australian censuses could be drawn on to devise a suitable question (cf. Shryock and Siegel 1975:252–82; Richmond 1980).

  These proposed questions have not been tested in empirical research, but are included here as an important contribution to the continuing search for a satisfactory indicator of race and ethnicity in social investigation.

Changing terminology and conceptualization

The seventeen studies make clear that there is no uniformity either in the way in which race is conceptualized nor in how it is measured. By contrast with social class, there is neither an available set of classic theoretic definitions, nor an operational handbook such as the OPCS *Classification of Occupations*. Instead, there is very considerable diversity, though an intuitive sense of being concerned with a common phenomenon.

Changes in terminology over time reflect both historical development and the changing politics of 'race' in Britain. Since the late 1950s black immigration to Britain and its social effects has been a matter of continuing political debate. Just as the terminology used (or not used) in early studies was influenced by the aftermath of Nazism, that in later studies was affected by the changing political climate of the times. Diversity was the result. This diversity is apparent in variations in terminology and underlying conceptualization, in turn probably affecting question response. Apparently minor differences in wording can loom large in people's minds. One group of terms relate to physical attributes. The use of 'negro', in contrast to the United States, has been rare; the only studies to use it were Little and Banton. 'Coloured' has been more widely used, though with some unease (cf. Patterson 1963:13; Allen *et al.*, 1977).

In recent years the term has come to have pejorative overtones, being replaced much more widely by 'black'. The term 'black', however, does not necessarily identify all racial or ethnic groups in Britain. It may be an accurate way of typifying Afro-Caribbean, but does it apply to Indians and Pakistanis, to Chinese or to Arabs? There has been resistance among some racial minorities to its use, leading to terminology such as 'black and Asian' or 'black and brown' to describe the main minority groups. But 'brown' is an ambiguous term too, so that attempts to provide a consistent terminology in terms of colour have not been very successful. 'Black' remains politically resonant for people of West Indian origin, and one way of identifying second generation British-born West Indians is as 'Black British'.

At one period the term 'immigrant' was ubiquitous both in sociological and official studies of racial minorities. (For an example of the latter, see Moser, 1972.) This reflected the recency of the mass movement of West Indians, Indians, Pakistanis and later East African Asians to Britain, and for a period was an accurate description. 'Immigrant' is also widely used in colloquial English as a synonym for members of racial minorities, and as such has acquired pejorative overtones. The political climate of race relations in Britain, with its obsession with numbers of immigrants and the continual linking of government action to limit entry with legislation to 'improve' race relations, largely ignores the fact that almost half of the black and Asian population are now British-born; 'race' and 'immigrant' no longer coincide. The term has therefore fallen from use in sociology. 'Migrant' continues to be used, for example, by Richmond (1973), Watson (1975) and Jeffery (1976) where the focus is specifically upon the process of migration and the connections between the country of origin and the country of settlement. As a way of designating racial minorities, however, 'migrant' is not satisfactory.

The most common terminology in the studies reviewed is a designate race in terms of area of origin, 'West Indian', 'Indian', 'Pakistani', 'African Asian' and so on. This involves the assumption that the composition of such groups is relatively homogeneous and that, in the case of Indians and Pakistanis, they do not include white Europeans with a substantial connection to those countries. These limits are illustrated by the use of 'African' unqualified, which could refer to black Africans, Africans of Asian descent, or white Africans. For some years, area of origin operated as a relatively satisfactory proxy for race, rather in the way that occupation has done for social class. The official compilation of demographic data about the population of 'New Commonwealth and Pakistani ethnic origin' (Moser 1972; OPCS 1975; OPCS 1977) was one example of this. The studies of Glass (1960), Daniel (1968) and Smith (1976) all embodied this approach in terms of area of origin.

More recently a shift has occurred to an emphasis on descent which extends the concept beyond one of a simple equation between racial identification and area of origin. In part this has occurred because members of the second and third generation may prefer to identify themselves in terms such as 'black British' rather than 'West Indian' or 'Asian'. It also links to the use of the terms 'racial group' or 'ethnic group', which explicitly acknowledges the existence of groups recognized as races in society. This shift from oblique to direct terminology is an important one and one likely to be carried further in the future. The main problem is to develop a terminology which is consistent and meaningful to respondents, a problem which OPCS methodological work for the 1981 Census and the House of Commons Select Committee have been struggling with. It is interesting to note that in the question on race asked in the 1980 US Census the wording 'race or colour' (used in 1970) was dropped, and the question simply asked: 'Is this person? White/Black or Negro/Japanese/Chinese/Filipino/

Korean/Vietnamese/Indian (American) (print tribe)/Asian Indian/
Hawaiian/Guamanian/Samoan/Eskimo/Aleut/Other (specify) (Bulmer 1983:140–1). This US question also demonstrates the points made
earlier that the classification used is specific to a particular society.

The adequacy of different indicators of race in empirical research

Choice of indicator and its embodiment in particular questions asked
of respondents has to be judged not only in terms of conceptual
criteria but also in terms of the reliability and validity of the resulting
data. In the field of race, the political acceptability of asking particular questions is also a factor to be considered.

One possible indication of race might be a person's legal status. In
practice this does not yield reliable or valid data, and is also open to
political objections. The 1961 Census included a question on
nationality which was answered so poorly that the data were un-
usable. British nationality law is exceptionally complex, as well as
politically contentious, and attempts to use this as an indicator are
best avoided. Questions on immigration status also yield data of
doubtful value, and are of exceptional political sensitivity, since they
link directly to political scares about numbers of immigrants and
right-wing calls for repatriation policies. In theory questions about
passport held might yield a more reliable response. This too should be
avoided since it is a matter of great political sensitivity, and moreover
does not yield a valid measure of race, since there is no necessary
connection between passport held and ethnic origin. In general, legal
status is a poor guide to race and ethnicity.

The standard method of identifying members of racial minorities in
the early years of mass Commonwealth immigration was by recording country of birth. Much of the quantitative data in standard
sources such as Rose (1969) and the Runnymede Trust (1980) use a
variable of this kind. Country of birth data are generally thought to be
of high reliability since the information is of a factual kind known to
most respondents and not liable to distortion, although a caveat
should be entered about various distortions which may occur in
distinguishing between people coming from India, Pakistan and
Bangladesh on the sub-continent.

The validity of country of birth data is more problematical. Its
value as a proxy indicator for race or ethnicity depends on the

assumptions that one makes, for example that all persons born in the West Indies are black. Such assumptions are less sound for persons born in India or Pakistan, a small proportion of whom are white Europeans whose families were in the civil service, army or business on the sub-continent. Nor does it permit separate identification of African Asians.

The main limitation of country of birth data, however, is that as more and more second and third generation members of racial minorities are born in Britain, such a question no longer validly identifies the variable it is used to measure. For this reason, the 1971 Census also included a question on parents' country of birth, which was used in conjunction with country of birth to produce demographic estimates of the size of the population of 'New Commonwealth (NCW) ethnic origin'. Various groups were defined as NCW ethnic origin, for example, people born in Britain with both parents born in the NCW. Non-response on this question was approximately 3 per cent, indicating a lower level of reliability than country of birth. Despite political objections at the time of the 1971 Census, and some technical limitations, during the 1970s parents' country of birth provided a reasonably good indicator of the ethnicity of members of a family or household, and was used by Richmond (1973), Smith (1976), Rex and Tomlinson (1979) and Ratcliffe (1981). The ethnicity of British-born children was inferred from that of their parents. In the 1980s, with the birth of third-generation black Britons, this approach will be increasingly limited (cf. OPCS 1978a, pp.35–43). It was recognition of this that led to the OPCS methodological work on the Census question. A further defect of country of birth and parents' country of birth data is that inferring the ethnicity of those of mixed origin (e.g. one parent born NCW, one parent born UK) is particularly hazardous, telling one little about the proportion of the population of mixed racial origin.

Recognition of these deficiencies led in several different directions. A few attempts have been made to infer ethnicity from people's names on the electoral register. While persons of Indian and Pakistani origin may be readily identifiable, those of West Indian origin are not, as they do not have distinctive names. It is not, therefore, an effective method. A different approach has been the direct observation of the colour of the respondent, used in the first phase of the Smith and Brown PSI survey as a supplementary procedure for identifying members of racial minorities, and as a general method in the OPCS General Household Survey. In the latter, the interviewer records whether the respondent is 'white' or 'coloured', and data are published broken down on this variable. It relies entirely on the judgment of the interviewer and produces very rough and ready results. The dichotomous classification does not permit important differences between different minorities (such as West Indians and Asians) to be identified. The classification of people of Maltese, Cypriot, or Arab descent or of mixed origin is particularly unclear. Respondents are given no opportunity to say how they identify themselves. As a method, it is not recommended. A third approach, in terms of language spoken, may serve to identify first-generation members of Asian minorities, but does not identify first-generation West Indian or West African immigrants, who come from English-speaking countries, or second or later-generation children of any origin, unless a different language is spoken in the home. It may, however, be a valuable subsidiary question to ask respondents of Asian origin.

The deficiencies of these various measures have led to the development of different forms of a direct question asking the respondent to identify themselves in terms of race and ethnicity. Such questions have been used successfully in other countries' censuses (Bulmer 1980) and in surveys in Britain. Their prospective use in future British censuses is highly contentious, and was recently the subject of the attention of the House of Commons Home Affairs Committee (1983a,b,c). They received evidence from, among others, a number of social scientists, who were divided in their views of the scientific validity and political desirability of such a question. Members of the S.S.R.C. Ethnic Relations Research Unit, for example, were equally divided between those favouring and those opposing the question. The census poses special problems, and the use of such self-identification questions in surveys and smaller-scale inquiries has had fewer problems. The experience of the National Dwelling and Housing Survey in 1976 and the Cross-Johnson S.S.R.C. Ethnic Relations Unit study suggests that such a question can be successfully asked.

British evidence about the reliability of such a question is lacking. American evidence suggests that such questions provide a high degree of reliability for the identification of *black* ethnic minorities, with consistency in reporting race more than 90 per cent from one occasion to another (Johnson 1974). Less satisfactory results for members of white ethnic groups have been achieved, suggesting that the boundaries of group membership are less sharply defined in the absence of an attribute such as skin colour (Petersen 1979; Smith 1980a). It is also possible that members of different racial and ethnic groups identify more or less strongly with their own particular group. 'Chinese' may identify in terms of appearance and descent more strongly as members of a single group (cf. Clammer 1982:128–9) than 'Indians' who tend to think of themselves in terms of region of origin or religious affiliation. At the time of writing, 1983, the use of such questions is still at an early stage in Britain and no firm recommendations can be made for the best type of question. The questions used in (1), (m), (q) and (v) above may be consulted. One particular problem is whether to include a category such as 'black British' which enables second and third generation minority group members to identify themselves in terms of colour. The House of Commons Home Affairs Committee (1983a:xxxii) divides respondents into 'white', 'black', 'Asians' and 'other', but whether this is adequate is doubtful. Their injunction to tick more than one box in answer to certain questions is also contrary to the usual canons of classification and measurement. It may be that such a difficult variable requires exceptions to the rules, but the case has not been clearly made out.

What is clearly needed is more methodological research into racial and ethnic identification. This should include unstructured group discussions with members of ethnic minorities as a start, but should proceed to more rigorous experimental comparisons with a test/retest design, using interpenetrating or split sampling to try out various modes of obtaining the data including questions on country of birth and parents' country of birth, religion, subjective identification, interviewer observation, etc. The nature and intensity of people's identification needs to be probed, perhaps using the twenty-statement 'who am I?' test. The test/retest reliabilities and multiform comparisons would enable one to see which type of question seemed most effective and to estimate reliabilities.

In the writer's view, the route to the valid measurement of race in the 1980s and beyond lies in some form of self-assessment question, in line with the subjectivity of the phenomenon as defined in theoretical terms. Race and ethnicity are in the last resort subjective phenomena (cf. Smith 1980b) though this fact greatly complicates their empirical study.

Conclusions

No very definite conclusions are possible, other than that race and ethnicity as variables pose particularly difficult problems for the social investigator. 'Of all basic background variables, ethnicity is probably the most difficult to measure' (Smith 1982:18) and the same is true of race. Some indication of the variability both in conceptualization and measurement has been given in this chapter. The discussion has focused upon quantitative studies because these have dealt with the problem explicitly in the formulation of survey questions. The qualitative studies tend to gloss over problems of definition and measurement to a greater extent. Race and ethnicity, unlike social class, lack clear objective criteria in terms of which they can be measured, though nativity or country of origin of one's family is of partial use in this respect. Unlike sex and gender, on the other hand, which is also a politically contentious area of research with an emotive penumbra, classification and measurement is complex. Though apparently 'black' and 'white' may seem as clear cut as 'female' and 'male', in reality they are not. The social and subjective element in their definition is far greater, and the element of arbitrariness in any final classification not insignificant (Kruskal 1981:512–13).

> One of the most frequent routes from theory to research is the selection of an indicator appropriately paired with a concept. . . . (T)he unwary researcher easily falls into traps hidden in the deceptively simple definitions of such designations as 'race' . . . There is no uniquely correct way to define terms like these. . . Only painstaking care can help one avoid such traps . . . (But) there is no reason to deduce from the complexity of an ethnic structure that no classification is feasible (Petersen 1969b:873, 875).

The struggle for a satisfactory classification will continue, made more necessary by the general recognition that Britain is now, as it was not in 1950, a multi-ethnic society whose racial minorities are preponderantly indigenous and British.

References

Allen, S., Bentley, S. and **Bornat, J.** (1977), *Work, Race and Immigration*, Bradford, Yorks., University of Bradford.

Banton, M. (1955), *The Coloured Quarter: negro immigrants in an English city*, London, Cape.

Brown, C. (1984) *Black and White Britain*, London, Heinemann.

Brown, C. and **Ritchie, J.** (1981), *Focussed Enumeration: the development of a method for sampling ethnic minority groups*, London, P.S.I. and S.C.P.R. mimeo).

Bulmer, M. (1980), 'On the feasibility of identifying "race" and "ethnicity" in censuses and surveys', *New Community* 8(1), (Spring-Summer), pp.3–16.

Bulmer, M. (1983), 'Memorandum', in House of Commons Home Affairs Committee (1983c), vol. III, pp.138–45.

Bulmer, M. and **Warwick, D.P.** (eds) (1983), *Social Research in Developing Countries*, London, Wiley.

Clammer, J. (1982), 'The institutionalisation of ethnicity: the culture of ethnicity in Singapore', *Ethnic and Racial Studies* 5(2) (April):127–39.

Cohen, A. (1981), 'Variables in ethnicity', in Keyes, C. (ed.), *Ethnic Change*, Seattle, University of Washington Press, pp.307–31.

Daniel, W.W. (1968), *Racial Discrimination in England*, Harmondsworth, Penguin.

Glass, R., with **Pollins, H.** (1960), *The Newcomers: West Indians in London*, London, Allen & Unwin.

Gossett, T.F. (1963), *Race: the history of an idea in America*, Dallas, Southern Methodist University Press.

House of Commons Home Affairs Committee (1983a,b,c), *Ethnic and Racial Questions in the Census*, London, HMSO, House of Commons Paper HC 33–I, II and III, Session 1982–83, volume 1, Report; volume 2, Minutes of Evidence; volume 3, Appendices.

Jeffery, P. (1976), *Migrants and Refugees: Muslim and Christian Pakistani families in Bristol*, Cambridge, Cambridge University Press.

Johnson, C.E. (1974), 'Consistency of Reporting of Ethnic Origin in the Current Population Survey', Washington DC, US Bureau of the Census, Technical Paper no.31.

Johnson, M. and **Cross, M.** (1984), *Surveying Service Users in Multi-Racial Areas: the Methodology of the Urban Institutions Project* (University of Warwick, Centre for Research in Ethnic Relations, RVER Research Papers in Ethnic Relations No.2).

Kruskal, W. (1981), 'Statistics in Society: problems unsolved and unformulated', *Journal of the American Statistical Association* 76 (no.375): 505–15.

Lawrence, D. (1974), *Black Migrants, White Natives: a study of race relations in Nottingham*, Cambridge, Cambridge University Press.

Little, K. (1948), *Negroes in Britain: a study of racial relations in English society*, London, Routledge & Kegan Paul.

Moser, C.A. (1972), 'Statistics about immigrants: objectives, sources, methods and problems', *Social Trends* 3, London, HMSO, pp.20–30.

National Dwelling and Housing Survey Report (1978), London, HMSO, for the Department of the Environment.

OPCS(1975), 'Country of birth and colour', *Population Trends* 2:2–8.

OPCS (1977), 'New Commonwealth and Pakistani population estimates', *Population Trends* 9:4–7.

OPCS (1978a,b,c), *Ethnic Origins 1, Ethnic Origins 2, Ethnic Origins 3*, London, OPCS Information Branch.

OPCS (1981), *Ethnic Origins 4*, London, OPCS Information Branch.

Park, R.E. (1950), *Race and Culture*, Glencoe, III., The Free Press.

Patterson, S. (1963), *Dark Strangers: a study of West Indians in London*, Harmondsworth, Penguin.

Patterson, S. (1983), Personal communication.

Petersen, W. (1969a), *Population*, New York, Macmillan, second edition.

Petersen, W. (1969b), 'The classification of subnations in Hawaii: an essay in the sociology of knowledge', *American Sociological Review* 34:863–77.

Petersen, W. (1979), 'The protection of privacy and the United States Census', in M. Bulmer (ed.), *Censuses, Surveys and Privacy*, London, Macmillan, pp.176–83.

Petersen, W. (1982), 'Concepts of ethnicity', in W. Petersen *et al.*, *Concepts of Ethnicity*, Cambridge, Mass., The Belknap Press of Harvard University, pp.1–26.

Price, C. (1980), 'What's in a name: Australia ponders', *New Community* vol. 8 (1–2), pp.17–18.

Pryce, K. (1979), *Endless Pressure: a study of West Indian life-styles in Bristol*, Harmondsworth, Penguin.

Ratcliffe, P. (1981), *Racism and Reaction: a profile of Handsworth*, London, Routledge & Kegan Paul.

Rex, J. and **Moore, R.** (1967), *Race, Community and Conflict: a study of Sparkbrook*, London, Oxford University Press.

Rex, J. and **Tomlinson, S.** (1979), *Colonial Immigrants in a British City: a class analysis*, London, Routledge & Kegan Paul.

Richmond, A. (1973), *Migration and Race Relations in an English City: a study in Bristol*, London, Oxford University Press.

Richmond, A.H. (1980), 'Ethnic questions in the Canadian census', *New Community*, vol.8 (1–2), pp.19–24.

Rose, E.J.B. *et al.* (1969), *Colour and Citizenship: a report on British Race Relations*, London, Oxford University Press for the Institute of Race Relations.

Runnymede Trust and Radical Statistics Group (1980), *Britain's Black Population*, London, Heinemann.

Schermerhorn, R.A. (1978), *Comparative Ethnic Relations: a framework for theory and research*, Chicago, University of Chicago Press.

Shryock, H.S. and **Siegel, J.S.** (eds) (1975), *The Methods and Materials of Demography* (Washington DC: US Government Printing Office), volume 1.

Sillitoe, K.K. (1978), 'Ethnic origins: the search for a question', *Population Trends* 13, pp.25–30.

Smith, D.J. (1976), *The Facts of Racial Disadvantage: a national survey*, London, PEP Broadsheet no.560.

Smith, T.W. (1980a), 'Ethnic measurement and identification', *Ethnicity* 7:78–95.

Smith, T.W. (1980b), 'The subjectivity of ethnicity', National Opinion Research Center, University of Chicago, mimeo.

Smith, T.W. (1982), 'Problems in ethnic measurement: over-, under- and misidentification', National Opinion Research Center, University of Chicago, mimeo.

Thompson, J.H. and **Lewis, C.G.** (1983), 'Sources of statistics on ethnic minorities: a discussion', *Journal of the Royal Statistical Society A*, vol.146(2), pp.99–114.

Watson, J.L. (1975), *Emigration and the Chinese Lineage: the 'Mans' in Hong Kong and London*, Berkeley, University of California Press.

Wright, T.P. (1983), 'The ethnic numbers game in India: Hindu-Muslim conflicts over conversion, family planning, migration and the census', in W.C. McCready (ed.), *Culture, Ethnicity and Identity: current issues in research*, New York, Academic Press, pp.405–27.

Health and illness   5

Sally Macintyre

Introduction: health and illness as key variables

Viewed from a broad-ranging historical or cross-cultural perspective, health is obviously a key variable in human affairs. Our expectation of life; the incidence and prevalence of infectious killer diseases, debilitating parasitic disease, nutritional deficiency diseases, or chronic and degenerative diseases; and the mortality or morbidity associated with events such as childbirth, or with our patterns of living such as our occupation or residence: all these shape and set limits to social life. Modern western societies are very different from their predecessors in the middle ages, when plagues periodically ravaged Europe (Shrewsbury, 1970). Life in industrialized societies now differs markedly even from life in the nineteenth century, when many children were born per family but few survived into adult life, young adults died from diseases such as tuberculosis, the expectation of life was shorter, and women's shorter than men's because of the mortality and debility associated with childbirth (Wrigley, 1969 and 1972; Laslett, 1972; Anderson, 1971; Howe, 1972; see also Finch in this volume).

Similarly much of the Third World shows a pattern of health very different from industrialized countries. There is a high prevalence of infectious diseases (intestinal parasitic and diarrhoeal disease; airborne diseases such as tuberculosis or measles; and vector borne diseases such as malaria, schistosomiasis or sleeping sickness) and nutritional deficiency diseases, which are associated with high infant mortality rates, short life expectancy, and widespread debility (Doyal, 1979; Bryant, 1969; PAHO, 1974; Muller, 1982). Such varying patterns of morbidity and mortality have implications not only for the demographic structure of society, but also for social institutions such as marriage and the family; industry, commerce and agriculture; residence and migration patterns; and the GNP (Gross National Product). They also have profound implications for our world views.

However, it may only be during periods of rapid change in the population's health, or when we compare ourselves with other parts of the world, or with our own countries in earlier times, that we are at all struck by the importance of prevailing patterns of mortality and morbidity for the organization of social life and our plans for our lives. Within a particular community or society at a given point in time such prevailing patterns of disease and death may be taken completely for granted as constituting part of the natural order of things, and may not be perceived as being 'key' variables at all. We all know, for example, in Europe and America, that women tend to live longer than men: it is simply a background expectation that we take for granted because we forget that this has not always been the case and is not everywhere the case now (Waldron, 1976 and 1983; El-Badry, 1969). Thus health and its impact on social organization has tended to be invisible, and typically there has been no, or little, consideration of health and illness in community studies or in general sociological texts. It is therefore pleasing that this topic has now been introduced into this volume.

Health and illness may be extremely important variables, but they are also extremely difficult to define and indeed there are no universally valid, comprehensive and agreed definitions of either concept. Definitional issues bedevil much discussion of health and illness, and will therefore be dealt with first in this chapter.

Disease and illness

Following Field (1976) and others, we can distinguish between the concepts of *disease* and of *illness*. *Disease* refers to a medical conception of an abnormality in function or structure of any part, process or system of the body. As Dingwall (1976) has suggested, it is possible to imagine medical practitioners using only signs based on objective indices of biological structure or function to decide whether disease is present or absent – regardless of whether the affected person actually feels ill at all. There are at least three main problems with this 'objective' view of disease. First, it is actually very difficult to develop universally valid norms of physical functioning because of the range of variability among humans. What is apparently normal for one individual may not be for another, or for the same person at a different

age or under different circumstances. For example, screening prog-
rammes on normal populations have found it very difficult to designate cut-off points between normality and abnormality in continuous
variables such as blood pressure. Some people with what was previously considered 'high' blood pressure have none of the commonly
associated correlates of pathological high blood pressure and are
perfectly 'well' according to other organic signs let alone symptoms.[1]

Second, indices of disease thus defined may bear very little relationship to subjective experience of pain, distress, debility, etc., or
to causes of death. Third, objectively defined disease may be so
prevalent that most of any human population would have to be
defined as 'diseased'. (These two points are discussed below.) These
last two points make the medical conception of disease as a major
criterion of ill health highly problematic in that, if even in the abstract
this notion of disease is clear-cut and sensible – that is, if we could
agree norms of bodily structure and functioning – this is not very
useful as a practical classification if it does not predict subjective
experience, or if it includes nearly everyone.

Illness refers to people's feelings of pain, discomfort, disability etc.
With the concept of disease the focus is objective and seen in terms of
the specific impaired state; with the concept of illness the focus is on
the subjective and on the diffuse consequences of the disease process.

The importance of the distinction between disease and illness is
that the relationship between disease and illness is not isomorphic but
highly complex and depends on a number of social and psychological
factors. It is possible to feel ill without having a disease, or to be
diseased without feeling ill. Many illness experiences – pain, aches,
discomfort, nausea, giddiness, weakness – are unaccompanied by
obvious signs of disease, or at least by any organic lesions discoverable with current investigative techniques. Some of these same
experiences – e.g. headaches, neuritis, stomach aches, chest pains –
may actually be related to the onset of chronic or degenerative disease
but observable features of the disease process may not become
apparent for an appreciable period of time (as, for example, with
multiple sclerosis). This may pose problems for the lay person who
can find it difficult to distinguish between self-limiting minor illness
and the signs and symptoms of potentially serious diseases
(A.R.M.S., 1983).

Ackernecht (1947) describes a skin disease (dichromic spirochetosis) that was so common among some South American tribes that *not*
having the condition was seen as pathological – to the extent that men
without it were excluded from marriage. This neatly illustrates the

point that – taking the western medical definition that dichromic spirochetosis is a disease – having the disease does not necessarily mean that someone feels ill, and that someone can be defined as ill in the absence of what we regard as disease. It also raises the more general question of whether we should adopt the outsiders' perception of this condition as a pathology, or the insiders' view of it as normality – particularly since the social consequences of the condition stem from the insiders' view.

It is in fact empirically much more common to be diseased without feeling ill than vice versa (Williams, 1983). People who have never experienced any 'illness' have been discovered on post mortem examination to have had serious organic pathology – such as advanced malignant neoplasms or circulatory abnormalities – which were not the cause of death (Tuckett, 1976). Some diseases may have latent phases (e.g. herpes or syphilis) or periods of remission (e.g. leukaemia) during which the affected person may be 'well' though still 'diseased'. Signs or symptoms may be unrecognized, denied or viewed as being part of normal life, and therefore not incorporated into a view of oneself as ill. Morris (1941) found, for example, that many people think decayed teeth are normal; Holland and Waller (1971) found that smoker's cough was often considered normal; and Clarke (1969) reported that chiropodists' estimates of unmet need for feet treatment far exceeded people's perceived needs. Fabrega and Manning (1972) suggest that there are certain dimensions along which experiences of disease vary and which may determine the responses made by sufferers and those around them to conditions potentially classifiable as illness. These are:

(1) Duration
(2) Prognosis (i.e. extent and possibility of cure)
(3) Severity (i.e. degree of discomfort, incapacity and disability)
(4) Stigmatization

It is these factors, plus the social framework of theories of disease causation, that are likely to be used to differentiate similar signs and symptoms – headache and vomiting, for example – into different 'diagnoses' with varying social and medical implications – a hangover, for example, rather than meningitis.[2]

The importance of the definition of illness – by self or others – is that it is this definition, rather than the experience of disease, which leads to significant action, such as going to the doctor, taking sick leave, or adopting the sick role (Parsons, 1951). Disease and illness can thus be viewed within the framework of Lemert's (1964) notion of primary and secondary deviation, the former referring to those slight deviations from normal (or ideal) functioning which are dealt with as part of routine social life, and the latter referring to those which are interpreted as illness and lead to alterations in conduct. The processes of interpretation of bodily states as 'illness', and the varying actions taken on the basis of such interpretations, have been extensively studied by sociologists under the general label of 'illness behaviour' (see Mechanic, 1968; Tuckett, 1976; Locker, 1981).

Screening studies of random cross-sections of the population have tended to show that very few people are without some abnormalities that can be defined as 'disease', even though many of the affected individuals are unaware of the disorders. As part of the Peckham Experiment in the 1930s, health overhauls were conducted on 1,206 families (4,002 individuals). Not more than 10 per cent at all ages were without discoverable pathological conditions: all the rest had one or more clinically recognizable disorders. Of those in whom disorders were detected, only around 30 per cent were aware of them (Pearse and Crocker, 1943). In Southwark the Medical Officer of Health screened 1,000 randomly selected individuals living in the Borough. The screening consisted of a physical examination and tests, plus social and medical history. Fifty-two per cent of the sample were regarded by the doctor as needing further investigations – and possibly treatment – which they were not currently receiving (Epson, 1969). In another early study of employees of a Midlands corporation, involving a questionnaire and medical examination, 7 per cent of those studied had major disorders, and most had minor disorders. Many of the major disorders were symptomless or did not interfere with daily work. The minor disorders were usually quite obvious: they were apparent, but not perceived (Morris, 1941).

Studies of self-reported complaints have similarly found that few people are without some disorders over any given period, even though few of these disorders may be defined as illness or form the basis for actions such as seeing a doctor or taking time off work. In a study of 514 families (2,204 persons) in a small town in New York State just after the Second World War, Koos (1954) divided illness into two types – disabling and non-disabling (the former involving disruption of normal duties in school, home, work etc., and the latter not so doing). Fifty-seven per cent of individuals reported some disabling illness in the twelve months prior to questioning (of which 75 per cent was treated in some form or other and 25 per cent was not), and 43 per cent reported no such disabling illnesses, although 6 per cent reported symptoms they did not regard as comprising 'illness'. Seventy-five per cent reported some non-disabling illnesses over the same period (of which 36 per cent were treated and 64 per cent not) and 25 per cent reported no non-disabling illnesses.

In another community based study, this time in Bermondsey and Southwark, London, Wadsworth, Butterfield and Blaney (1971) studied a random sample of 2,500 adults. Almost 5 per cent reported no health complaints at all in the previous fourteen days. This is an extremely low figure but the authors think that their method of cross-checking information by the use of correlated checklists not only of symptoms but also of medicines, actions taken, chronic diseases, impairments etc. prompted memories and therefore rendered their findings very accurate. 18.8 per cent reported complaints for which no action was taken, and 76.3 per cent reported complaints for which some action was taken. What is interesting about these findings – apart from this very high prevalence of complaints – is that this high prevalence co-existed with optimistic self-evaluations of general health. Thirty-five per cent of respondents assessed their state of health as 'perfect', 34 per cent as 'good', 21 per cent as 'fair', and only 10 per cent as 'poor'.

These findings are similar to those of the UK General Household Survey. The General Household Survey (an inter-departmental survey sponsored by the Central Statistical Office and conducted every year since 1971) asks three main types of questions about health status. It asks for a general evaluation of the individual's state of health over the last twelve months; about chronic illness conditions; and about short term illness conditions (i.e. in the previous fourteen days).

In 1978, 56 per cent of men and 70 per cent of women reported that they had a chronic health problem (as is usually the case, the proportion reporting chronic ill health was greater among women than among men, among the older rather than younger respondents, and among the lower socio-economic groups). Forty-nine per cent of men and 54 per cent of women reported no health problems at all (i.e. neither chronic nor short term). Despite the high prevalence and incidence of reported health problems, however, evaluations of health over the past year tended to be rather positive: 64 per cent of men and 54 per cent of women rating their health as 'good', 26 per cent of men and 33 per cent of women rating their health as 'fairly good' and 9 per cent of men and 13 per cent of women rating their health as 'not good'. Although evaluations of general health are associated with reported chronic and short term health problems, the associations are very weak: for example, while 89 per cent of men who reported no health problems at all rated their health as good, so did 46 per cent of men who reported both short term and chronic health problems (OPCS, 1980).

That disease is defined in terms of objectively discoverable abnormalities, as contrasted with illness which is defined in terms of subjective experience, should not be taken to mean that trained observers will necessarily agree on the presence or absence of the former. In fact studies have shown a magnitude of observer variation in many areas of diagnosis and interpretation of laboratory tests which is extremely surprising – especially to the clinicians concerned who often find it difficult to believe such results (Garland, 1959). A classic study reported by Bakwin (1945) took 1,000 New York schoolchildren, 61 per cent of whom had already lost their tonsils. The remaining 39 per cent were referred to a group of physicians responsible for assessing E.N.T. symptoms among schoolchildren. Forty-five per cent of the children were recommended for adenotonsillectomy and the rest were rejected. Those rejected were referred to a second group of school physicians who recommended adenotonsillectomy for 46 per cent of them. Those twice rejected were referred for a third assessment to yet another group of school physicians, and 44 per cent of those were selected for surgery. In the end there were sixty-five children, out of the original 1,000, whose tonsils had not been removed or recommended for removal. Economic factors apparently played no role in the recommendations for this series, and Bakwin concluded that there were virtually no correlations between physicians in their estimates of the advisability of tonsillectomy.

Similar variations between observers (and between one observer at different times) have been demonstrated in the interpretation of diagnostic aids such as x-rays, electrocardiograms, and clinical laboratory samples, and in various clinical diagnoses such as myocardial infarct and bronchitis (see Garland, 1959 and Maddox, 1973 for a review of variations in diagnosis). Self-reports of illness are sometimes criticized for being unreliable since they are 'only subjective' and therefore subject to variations between individuals in what they mean by illness; it is often forgotten that objective diagnoses of disease may equally be subject to variations between observers and hence be unreliable too.

Health

Thus far we have mainly dealt with problems of defining disease or illness, but the investigations by Wadsworth *et al.* (1971) and the General Household Survey lead us to consider what people mean by health.

If it is difficult to reach agreement on definitions of disease and illness, it is even more difficult to devise an agreed definition of health. To define it as the absence of disease is to encounter the problems discussed above; to define it as the absence of illness is to produce a circular definition since illness itself is often defined as the absence of health.

Koos (1954) has a subheading 'Health is an imponderable', in a chapter on illness. He states: 'Not only was illness difficult to define for the purposes of the study, but health – the soundness of body and freedom from disease or ailment – proved to be equally so (p.31).

Various types of definitions have been proposed. In reviewing these, Culyer (1981) lists four approaches: health as absence of disease (the 'medical model'); health as absence of illness (the 'sociological model'); health as an ideal (the WHO model); and health as pragmatically defined in terms of particular characteristics.

The medical model is useful for certain purposes but fails to take into account notions of positive health or psychiatric health, or to deal with the complicated relationship between objective disease and subjective perceptions. The sociological model, depending as it does on the reactions of self or others, may only enable us to define health *post hoc*, and it may be too relativistic to be used for comparative purposes since it is so dependent on individual or social thresholds and circumstances.

The WHO definition of health, as 'a state of complete physical, mental and social well-being, not merely the absence of disease or infirmity', is the best known attempt to propose an idealized definition of health. It has not proved particularly useful, however, perhaps because it is too broadly defined. As Culyer comments:

> Moreover, whether such a state can actually be described in a non-relativist fashion (let alone measured) seems to be in doubt: if health is conceived as a continuum of states of which one extreme is 'perfect health', it seems both analytically more manageable and practically more relevant to focus on the in-between states and on improvements (movements towards the state of 'perfect health') than upon the extreme

state itself which may be unattainable and even unimaginable. (1981,p.10)

What Culyer calls the 'characteristics approach' defines health or ill health according to characteristics of the individual which are relevant to the investigator's current concerns, e.g. functional capacity, pain, emotional state, etc. It is this approach, he argues, that has become the most important one in the development of health indicators (see later for a discussion of health indicators).

Lay definitions of health and illness

Thus far we have mainly dealt with attempts by observers or investigators to define or conceptualize health and illness. It is clear from some of the material discussed above that the sociological definition of health and illness – i.e. those states recognized by self or others as being health or illness – requires us to explore what ideas members of a particular society, or subculture, or family have about health and illness. Probably partly for the reasons mentioned at the beginning of this chapter – that we generally take for granted health and illness, and ideas about them, as part of the natural order of things – until recently more interest has been shown in concepts of health and illness among non-western or tribal societies than in our own society (see, for example, Carstairs, 1955; Frake, 1961; Fabrega and Silver, 1973; Lewis, 1975).[3] Two recent studies – one in Paris and one in Aberdeen, Scotland – have helped to redress the balance and to give us a clearer idea about the distinctions made in modern western societies between the various components and dimensions of health and illness.

The Parisian study, conducted by Claudine Herzlich, was based on the premise that: ' . . . in the study of the response to illness we need a psycho-social orientation centred upon the articulation of the person and the socio-cultural system' (Herzlich, 1973, p.10), and relied on interviews with eighty middle-aged and middle-class respondents. She found that among her respondents there was no single concept of health, but rather at least three concepts of health. First, there was 'health in a vacuum', which was seen as a state of *being*, involving absence of illness. This concept was marked by a lack of positive content and was regarded as an impersonal, all-or-nothing fact. Second, there was the notion of a 'reserve of health', which was seen as a state of *having*, involving robustness or strength and a resistance to the assaults of illness or injury. This was seen as a permanent personal characteristic, though variable over time. Third, there was health as 'equilibrium', seen as a state of *doing*, involving physical well-being, good humour, good relations with others, activity, and the assimilation of disorders. Later in her analysis she suggests that within the social representations she was studying illness could be regarded as a state of an individual, as an object external to the person, and as the conduct of a sick person. Health, similarly, could be thought of as a state, as something belonging to the individual, and as the conduct of the healthy person (Herzlich, 1973).

Rory Williams found three rather similar ideas among a sample of middle and working class elderly Aberdonians (Williams, 1983). The first concept of health he found among his informants was health as the absence of illness or disease – the distinction made between illness and disease being similar to the orthodox medical distinction between symptoms and objectively discoverable disease. The second idea was of health as strength, a much more positive concept than the first. People who are well, strong, fit or healthy have the power to 'come through' and could describe themselves as having always been healthy despite perhaps having experienced much disease. A corollary to the idea of strength is the idea of weaknesses in particular organs or locations (e.g. in the chest), or the idea of being 'done up', having exhausted all one's strength. As Williams points out:

> Bad health therefore can exist in the absence of disease, just as disease can exist without compromising good health. Health and illness are in this sense separate dimensions, each dimension having its own poles of well-being and misfortune; and deterioration on one dimension need not be accompanied by deterioration on the other, though as a matter of contingent fact this is more likely than not – for claims to poor health in the absence of *any* pathological history are limited by fear of being seen as a hypochondriac, and claims to good health unlikely in the presence of severe disability. (Williams, 1983, p.14)

The third idea about health held by Williams' respondents concerned functional fitness – fitness in regard to conventional activities such as paid work or work in the home or garden. He found that this concept was, again, not related in any simple fashion to the other two; while to be accepted as unfit for normal obligations implied sickness or disabling disease, it was not necessarily related to weakness in health, which was not, in turn, accepted as sufficient grounds for being recognized as unfit.

Williams points out that the three dimensions of health he elicited from Aberdonians are very similar to those elicited by Herzlich from her Parisian sample (although he also analysed interesting differences) and he argues that these similarities across ages, classes and nationality suggest that fairly fundamental ideas are involved.

Other studies have also pointed to the existence of different axes along which people may range 'health', 'illness', 'disease' and 'fitness' and which may be only loosely associated with each other, e.g. self-ratings of 'perfect health' co-existing with reports of disorders in the Bermondsey and Southwark study (Wadsworth *et al.*, 1971). Blaxter and Paterson (1982) reported that working class middle-aged to elderly women in Aberdeen could regard their health as good even when, to the investigators, they appeared to have had troubled histories of both chronic and acute disease. Health is, of course, relative to expectations,and Blaxter and Paterson, with their social class IV and V sample, may have been tapping the same low expectations that Koos (1954) found in his lower social class respondents in 'Regionville' who, when presented with a list of symptoms and asked which merited medical attention, showed: 'a marked indifference to most symptoms' (1954, p.33). As a local public health nurse commented on these findings of Koos: 'As for backache, tiredness and stiffness, why should they worry about those? Heavens, they're second nature to poor people with bad diets, poor postnatal care, too much work, and all the rest' (1954, p.33).

This topic of class (and other) variations in thresholds of tolerance for particular disorders or disorders in general, has been discussed extensively in the literature on illness behaviour (e.g. Mechanic, 1968; Tuckett, 1976).

Measurements and indicators of health

Despite all the conceptual problems mentioned above, and the apparently multidimensional ideas that people have about what constitutes 'health', 'illness', 'disease', and 'fitness', it is obviously useful at times for social investigators to try to develop and use measurements or indicators of health. We might want to enquire whether healthier individuals are more likely than their less healthy peers to be socially or geographically mobile; whether health is a mediating factor in the better school performance of middle rather than working class children; or whether the social and health insurance systems introduced in Britain in the 1940s have had any effect on the health of the population or on inequalities between classes (Townsend and Davidson, 1982). To begin to answer any of these questions we would need to develop simple measures of health status that could permit comparisons across individuals, groups, or time periods.

The earliest used health indicators were the London Bills of Mortality, mortality statistics first collected in sixteenth century London in connection with epidemics of plague. From 1603 these were published weekly and were an important basis for the development of statistics and epidemiology in the century following. Sir William Petty argued in his 'Treatise on Taxes and Contributions' (1662) for demographic data to be used in policy making, and John Graunt in his 'Observations on the London Bills of Mortality' (1662) was able to make observations about the patterning of mortality rates.[4] Since the sixteenth century the amount of data routinely collected on health matters has grown enormously in all countries of the world (and there is pressure for yet more to be collected). Health indicators are of interest not only to epidemiologists and public health workers, but to many other investigators, administrators, and policy makers, at local, national and international levels. The field of health indicators is now extensive and still growing fast. Increasing interest in this field seems to have arisen out of the conjunction of a number of initially separate strands, for example, the development in the 1960s of a social indicators movement (Carley, 1981); realization that traditionally used indicators based on death were no longer appropriate as measures of health trends (see below) and an increasing need for sophisticated outcome measures for clinical trials in medicine (Culyer, 1981). For a review of developments in the health indicator field Culyer (1981) and Alderson and Dowie (1979) are among the most useful sources. In a chapter such as this we can do no more than sketch in some of the main issues.

The idea of a health indicator is simply that statistics such as the incidence of a disease, days lost from work because of sickness, or a mortality rate, can indicate a state of health. Health indicators can be used for a number of purposes: to evaluate services or procedures; to monitor health or health services; to forecast at an individual, group or national level; to study the distribution and cause of disease; to allocate resources for health related services; or to adjudge compensation for injury or death. They may be used by a range of persons and institutions including health service providers, planners and managers, the community (whether as consumers or providers of care), disease surveillance experts (whether professional – as at the communicable disease center, Atlanta – or lay, as in certain pressure groups), the legislature, judiciary, and international organizations (the UN agencies, WHO and ILO, for example) (Culyer, 1981).

Health indicators may also be required as independent, intervening or dependent variables in social investigation, as illustrated in the first paragraph of this section. Here the interest is in health, *per se*, as an important variable in social processes. Health indicators are also used, however, as indirect measures of social processes, the most common example being the use of measures such as infant mortality rates or life expectancy to indicate the relative stage of development of various countries. Worldwatch have recently claimed, for example, that current changes in infant mortality rates are as important as the Gross National Product in monitoring national progress (Newland, 1981). Here health or mortality measures based on individuals are being used to indicate the 'health' of the society to which the individuals belong.

Health indicators can be composed of many different sorts of measurements. A WHO study group on measurement of levels of health suggested two broad types of classification. The first divided indicators into three types:

(a) Those associated with the health status of persons or populations in a given area (e.g. vital statistics)
(b) Those related to physical environmental conditions that may bear on health status (e.g. air pollution, accessibility of clean water supplies)
(c) Those concerned with health services and their activities (e.g. availability and use of hospitals and doctors)
      (WHO, 1957)

The potential value of indicators of each of these types obviously depends on the purposes for which the indicators are required and the level of analysis being undertaken. Because it is sometimes fallaciously assumed that the three types will co-vary, the wrong type and level can be used for the purpose at hand, and this selection may be based on and reinforce incorrect inferences about causal relationships or social processes. Data on health services or their activities (for example, proportion of births taking place in hospitals) are sometimes used as surrogate indices for something to do with the health of the relevant population, as if they bore an undisputed and linear relationship to the health measure in which the investigator is really interested (for example, in this case maternal and perinatal mortality and morbidity) and as if these measures were unaffected by factors relating to the social and physical environment (e.g. in this case maternal nutrition, domestic division of labour, hazards at work, etc.). As Carr-Hill and Blaxter (1982) note, most practical indicators confuse the levels and types being used.

Traditionally, the most commonly used – and useful – indicators have been those based on death, such as life expectancy at a given age, infant or perinatal mortality, and disease specific mortality rates (often standardized by age or sex). These tend to be the most easily available statistics and to be less ambiguous than other measures. Life expectancy is a useful comparative measure, e.g. between countries, but although it appears to say something about the future it is of course based on extrapolation of past mortality rates and therefore is least useful when these rates are subject to rapid change. With changing patterns of disease and increased longevity in the developed world indicators based on mortality are increasingly regarded as less useful. The death rate for some conditions (e.g. maternal mortality) is now so low that rates are subject to small number fluctuations which make any comparative analysis meaningless. With the decline in commonly fatal communicable diseases and the related increase in chronic, degenerative, multi-caused disease and disability, general or disease specific death rates become less and less useful as indicators of levels of health because (a) morbidity and disability may be rising while mortality rates decline; (b) it becomes more and more difficult unequivocally to diagnose cause of death; (c) thresholds of acceptable illness or disability could change such that the severity with which a particular statistic is regarded might increase while the rate of the statistic is falling (Carr-Hill and Blaxter, 1982; Culyer, 1981; Alderson and Dowie, 1979). An example might be that perinatal mortality could fall, but at the expense of an increase in handicapped survivors; that with low birthweight babies, in whom most of the mortality occurs, it may be impossible to know why the mother went into labour early or of what organ failure the baby died; and with decreasing perinatal and infant mortality parents now expect all their children to live, and therefore death in childhood may be regarded as more of a tragedy than it would have been a century ago.

Increasing attention, therefore, is being given to measures of morbidity. These pose great problems compared with mortality statistics. Health examination surveys (e.g. Epson, 1969; Morris, 1941; the US National Health Examination Survey) are time consuming and costly and can therefore only usually deal with small samples or subgroups of interest, or with relatively 'captive' populations such as recruits to the armed service, school children, etc. They face the problems discussed in earlier sections, e.g. of deciding what are to count as abnormalities, and of uncovering disorders of which the 'sufferers' may know nothing (Culyer, 1981). Health interview studies may be better at eliciting illness than disease, which is sometimes seen as a problem to those concerned with 'real' prevalence of disease: again, they are rather expensive and can only be done on a sample basis (e.g. the UK General Household Survey; Wadsworth *et al.*, 1971). The Survey of Sickness, which was carried out in the UK between 1945 and 1952, was suggested by the General Register Office as a means of monitoring the health of the civilian population, which it was feared had deteriorated since the start of the War. The health questions in the General Household Survey (1971-continuing) are similarly intended to monitor morbidity among the population and to detect changes in total morbidity.

In addition to data collected from health examination or interview surveys, in all countries some other data are routinely collected by governments, hospitals, practitioners, etc. and can be used as health indicators. In Britain there is routine, statutory notification, collation and publication of data on: mortality, abortions, cancer, congenital abnormalities, handicapped persons, hospital inpatient data for admission to acute, chronic and psychiatric hospitals, certain infectious diseases, morbidity in school children, and sickness absence from work (Alderson and Dowie, 1979). The registration of particular notifiable diseases or conditions may depend on the illness behaviour of sufferers or their families (i.e. whether people with cancer or sexually transmitted disease attend for diagnosis), the extent to which the condition is stigmatized, the level of service provision available, the accuracy and certainty of diagnosis, and social and administrative processes encouraging or discouraging notification. Rates of contact with the health services (i.e. outpatient or inpatient attendances) are a product not only of need for services but also of the supply of services, the admission or referral policies of doctors, and the demand for services. The most important variable affecting use of health services at an aggregate level seems in fact to be the supply of health services (Airth and Newell, 1962; Kohn and White, 1976). Rates of sickness absence from work, or sickness benefits claimed, are heavily dependent on administrative and social factors as well as on illness behaviour and the personal circumstances of individuals.

Much interest has been shown in recent years in the conceptualization and measurement of 'disability' as opposed to 'morbidity' (e.g. see Williams, 1981). With the concept of disability, health can be conceived of in terms of fitting people to a greater or lesser extent for their conventional roles and activities, and therefore it is perhaps the most sociological conceptualization (e.g. Parsons' definition of health as 'the state of optimum capacity of an individual for the effective performance of the roles and tasks for which he has been socialized' (1951)). It also has the advantage that degree of handicap can be treated as a more or less continuous variable, rather than a dichotomy such as 'able-bodied/disabled'. Unfortunately, the sorts of measures available from routinely available administrative statistics (e.g. persons registered as disabled) are often too crude to be useful, so estimates of the prevalence of varying degrees of disability have to be based on sample surveys such as the General Household Survey.

Hunt and McEwen (1980) describe four strands in recent attempts to improve the validity and reliability of morbidity statistics. First, there have been attempts to produce refined indices (incidence and prevalence of specific conditions, absence from work, illness episodes, etc.). Second, there has been the development of disability indices (e.g. the Activities of Daily Living Index, Katz *et al.*, 1963). Third, there have been symptom or function indices, describing clinical symptoms (e.g. the Cornell medical index, Broadman *et al.*, 1951), ability to function in one's role (e.g. the Function Status index, Reynolds *et al.*, 1974) or the effect of illness or disability on one's life activities (e.g. the Sickness Impact Profile, Bergner *et al.*, 1978), most of these being based on a professional observer's judgment. Fourth, there are measurements of consumer satisfaction with health care (not usually related either to the individual's health problem or to the level of functioning). Hunt and McEwen argue cogently that what is missing is an attempt to incorporate subjective health indicators, and they describe an attempt to develop such a subjective health indicator, the aim being to produce an instrument that can be used in population surveys to supplement the already used indices of health. Their piloting of this instrument sounds promising but at the time of writing it is not generally available for others to use.

Thus far I have dealt almost exclusively with indicators of physical morbidity rather than of psychiatric morbidity. There is insufficient space to review all the literature on psychiatric epidemiology and on attempts to measure mental health, but one or two general points can be made. First, if concepts such as 'health', 'disease' and 'illness' are difficult to define, conceptualize, and measure in relation to physical states, they are even more so in relation to mental states. This is not necessarily to suggest that the problems are of a different order. As Sedgewick (1972) pointed out, the 'anti-psychiatry' movement in the 1960s tended to criticize the concept of mental illness without appreciating that many of the same definitional and social issues applied to the definition of any sort of illness. Second, sociologists have often fought shy of any biophysiological or biochemical explanations of mental illnesses, or even of any suggestion of interactions between social or emotional and organic processes in mental states. They have thus tended to focus on the more obviously socially related mental conditions, in particular on neuroses rather than psychoses (though Brown's work on schizophrenia is an honourable exception: e.g. Brown and Birley, 1968; Brown *et al.*, 1966). Taken together, the consequences of these two points are that much of the sociological literature either attacks the concept of mental illness (e.g. Szasz, 1962), deals with conditions such as depression or anxiety (e.g. Oakley, 1980; Brown and Harris, 1978) or examines stress and its relationship with physical or mental well-being (e.g. Dohrenwend and Dohrenwend, 1974).

Banks *et al.* (1980) distinguish two uses of the term 'mental health'; one referring to life satisfaction or happiness and having no necessary connection with mental illness in a clinical sense, and the other referring to the absence of clinically defined mental illness. Outside the clinical psychiatric field there seem to be more studies of mental health in the former than in the latter sense.

In recent years there has been considerable interest, particularly in the USA, in the measurement of life satisfaction and related themes such as morale, well-being, and happiness. In reviewing the existing scales and measurements in this area Ford (1979) notes two main traditions: one explains satisfaction as an inner quality of the person (e.g. Bradburn, 1969) while the other tends to look outward to the person's circumstances (e.g. Campbell *et al.*, 1976). An interesting empirical finding to emerge from examination of the Positive Affect and Negative Affect Scales (five item dimensions derived from cluster analysis) developed by Bradburn and Caplovitz (1965) was that positive and negative affect were not inversely correlated: that is that the absence of negative affect does not ensure happiness, and vice versa. For reviews the theoretical, conceptual and methodological underpinnings of the American scales, pointing out that although interest in life-satisfaction measures has been increasing in Britain, there have been few applications of them in the UK, and that in any case, life satisfaction scales 'seem to be more promise than achievement' (1979, p.24).

It might be thought that combining different indicators – for example, mortality, morbidity, disability, subjective health indicators, mental health measures, life satisfaction scores – into a single summary measure of 'health' would be useful. Although there has been much interest in developing such composite measures for international comparisons, it is thought that such a task is likely to prove extremely difficult, not least because there is little agreement on weighting factors for the units of measurement to be combined. As Carr-Hill and Blaxter (1982) have recently noted, the British health system has still found no better measure for distributing its resources between regions than mortality rates combined with demographic profiles. While this is seen as inadequate (e.g. by Townsend and Davidson, 1982), the development of summary indicators is still some way off. In the meantime, the most useful approach among those wishing to use health indicators in social investigation is to be as clear and specific as possible about the purpose for which the indicator is required, the level of analysis involved, and the nature and derivation of the indicator being used.

Concluding remarks

Like age, gender and race, health and illness are social categories with physical foundations. While the biological basis can shape and set limits to human experience, it may tell us little about the social meaning and significance ascribed to such categories (Sontag, 1979; see also Finch, Morgan and Bulmer in this volume). Definitions and diagnoses of disease, illness and health may vary between cultures, between historical periods, between individuals and between the same individual at different times. Unlike variables such as age or gender, 'healthiness' is unlikely to appear as a standard face sheet variable in most survey research, and there would be great difficulties in devising a simple composite measure that could be elicited easily by an interviewer in the way that age or gender are. Despite the difficulties of defining and measuring it, health can nevertheless be viewed as being a key variable, whether relating to individuals or social groups, which can interact with or overshadow other characteristics such as age, gender, race or class to exert a major influence on people's life chances and experiences.

Notes

1 A 'sign' usually refers to something outwardly manifested or detectable by others or by measurement techniques: a 'symptom'

refers to something privately experienced and not necessarily communicated to anyone else.

2 See Field, 1976, for a discussion of these dimensions and particularly stigmatization.

3 For a spoof on the tendency only to look at 'strange' cultural ideas about health, see Horace Miner's (1956) article 'Body ritual among the Nacirema'.

4 For a discussion of the history of social statistics see Shaw and Miles, 1979.

References

Ackernecht, E.W. (1947), 'The Role of Medical History in Medical Education', *Bulletin of the History of Medicine*, vol.21.

Airth, A.D. and **Newell, D.J.** (1962), 'The Demand for Hospital Beds'. Results of an Enquiry on Teesside, Newcastle upon Tyne, University of Durham, Kings College.

Alderson, M.R. and **Dowie, R.** (1979), Health Surveys and Related Studies, SSRC/RSS Reviews of UK Statistical Sources, vol.IX, Oxford, Pergamon Press.

Anderson M. (1971), *Family Structure in Nineteenth Century Lancashire*, Cambridge, Cambridge University Press.

A.R.M.S. (1983), Action for Research into Multiple Sclerosis; Research Unit, Brunel, General Report No.3, *Discovering the Diagnosis of MS*, Department of Sociology, Brunel University.

Bakwin, H. (1945), 'Pseudocia Pediatrica', *New England Journal of Medicine*, vol.232, pp.691–7.

Banks, M.H., Clegg, C.W., Jackson, P.R., Kemp, N.J., Stafford, E.M. and Wall, T.D. (1980), 'The Use of the General Health Questionnaire as an indicator of mental health in occupational studies', *Journal of Occupational Psychology*, vol.53, pp.187–94.

Bergner, M., Bobbitt, R.A., Kressel, S., Pollard, W.E., Gibson, B.S. and **Morrice, J.R.** (1978), 'The sickness impact profile: Conceptual formulation and methodology for the development of a health status measure', *International Journal of Health Services*, vol.6, pp.393–415.

Blaxter, M. and **Paterson, E.** (1982), *Mothers and Daughters: A Three Generational Study of Health Attitudes and Behaviour*, London, Heinemann.

Bradburn, N.B. (1969), *The Structure of Psychological Well-Being*, Chicago, Aldine Press.

Bradburn, N.M. and **Caplovitz, D.** (1965), *Reports on Happiness: A Pilot Study of Behaviour Related to Mental Health*, Chicago, Aldine Press.

Broadman, K., Erdman, A.J., Lorge, I. and **Wolff, H.G.** (1951), 'The Cornell Medical Index Health Questionnaire II as a diagnostic instrument', *Journal of the American Medical Association*, vol.145, no.3, pp.152–7.

Brown, G.W., Bone, M., Dalison, B. and **Wing, J.K.** (1966), *Schizophrenia and Social Care*, London, Oxford University Press.

Brown, G.W. and **Birley, J.L.T.** (1968), 'Crises and Life Changes and the Onset of Schizophrenia', *Journal of Health and Social Behaviour*, vol. 9, pp.203–14,

Brown, G.W. and **Harris, T.** (1978), *The Social Origins of Depression: A Study of Psychiatric Disorder in Women*, London, Tavistock.

Bryant, J. (1969), *Health and the Developing World*, Ithaca, New York, Cornell University Press.

Campbell, A., Converse, P.E. and **Rodgers, W.L.** (1976), *The Quality of American Life*, New York, Russell Sage Foundation.

Carley, M. (1981), *Social Measurement and Social Indicators*, London, Allen & Unwin.

Carr-Hill, R.A. and **Blaxter, M.** (1982), 'Indicators of Health, Poverty and Their Joint Variation'. Paper presented at WHO Consultation on Poverty, Unemployment and Health, mimeo, Institute of Medical Sociology, Aberdeen.

Carstairs, G.M. (1955), 'Medicine and Faith in Rural Rajasthan', in B. Paul (ed.), *Health, Culture and Community*, New York, Russell Sage Foundation.

Clarke, M. (1969), 'Trouble with Feet', *Occasional Papers on Social Administration*. no.29, London, Bell.

Culyer, A.J. (1981), 'Health and Health Indicators. Proceedings of a European Workshop'. A report to the British Social Science Research Council and the European Science Foundation, York, University of York.

Dingwall, R. (1976), *Aspects of Illness*, London, Martin Robertson.

Dohrenwend, B.P. and **Dohrenwend, B.S.** (1974), *Stressful Life Events: Their Nature and Effects*, New York, John Wiley.

Doyal, L. (with **Pennell, I.**) (1979), *The Political Economy of Health*, London, Pluto Press.

El-Badry, M.A. (1969), 'Higher Female than Male Mortality in some countries of South Asia: A Digest', *American Statistical Association Journal*, vol.64, pp.1234–44.

Epson, J.E. (1969), 'The Mobile Health Clinic: an interim report on

a preliminary analysis of the first 1,000 patients to attend',
mimeo, London, London Borough of Southwark.

Fabrega, H. and **Manning P.** (1972), 'Health Maintenance among
Peruvian Peasants', *Human Organisation*, vol.31, pp.243–56.

Fabrega H. and **Silver, D.B.** (1973), *Illness and Shamanistic Curing in
Zinacantan: An Ethnomedical Analysis*, Stanford, California,
Stanford University Press.

Field, D. (1976), 'The Social Definition of Illness', in Tuckett, D.
(ed.), *An Introduction to Medical Sociology*, London, Tavistock.

Ford, G. (1979), 'A Review of Life SatisfactionMeasurement'.
Scottish Home and Health Department Working Party on the
Elderly – Sub Group on measurement of Health Status, mimeo,
Institute of Medical Sociology, Aberdeen.

Frake, C.O. (1961), 'The Diagnosis of disease among the Subanun
of Mindanao', *American Anthropologist*, vol.63, pp.113–32.

Garland, L.H. (1959), 'Studies on the Accuracy of Diagnostic
Procedures', *American Journal of Roentgenology*, vol.82, no.1, pp.25–
38.

Herzlich, C. (1973), *Health and Illness*, London, Academic Press.

Holland, W.W. and **Waller, J.** (1971), 'Population Studies in the
London Borough of Lambeth', *Community Medicine*, vol.126,
p.153.

Howe, G.M. (1972), *Man, Environment and Disease in Britain: A
Medical Geography Through the Ages*, Newton Abbot, David and
Charles.

Hunt, S.M. and **McEwen, J.** (1980), 'The Development of a
Subjective Health Indicator', *Sociology of Health and Illness*, vol.2,
no.3, pp.231–46.

**Katz, S., Ford, A.B., Moskowitz, R.W., Jackson, B.A., Jaffe,
M.W.** and **Cleveland, M.A.** (1963), 'Studies of illness in the
aged. The index of ADL. A standardised measure of biological
and psychological function', *Journal of the American Medical
Association*, vol.145, no.3, pp.152–7.

Kohn, R. and **White, T.** (1976), *Health Care: An International Study*,
London, Oxford University Press.

Koos, E.L. (1954), *The Health of Regionville: What the People Thought
and Did About It*, New York/London, Hefner Publishing Co.

Laslett, P. (1972), *Household and Family in Past Time*, Cambridge,
Cambridge University Press.

Lemert, E.M. (1964), 'Social structure, social control and
deviation', in Clinnard M.B. (ed.), *Anomie and Deviant Behaviour*,
New York, Free Press.

Lewis, G. (1975), *Knowledge of Illness in a Sepik Society*, London, Athlone Press.

Locker, D. (1981), *Symptoms and Illness: The Cognitive Organisation of Disorder*, London, Tavistock.

Maddox, E.J. (1973), 'The Diagnostic process: a sociological approach to some factors affecting outcomes with special reference to variations', unpublished M.Litt dissertation, University of Aberdeen, Scotland.

Mechanic, D. (1968), *Medical Sociology*, New York, Free Press.

Miner, H. (1956), 'Body ritual among the Nacirema', *American Anthropologist*, vol.58, pp.503–7.

Morris, J.N. (1941), 'A medical examination of 1592 workers', *Lancet*, vol.1, p.51.

Muller, M. (1982), *The Health of Nations: a North-South Investigation*, London, Faber & Faber.

Newland, K. (1981), 'Infant mortality and the health of societies', Worldwatch Paper, no.47, December, Worldwatch Institute, Washington DC, (quoted p.371 in *Midwives Chronicle*, vol.95, no.1, p.137).

Oakley, A. (1980), *Women Confined: Towards a Sociology of Childbirth*, Oxford, Martin Robertson.

Office of Population Censuses and Surveys (Social Survey Division) (1980), *General Household Survey 1978*, London, HMSO.

Pan American Health Organisation (1974), *Health Conditions in the Americas 1969—72*, Scientific Publication no.287, World Health Organisation, Washington, D.C.

Parsons, T. (1951), *The Social System*, London, Routledge & Kegan Paul.

Pearse, I.H. and **Crocker, L.H.** (1943), *The Peckham Experiment: A Study of the Living Structure of Society*, London, Allen & Unwin.

Reynolds, W.J., Rushing, W.A. and **Miles, D.L.** (1974), 'The validation of a function status index', *Journal of Health and Social Behaviour*, vol.15, pp.271–83.

Sedgewick, P. (1972), 'Mental illness *is* illness', Paper presented to the 10th National Deviancy Symposium, York.

Shaw, M. and **Miles, I.** (1979), 'The social roots of statistical knowledge' in Irvine, J., Miles, I., and Evans, J. (eds), *Demystifying Social Statistics*, London, Pluto Press.

Shrewsbury, J.F. (1970), *A History of Bubonic Plague in the British Isles*, Cambridge, Cambridge University Press.

Sontag, Susan (1979), *Illness as metaphor*, London, Allen Lane.

Szasz, T.S. (1962), *The Myth of Mental Illness*, London, Secker & Warburg.

Townsend, P. and **Davidson, N.** (1982), *The Black Report: Inequalities in Health*, Harmondsworth, Penguin.

Tuckett, D. (1976), 'Becoming a patient', in Tuckett, D. (ed.), *An Introduction to Medical Sociology*, London, Tavistock.

Wadsworth, M.E.J., Butterfield, W.J.H. and **Blaney, R.** (1971), *Health and Sickness: The Choice of Treatment. Perception of Illness and Use of Services in the Urban Community*, London, Tavistock.

Waldron, I. (1976), 'Why do women live longer than men?', *Social Science and Medicine*, vol.10, pp. 349–62.

Waldron, I. (1983), 'Sex differences in illness incidence, prognosis and mortality: issues and evidence', *Social Science and Medicine*, vol.17, no.16, pp.1107–23.

Williams, R.G.A. (1981), 'Disability as a health indicator', in Culyer, A.J. (ed.), *op. cit.*

Williams, R.G.A. (1983), 'Concepts of health: an analysis of lay logic', *Sociology*, vol.17, pp.185–205.

World Health Organisation (1957) *Measurement of Levels of Health: Report of a Study Group*, WHO Technical Report Series no. 137, Geneva, World Health Organisation.

Wrigley, E.A. (1969), *Population and History*, New York, McGraw-Hill.

Wrigley, E.A. (1972), *Nineteenth-Century Society. Essays in the Use of Quantitative Methods for the Study of Social Data*, Cambridge, Cambridge University Press.

Education* 6

Robert G. Burgess

Although there is a vast literature on 'education' and the 'sociology of education' it appears that researchers are far from clear as to what counts as 'education' and the 'educational process'. A brief glance at a range of basic texts devoted to social science and educational studies indicates that the term 'education' is often ill-defined and used to apply to a narrow range of social circumstances. Despite the fact that 'education' is a life-long experience that can be acquired through the family, the peer group, the church, the trade union, the workplace and so on, it is often the case that education is equated with schools, colleges, classrooms, curricula and examinations. In these circumstances, we need to consider *how* researchers have defined 'education' and for what purpose. This chapter therefore focuses on the way in which 'education' has been defined within major areas of the sociology of education. As 'education' is in part defined by social legislation there are numerous differences between the structure of the educational systems of different societies and in turn this influences the ways in which researchers define 'education'. Accordingly, much of the discussion provided in this chapter together with examples of empirical evidence will be drawn from the United Kingdom and in particular from the English educational system.

Education as an area of study

As a recent review of social science and educational studies by Hartnett (1982) indicates, 'education' is the subject of research by

---

* I am grateful to Alison Andrew, Janet Finch, Betty Gittus and Aubrey Weinberg who were kind enough to provide written comments on an earlier version of this chapter.

anthropologists, psychologists, historians and philosophers as well as sociologists. Indeed, the field of study is one in which researchers have applied their disciplines to 'education'. Among sociologists this has resulted in a preoccupation with the policy concerns of governments and the professional problems of educators (cf. Young, 1971; Karabel and Halsey, 1977). Nowhere is this more apparent than in Britain where Bernstein (1974) has argued that the sociology of education in the immediate post-second world war period 'bore the hallmarks of British applied sociology; atheoretical, pragmatic, descriptive and policy focussed' (1974, p. 149). Such an approach, as Archer (1981) has commented, overlooks the contribution that Weber, Marx and particularly Durkheim made to the study of education as a social institution. While she acknowledges that education was never a major field of study for Marx and Weber, she argues that with Durkheim they developed a common orientation to this area by treating education as a macroscopic social institution, by placing the educational institution in the wider social structure and by focusing on education, social structure and other social institutions in examining the dynamics of educational change. Archer considers that from this tradition a sociology of educational systems can be developed (cf. Archer, 1979), but this has been a minority interest in sociology (Banks, 1982). Accordingly, we need to ask: what constitutes the sociological study of education? How is 'education' defined? How have researchers interpreted 'education' as a variable in social investigation?

There have been numerous reviews of the sociology of education in Britain over the last thirty years (cf. Floud and Halsey, 1958; Bernbaum, 1977; Banks, 1982; Burgess, 1984a); all of which indicate that it has departed radically from sociological theory. Indeed, the traditional or 'old' sociology of education of the 1950s and 1960s was dominated by studies of social stratification and social mobility in relation to education. Such developments are characterized by Archer as:

> 'methodological empiricism' where social structure was disaggregated into a series of atomized inputs (social class, for example, ceased to refer to active groups and was translated into a static membership characteristic of individuals). Education itself was reduced to a set of equally atomized outputs (x school-leavers with y certificates). Educational processes became a black box whose contents, the definitions of instruction, knowledge and achievement, were treated as timeless 'givens', unproblematic and immutable (Archer, 1981, p. 262).

This focus on inputs and outputs rather than upon the content of education drew criticism from Young (1971) who argued that sociologists needed to turn their attention to the content of education and to consider such questions as: what counts as education? What does it mean to be educated? It was Young and his associates who took up this approach which became known as the 'new' sociology of education where schools, classrooms and curricula were the basic units of study. However, this polarization into an 'old' and a 'new' sociology of education resulted in different areas of study, different research questions about 'education' and concentration on some topics at the expense of others. For example, neo-Marxists have argued that schools and classrooms need to be placed in the context of the wider social structure (cf. Sharp and Green, 1975; Bellaby, 1979), while feminists have shown that the kinds of questions and concepts which have been used to address education and educational experiences have systematically underplayed the position of girls and women (cf. Byrne, 1978; Deem, 1978; Delamont, 1980). Indeed, Acker (1981) reviewed the British sociology of education in the period 1960–79 and concluded that its concerns are such that it is 'no woman's land'. From a different perspective Archer (1981) has argued that both the 'old' and 'new' sociology of education have neglected the social origins and operations of educational systems. She considers this to be a serious omission as the educational system shapes the pattern of social relationships between teacher and pupil by contributing to the definition of their respective roles, the distribution of authority between them and the allocation of sanctions. The main subject matter of the 'old' and 'new' sociology of education would, therefore, appear to carry a set of basic problems that we need to explore before turning to examine 'educational' data.

Some problems in educational study

As sociologists have neglected the educational system it means that in much traditional sociology of education the data appears as a timeless 'given' where the origins of educational activities are ignored. Meanwhile, the 'new' sociology of education (based broadly on symbolic interactionism) was concerned with the 'here and now' and did not take into account the constraints within which schools and classrooms operated (Woods, 1983). As a consequence sociologists have called for greater attention to be given to the collection of historical data and to the study of educational politics in order to take account of the links between the past and the present. Indeed, Salter and Tapper (1981) have argued that it is essential to understand the dynamics of educational change.

Essentially there is a concern here with the unit of study, the time at which the units are studied and the level at which the study is conducted, all of which have implications for the ways in which data are collected, analysed and compared. Even within the United Kingdom these problems are apparent. If the unit of study is the educational system some account has to be taken of the differences between the educational system of England and Wales and the Scottish system with its different age of transfer between primary and secondary school, examination system and terminal education age before university (cf. Gray, McPherson and Raffe, 1983). Meanwhile, in Northern Ireland, there is a marked difference from England and Wales given the predominance of selective and non-selective secondary schools and the high density of denominational schools as religion permeates the whole of the educational process (cf. Cormack and Osborne, 1983). Accordingly, when comparisons are made within the United Kingdom care needs to be exercised over the similarities and differences that exist within the systems (cf. Burgess, 1984c).

While it may appear relatively straightforward for researchers to use terms such as 'primary education' and 'secondary education' care needs to be exercised over such terminology even within an educational system such as England and Wales where variations may exist between different local education authorities. For example, among authorities that border one another differences may exist in terms of the age of transfer between primary and secondary education, and arrangements for primary and secondary education in schools that cover different age ranges. Researchers who wish to pose questions about respondents' education in schools and colleges cannot merely adopt the administrative terminology as it may have different meanings in different geographical areas. However, further difficulties arise when comparisons are made in different historical periods as depending on the historical period involved, 'education' and educational activities may have different meanings. For as Andrew (1985) remarks in relation to her study of working class educational activity in nineteenth century Preston ' "Education" need not mean schools and classrooms as we know them and much evidence has been produced which indicates that working class educational activity in the nineteenth century often explicitly challenged the dominant model' (1985, p.164). She argues that the kinds of questions posed must be relevant to the period under study. Certainly, the same point can be made with regard to English education in the twentieth century where the time period has significance for the questions asked and the data collected. Reid (1981) advises caution on the interpretation of educational data, for he indicates that throughout the twentieth century and especially in the last two decades, education has been marked by a period of reorganization in secondary and in higher education. He argues that social scientists need to interpret educational data in recent years in the light of the raising of the school leaving age, increased opportunities to take examinations and the development of the comprehensive system.

Such changes in the English educational system need to be considered when, for example, secondary education is examined between 1902 and the present day. Certainly, consideration needs to be given to legislation and in particular to the 1944 Education Act which has not only shaped our current conception of state education, but also heralded secondary education for all and the advent of the tripartite system. In turn, care needs to be exercised in comparing a grammar school education in the pre- and post-1944 period. However, English secondary education has undergone 'experiment' and change since the 1944 Act. In the early 1950s a small number of local education authorities who argued that they constituted a 'special case' began to experiment with bilateral, 'multilateral' and comprehensive schools. Subsequently with the issue of government circular 10/65 (DES, 1965) which requested that LEAs should submit plans for the reorganization of schools along comprehensive lines there has been some modification of former grammar and secondary modern schools into comprehensive schools. However, the terms 'comprehensive school' and 'comprehensive education' may refer to different forms of provision given that there are differences between purpose built and split site schools and between comprehensive schools that were established out of a grammar rather than a secondary modern school base. In turn 'education' may be defined in different ways within a comprehensive school (cf. Burgess, 1983) and may not be comparable when one comprehensive school has been in operation for twenty years, while another has only been comprehensive for five years.

While changes have occurred in the structure of English education in the twentieth century, some consideration has to be given to provision and opportunity. For example, the school leaving age was fixed at fourteen years in 1921, raised to fifteen years in 1947 and extended to sixteen years in 1972. Alongside these developments it should be recalled that in 1921 there was universal primary education in elementary schools with limited opportunity for secondary education in grammar, technical and central schools. By 1947 there was universal secondary education, but no possibility of taking external examinations in secondary modern schools until after 1954. The gradual abolition of the distinction between selective and non-selective secondary education, together with opportunities for taking examinations has changed the character of secondary education. Researchers should be aware of the social and political context in which education operates and the way it is defined. For example, asking respondents for their terminal education age when their dates of leaving school might include 1914, 1924, 1954 and 1974 means little unless viewed in relation to the legislation in force during the particular period.

When focusing on the examination system in England and Wales some account needs to be taken of the replacement of the School Certificate by the General Certificate of Education (GCE) in 1950 and the introduction of the Certificate of Secondary Education (CSE) in 1965. Each of these examinations were structured in different ways. The School Certificate unlike the GCE required passes in specified subjects. It is, therefore, not possible to equate a given number of Ordinary level passes in the GCE with the School Certificate. Indeed, Halsey, Heath and Ridge (1980, p. 110) point out that serious problems of comparability are involved as a single 'A' level cannot be equated with the Higher School Certificate and a group of five or more passes at Ordinary level (GCE) cannot be simply equated with a pass in the School Certificate. Further difficulties also arise in comparing CSE and GCE especially when considering grades and the pass rate over time.

When researchers use examinations as a measure of 'education' it has to be seen in the context of the educational system. For example, in 1976 15 per cent of all school leavers did not attempt public examinations, while three years earlier this applied to 40 per cent of secondary school pupils. In this instance, comparisons are being made before and after the raising of the school leaving age to sixteen so that in 1973 a proportion of the age group had left school before public examinations were taken, while in 1976 all sixteen year olds were retained in the school system. Some account has also to be taken of the numbers of students who enter public examinations after they leave school (cf. Blackburn, Stewart and Prandy, 1980; Raffe, 1979).

Public examination entries also reflect curriculum opportunities and some account has to be taken of these opportunities for boys and girls (cf. DES, 1979). For example, Wilkin (1982) suggests that we should ask: who defines and operates the educational system? What counts as educational success? Questions about the structure of education and what counts as 'education' need to be constantly addressed in substantive studies and when interpreting official data.

Some sources of educational data

Although much educational research is done by generating 'new' data there are also many existing data sets which can be used in secondary analysis. This section provides guidance on some of the major sources of educational data: population censuses, continuous and regular surveys such as the General Household Survey, national cohort or longitudinal studies (Douglas, 1964, Douglas, Ross, and Simpson, 1968; Fogelman, 1983) and *ad hoc* investigations using qualitative and quantitative data.

(a) The population census is unique to central government, is compulsory and has been used to collect basic data since 1851. Although systematic educational data have only been collected in recent years, a voluntary Education Census was carried out in 1851 and the census has carried some questions on education at home or school since 1851. However, it was only in 1951 and 1961 that individuals were asked about the age at which their full-time education was completed and since 1961 data have been collected on educational qualifications. Specific questions were posed on scientific and technical qualifications, qualifications obtained in higher education and elsewhere (cf. Hakim, 1982).

(b) Regular surveys: the General Household Survey is a continuous survey that was started by the Office of Population, Censuses and Surveys in 1971 which allows trends over time to be examined in particular areas of social life including education. Since 1971 the following topics have been examined: type of school, college and so on that the individual has attended, terminal education age, qualifications, current education and apprenticeships and the respondent's father's occupation. In addition, teacher training course experience was followed up in 1978 and 1979, the use of nursery schools for the under fives in 1979 and attendance at leisure or recreation classes and student's institutional accommodation in 1981. The survey covers broadly

similar areas to the census but in much greater depth. Indeed, when it was originally established the education section of the General Household Survey was designed to supplement existing data sources, to relate education to housing, job earnings and health, to compare the educational standing of different generations, to monitor changes in type and amount of education and to develop measures of unfulfilled need (OPCS, 1973).

In 1980 the data that were gathered included age on leaving school, education since leaving school, type of school, college or training establishment currently attended, the school or college attended full-time and qualifications obtained. The questions for those at school took the following form:

> 3 What type of school college or training establishment are you attending (in the college part of your course)?
> SECONDARY SCHOOL
> Local authority secondary school
> (inc. state grammar/secondary modern/ comprehensive/ Sixth Form College).
> Independent secondary school
> (e.g. Public school/private school/fee paying grammar)
> Other school (e.g. special school for Handicapped/ESN)
> (SPECIFY TYPE)
> FURTHER EDUCATION
> Nursing school or teaching hospital
> (GIVE NAME AND TOWN)
> UNIVERSITY
> Other college or training establishment
> (SPECIFY TYPE, NAME AND TOWN)
>
> (OPCS 1982, p. 246)

Here, education is equated with formal institutions, and also in a later question:

> 4 Now thinking just of your full-time education;
> What type of school or college did you last attend full-time?
> Was it:
> elementary or secondary school
> university
> nursing school or teaching hospital or some other type of college?
>
> (OPCS, 1982, p. 246)

Meanwhile, education also equals qualifications when individuals are asked what qualifications they possess and what examinations they have passed (OPCS, 1982, p.247). In this question importance is attached to making distinctions between different kinds of educational qualifications during different historical periods and to differences between school examinations in Scotland compared with other parts of the United Kingdom. On the basis of collecting such data OPCS have been able to report on trends in educational achievement over a ten year period (OPCS, 1982, pp. 117–31).

(c) *National cohorts (or longitudinal) studies* In Britain two of the largest cohort studies are directly concerned with education. The first by the Population Investigation Committee under the direction of J. W. B. Douglas which reported on 5362 children born during the first week of March 1946. In *The Home and the School* (1964) Douglas reports on the children's primary schooling until they sat the eleven plus examination for secondary school selection. Meanwhile, in a subsequent report (Douglas, Ross and Simpson, 1968) the progress of the cohort is discussed from entry to secondary school until they were sixteen and a half years old and focused upon ability and attainment, examination results and pupil progress and attainment in different kinds of schooling all of which were equated with the 'educational process'.

Meanwhile, a second longitudinal study on the physical, social and educational development of 16,000 children born in the first week of March 1958 has been conducted by the National Children's Bureau. This investigation (like that of Douglas) began as a medical study. In 1965 it continued with a follow-up at the age of seven and subsequent follow-ups at the age of eleven and sixteen. At each stage the cohort were given a medical examination, their parents interviewed, a questionnaire was completed by teachers at the schools the pupils attended, the pupils were given tests of attainment and ability and completed a questionnaire when they were sixteen. To date this study has given rise to several reports on primary and secondary education and the examination system (for a discussion of the main trends see Fogelman, 1983).

(d) *Other studies* There are numerous other sources of educational data and studies that focus on 'education' including reports by local education authorities, Her Majesty's Inspectors and researchers from a range of disciplines. The last decade has witnessed a number of major surveys that have contributed to sociological debates about education. These studies include the work of Halsey and his colleagues concerning family, class and education based on 10,000 adult men who were regarded as a representative sample of the adult male population in England and Wales (Halsey, Heath and Ridge, 1980) and Michael Rutter's work on twelve Inner London Education Authority non-selective secondary schools (Rutter *et al.*, 1979). In these studies 'education' is equated with 'schooling' and the authors rely on data derived from interviews and questionnaires rather than any observational or documentary evidence. Yet there are now many studies about schools that rely almost exclusively upon data collected by means of observation and participant observation. In Britain there have been observational studies of secondary schools: Lacey (1970) on a grammar school, Hargreaves (1967) and Woods (1979) on secondary modern schools and Ball (1981), Turner (1983) and Burgess (1983) on comprehensive schools. In turn, the classroom has been a focus of interest for many others (cf. Chanan and Delamont, 1975; Hammersley and Woods, 1976; Woods and Hammersley, 1977; Woods, 1980a; 1980b) and attention has recently turned towards empirical studies of the curriculum which bring us closer to understanding the nature of subject disciplines and the *content* of education (Goodson, 1982; Goodson and Ball, 1984). Such a range of quantitative and qualitative data on education leads us to consider how researchers have defined education and the problems of handling data on educational activities. For the purposes of this review four areas will be considered that have been identified as central concerns in the sociology of education: the study of schools and classrooms, the curriculum and examinations, education and occupation and education and social stratification. The materials that are to be examined will not focus on a review of findings, but concentrate on the way in which researchers have defined 'education'.

The study of schools and classrooms

Trend reports indicate that studies of schools and classrooms are a relatively recent interest among sociologists who had for some time regarded the school as a 'black box' where internal processes remained unquestioned. Indeed, Ottaway was able to comment in 1960 that no sociologist was familiar with the internal activities of schools. However, subsequent work on schools and classrooms, conducted in Britain and the USA has begun to fill this gap.

In Britain there have been a series of case studies of individual schools. But how have these researchers contributed to our understanding of 'education'? In many of these studies the interest has been upon school structures and informal social relationships *rather than* upon the content of education. Indeed, some have traced the influence of social class and educational achievement in the school.

The studies by Hargreaves (1967) and Lacey (1970) had a marked influence upon other research. Hargreaves' work on Lumley Secondary Modern School for boys focused on fourth year pupils (excluding the bottom stream) to study 'the structure of the informal groups of pupils and the influence of such groups on the educative process' (1967, p. x). In particular, Hargreaves identified two subcultures among fourth year pupils: the academic among A and B stream pupils who supported the norms and values of the school and the delinquescent where pupils predominantly from the C and D streams took the values of the higher stream boys and their teachers and inverted them. Yet we might ask: what counts as 'the educational process' among such groups? Lacey's study also focused on boys when he examined subcultures. On the basis of studying stratification and subcultural development in relation to streaming by ability, Lacey suggested a model of differentiation and polarization, where differentiation refers to the process by which pupils are ranked by teachers according to a series of academic values, and polarization to a subcultural formation by which the values of members of the school are opposed by this 'anti group' culture. He concludes from this evidence that those who want to do well in school will accept academic values, while those who do badly will reject the system, disobey teachers and support the anti-group. In short, the focus is upon the relationship between internal school organization and the development of pupil subculture, the social processes among boys in a grammar school and upon 'the social mechanisms that *account for the correlation between social class and educational achievement*' (Lacey, 1970, p. 19, my emphasis).

Alongside these ethnographic studies of schools have been investigations that have generated quantitative data. Studies by Monks (1968, 1970) and by Benn and Simon (1972) on patterns of internal organization in comprehensive schools focused upon the range of their facilities, the number, experience and qualifications of their staff and the sizes of their teaching groups. Meanwhile, at the end of the 1970s Rutter *et al.* (1979) were able to report on the influence of school upon children's behaviour and attainments paying particular attention to the way in which the schools functioned as social organizations. The Rutter Study followed the progress of a year group of pupils within twelve ILEA secondary schools. Among the outcome variables that were examined were: school attendance, pupil attainment in public examinations, school behaviour and delinquency. Inferences were made about the schools only after allowing for differences between their intakes, with the result that the authors could conclude that the pupil's experience of school may influence progress, that differences in schools are related to their ethos rather than their physical and administrative characteristics and outcomes were linked to the academic balance of the intake. Such evidence seemed to suggest that schools do make a difference. However, several reviewers (cf. Reynolds, 1980) did note that Rutter and his associates had not taken into account the micro-sociological accounts of schooling including evidence from ethnographic studies of classrooms.

Classroom studies have focused upon the participants' point of view: the meanings that are attached to a social context and the way in which the participants define, redefine, construct, interpret and negotiate the meanings of the classroom. An early investigation by Keddie (1971) looked at the way in which comprehensive school pupils were categorized on the basis of classroom knowledge and how teachers held distinct views on the type of knowledge available for different groups of pupils. Subsequent studies have focused on social processes. Hargreaves, Hester and Mellor (1975) examined deviance in the secondary school classroom and looked at the ways in which teachers construct rules and typify pupils. Meanwhile, Sharp and Green's study (1975) of a progressive primary school locates the school in a broader context by looking at the way in which external constraints, child centred ideology and social stratification are reproduced in the classroom. Woods (1979) has examined the strategies that secondary pupils use to define, negotiate and bargain within classrooms, while Burgess (1983) has looked at the definition and redefinition of situations between teachers and pupils. Studies of school classrooms have focused on how pupils and teachers define 'education' and what happens when teachers and pupils meet in the classroom. Several studies have highlighted the criteria that pupils use to evaluate teachers including how pupils 'size up' teachers and make judgments about their classroom effectiveness while others focus on the teacher's work (cf. Woods, 1980a; 1980b). It is qualitative accounts such as these that could be consulted by researchers in the course of framing questions about education and educational processes; a situation that might bring them closer to understanding educational activities and the content of education.

The curriculum and examinations

Despite the theoretical interest shown by sociologists in the curriculum (Young, 1971) it has taken some years for empirical studies to appear that focus on school subjects. Much of this material focuses on academic subjects: English (Ball, 1982), science (Layton, 1973; Kelly, 1981), and mathematics (Cooper, 1983). Even Goodson's account of environmental studies looks at the way an area becomes an academic subject thus making it available for examination (Goodson, 1982). Such a focus means that areas of the curriculum that are 'not proper subjects' and non-examinable are often omitted from view. However, Burgess (1983; 1984b) who focused on the Newsom curriculum for secondary school pupils regarded as less willing and less able found that even this area of the curriculum was defined in terms of examinations. It was regarded as 'suitable for those pupils whose maximum expectation of success in school examinations will be three CSE grade five's or less'. Furthermore, when pupils did take examinations in options that were followed in this area, they were regarded as 'not proper qualifications'.

Such evidence indicates the need to examine the close links between the curriculum and examinations as it is the equation of education and examination and education and qualifications that has dominated English education (Hargreaves, 1982). For as HMI state, schools 'are conscious of the degree to which (their) effectiveness is liable to be measured publicly by examination results' (DES, 1979, p. 262) as examinations are one of the few measures by which secondary schools can be made publicly accountable. However, several commentators have indicated that there are difficulties involved in using data on examinations to provide a 'measure' of education and to discuss patterns of education. Automatically such data exclude all pupils who are not entered for public examinations (cf. Philips, 1981). Furthermore, researchers need to consider several problematic issues: what counts as an examination result – the first result or the best result? Should separate analyses be conducted when looking at examination results in selective and non-selective schools? Do examinations highlight the attainment of the individual, reflect the policies of the school or the policies of the local education authority?

On the basis of their experience with ILEA Mortimore and Byford (1981) indicate some further problems associated with using examinations as a unit of educational study. First, they point to a target problem as only a minority of pupils take the examinations that are specifically designed for them. Second, there is a comparability problem given the number of syllabuses and examination boards. For example, Fogelman (1981) found that there were twenty-six paper titles to refer to 'Mathematics'. In these circumstances questions need to be asked about what constitutes a subject. Third, there are problems of comparing the results of girls and boys in subject areas as Harding (1981) found that girls appear to do less well than boys in science examinations where multiple choice questions are used. Finally examinations also raise a validity problem for researchers as they only test certain items. As a consequence, Mortimore and Byford (1981) point to the aims of examination monitoring in ILEA which attempts to handle some of these problems by reviewing entries as well as results, by comparing data from year to year, within geographical areas and between boys and girls. Finally, they indicate the importance of considering the social context against which to consider examination results. This point is also stressed by Gray (1981) who considers that it is important to compare schools with similar pupil intakes and to focus on progress as well as attainment. Such conclusions highlight the need for caution when collecting data on examinations and using them as a 'measure' of education. Nevertheless, examination results are commonly used to examine the relationships between education and occupation and have recently been used in discussing education and unemployment (Main and Raffe, 1983).

Education and occupation

Much basic data on education and occupation can be derived from the General Household Survey. Here, the occupational category of adults is related to their education, relationships are discussed between age, qualifications and occupations and it is shown that those individuals who possess educational qualifications are more likely to achieve high status occupations. On the basis of the evidence it has been concluded that those individuals with educational qualifications have increased life chances and that educational experience will have a marked influence on occupational opportunities. In turn, educational qualifications and a lack of them have been shown to influence unemployment and allocation to training schemes (OPCS, 1983; Main and Raffe, 1983). However, in each instance it is essential to consider what constitutes an 'educational experience' and to evaluate the influence of independent, state selective and non-selective school education.

When data are collected on pupil careers, researchers need to obtain sufficient material so that the experiences of boys and girls and pupils from different ethnic groups can be compared. The evidence from Willis' ethnographic study of boys in the West Midlands where he considers the question 'Why do working class kids get working class jobs?' provides supportive evidence about the experiences of low stream boys (Willis, 1977). Meanwhile, Helen Roberts' study of girls' transition from school to work in Bradford provides evidence that when girls leave school without examinations, they get jobs that are low paid with little training and few opportunities for promotion (Roberts, 1982). Indeed, Roberts' case study indicates that short term menial tasks are the lot of many girls, while opportunities for further training exist more often for boys than girls. Such evidence points to the importance of considering the educational experiences of boys and girls as they hold implications for different kinds of opportunities in the labour market and in higher education. However, much of the evidence focuses on social class and education and examines boys alone with the result that the relationship between education and other key variables such as 'gender' and 'race' remains hidden from view.

Education and social stratification

Of all the areas of sociological investigation in 'education' it is the relationship between education and social class which has been widely researched and reviewed (cf. Silver, 1973; Reid, 1981). Within this area of study, investigators have focused on 'educational performance', 'educational achievement', 'equality of educational opportunity' and 'selection strategies' in relation to social class. However, as Marsh has shown (this volume) there are problems surrounding the way in which researchers have operationalized the concept of class. On some occasions class is broadly defined in terms of socio-economic status, in others in terms of the registrar general's classification, while in some instances the term 'class' is defined in a particular way within the studies (cf. Douglas, 1964). There are difficulties involved in attempting to compare findings in studies where 'class' and 'socio-economic status' categories are used: How, might we ask may the findings in studies using these two categories be compared? Obviously the problem is magnified when further categories are compared. Further problems concern the way in which educational performance and educational achievement are 'measured' using tests for reading, arithmetic and intelligence (cf. Douglas, 1964; Fogelman, 1983). This section therefore focuses on some of these difficulties when collecting data on 'education' in relation to social class.

Research on social class and education was most commonly conducted in the 1950s and 1960s although large scale surveys have been recently reported for England and Wales (Halsey, Heath and Ridge, 1980), for Scotland (Gray, McPherson and Raffe, 1983) and for Northern Ireland (Cormack and Osborne, 1983). Some of the early work by Floud (1954) and Himmelweit (1954) arose out of the study of social mobility by Glass (1954) just as the more recent work of Halsey, Heath and Ridge was linked to the Oxford Mobility study.

Many of the early studies provide no evidence on the questions that were posed and the ways in which education was defined. However, caution needs to be exercised over conclusions on education and social class as studies dealt with particular sections of the population and specific problems. For example, Floud (1954) was interested in comparing the increase in educational opportunity afforded by a *grammar school* education in the 1930s compared with 1910, while Himmelweit (1954) focused on *boys* in grammar and secondary modern schools in London. However, even in this study the focus was on access to these schools and the activities of working class *boys* within them. Meanwhile, even the major study on social class and educational opportunity conducted by Floud, Halsey and Martin (1956) focused on the issue of selection for *grammar school* which was related to the social distribution of ability as measured by intelligence tests and the class chances of obtaining a grammar school education in South West Hertfordshire and Middlesborough. Further evidence on social class and education relating to the grammar school was provided in official reports on *Early Leaving* (Ministry of Education, 1954) and in *Fifteen to Eighteen* (Ministry of Education, 1959). In the studies reported by Bernstein in the early 1960s discussing class differences in education and linguistic ability similar trends can be seen. In a central discussion of language and class Bernstein contrasts the speech of post office messenger *boys* with public school *boys*. These results were used to generate ideas about the education of *children* although the evidence was based on *an all male sample* (Bernstein, 1960). Yet such crude generalization was not confined to Bernstein's work as other commentators have drawn attention to the way in which educational research has been carelessly summarized as relating to all children when many of the samples were confined to boys.

Indeed, in recent years we need look no further than the study by Halsey, Heath and Ridge (1980) where conclusions are drawn concerning children on the basis of an all male sample. Furthermore, this study has continued to look at issues concerning access to education and educational performance in selective and non-selective schools. Once more this highlights the narrowness of vision associated with studies of class and education (cf. Blackstone, 1980; Burgess, 1984a).

Much of this research on class and education has focused on elite forms of education: academic performances that would result in entry to grammar schools and subsequent entry to universities. However, it does not end there, for the educational performance of pupils has focused on the education of boys who performed well in grammar schools with the result that only a small sector of 'education' was examined. In a recent survey of the sociology of education from 1960 to 1979 Acker (1981) arrives at a similar conclusion. Her analysis concerns the absence of studies on girls and women in education but her findings also highlight the narrow focus in studies of education. She discusses what the proverbial visitor from Mars might conclude about British society and the English educational system from reading the available literature as girls and women are virtually absent from the schools and colleges represented.

Similar comments could be made about data on race and education. As Tomlinson (1983) indicates, we have numerous local studies concerning the educational performance of West Indian and Asian pupils, but we might ask: how can we compare performances between different groups when investigators have used different tests to 'measure' educational performance and education is perceived in different ways? In turn, we lack basic data on the educational experiences of pupils and students from different ethnic groups. For example, there is relatively little British observational research on the school experience of black pupils. The work of Mary Fuller (1980) provides one of the few accounts in this area. In turn, our knowledge of the educational performance of black pupils in public examinations is very sparse, so much so that the Rampton Committee (1981) had to conduct a special inquiry to obtain comparative data in six local education authorities. The result was that some useful base data were provided that could be utilized in further investigations by the Swann Committee (1985). However, if difficulties exist in looking at the schooling of ethnic groups, the problem is magnified when looking at higher education. Here, there are no data that provide national trends and patterns in Britain; a situation that has been the subject of critical comment by Craft and Craft (1983).

Conclusion

Such evidence demonstrates that the sociology of education has continued to work within a narrow field of vision. Accordingly, it suggests that there is much new work to be done by researchers in extending studies *of* education and studies *in* education. Indeed, future work on education needs to go beyond the narrow concentration on white, male, grammar school pupils which has been a central focus for over thirty years. Work on educational achievement needs to be complemented by work on the content of education, girls' education needs to be studied and compared with that of boys, and the implications of a multi-cultural society need to be considered for education. Furthermore, sociologists need to be aware that education does not equal qualifications, school structures and patterns of formal schooling. There are many open spaces for sociologists to focus upon as pre-school education, higher education and the politics of education are all under-researched. Furthermore, even more familiar areas demand empirical study as they are more often characterized by concept spinning than by data collection (Davies, 1983).

If social researchers are to extend the boundaries of what constitutes the study of education the following recommendations should be kept in mind:

1 The focus should be upon educational systems as well as schools and classrooms so that educational politics, decision making and its influence upon educational change can be taken into account.
2 Studies of education need to be time specific, as what constitutes education and what it means to be educated may vary depending on the period under study.
3 Researchers need to specify the unit of educational study with some care for in a hierarchical educational system the level at which data are collected may influence the scope of the analysis.
4 Data need to be collected about the education of girls and women as well as boys and men and researchers should refrain from making generalizations about the education of children when studies have focused only on boys. Indeed, for those engaged in secondary analysis, data from previous studies might be reinterpreted while common sense assumptions about the education of boys and girls need to be questioned in new investigations.

5 Data on 'education' should not merely focus on the academ-
ically successful elite groups and high achievers, as we need
to know more about the education of individuals who are
placed in non-academic, non-subject, non-examination
groups. In turn, we need to investigate the criteria that are
used to assign individuals in particular groups.

6 Among the minimum data that are required on academic
education are: terminal education age, number of years
stayed beyond the school leaving age, last school attended,
duration of further or higher education full or part time and
details of educational qualifications. (For the ways in which
questions may be posed on some of these topics see Weinberg, 1969.)

7 While the aspect of education studied will depend on the
purpose of the investigation it is important to collect data on
the curriculum that is followed and the activities that occur
in classrooms to complement other work.

8 Where possible researchers involved in local surveys and
small scale investigations might look at the categories used in
large scale national surveys such as the General Household
Survey, so that comparisons can be made between the local
and the national.

9 Wherever possible quantitative and qualitative data should
be collected to complement each other.

References

Acker, S. (1981), 'No woman's-land: British sociology of education
1960–1979', *Sociological Review*, vol. 19, no. 1, pp. 77–104.
Andrew, A. (1985), 'In pursuit of the past: some problems in the
collection, analysis and use of historical documentary evidence',
in R. G. Burgess (ed.) *Strategies of Educational Research: Qualitative
Methods*, Lewes, Falmer Press.
Archer, M. S. (1979), *The Social Origins of Educational Systems*,
Beverly Hills, California, Sage.
Archer, M. S. (1981), 'Fields of specialization: educational
systems', *International Social Science Journal*, vol. 33, no. 2,
pp. 261–84.
Ball, S. J. (1981), *Beachside Comprehensive: A Case Study of Secondary
Schooling*, Cambridge, Cambridge University Press.
Ball, S. J. (1982), 'Competition and conflict in the teaching of

English: a socio-historical analysis', *Journal of Curriculum Studies*, vol. 14, no. 1, pp. 1–28.

Banks, O. (1982a), 'The sociology of education, 1952–1982', *British Journal of Educational Studies*, vol. 30, no. 1, pp. 18–31.

Bellaby, P. (1979), 'Towards a political economy of decision-making in the classroom' in J. Eggleston (ed.) *Teacher Decision-making in the Classroom*, London, Routledge & Kegan Paul, pp. 93–117.

Benn, C. and **Simon, B.** (1972), *Half Way There: A Report of the British Comprehensive School Reform* (2nd edn), Harmondsworth, Penguin.

Bernbaum, G. (1977), *Knowledge and Ideology in the Sociology of Education*, London, Macmillan.

Bernstein, B. (1960), 'Language and social class', *British Journal of Sociology*, vol. 11, pp. 271–6.

Bernstein, B. (1974), 'Sociology and the sociology of education: a brief account', in J. Rex (ed.) *Approaches to Sociology: An Introduction to Major Trends in British Sociology*, London, Routledge & Kegan Paul, pp. 145–59.

Blackburn, R. M., Stewart, A. and **Prandy, K.** (1980). 'Part-time education and the "alternative route" ', *Sociology*, vol. 14, no. 4, pp. 603–14.

Blackstone, T. (1980), 'Falling short of meritocracy', *The Times Higher Education Supplement*, 18 January, p. 14.

Burgess, R. G. (1983) *Experiencing Comprehensive Education: A Study of Bishop McGregor School*, London, Methuen.

Burgess, R. G. (1984a), 'Exploring frontiers and settling territory: shaping the sociology of education', *British Journal of Sociology*, vol. 35, no. 1, pp. 122–37.

Burgess, R. G. (1984b) 'It's not a proper subject: it's just Newsom' in I. F. Goodson and S. J. Ball (eds) *Defining the Curriculum*, Lewes, Falmer Press.

Burgess, R. G. (1984c), 'Patterns and processes of education in the United Kingdom', in P. Abrams and R. K. Brown (eds) *UK Society To-day: Work, Urbanism and Inequality* (2nd edn), London, Weidenfeld & Nicolson, pp. 58–128.

Byrne, E. (1978) *Women and Education*, London, Tavistock.

Chanan, G. and **Delamont, S.** (1975) (eds) *Frontiers of Classroom Research*, Slough, NFER.

Cooper, B. (1983), 'On explaining change in school subjects', *British Journal of Sociology of Education*, vol.4, no. 3, pp. 207–22.

Cormack, R. J. and **Osborne, R. D.** (1983) (eds), *Religion, Education* *and Employment: Aspects of Equal Opportunity in Northern Ireland*, Belfast, Appletree Press.

Craft, M. and **Craft, A.** (1983), 'The participation of ethnic minority pupils in further and higher education', *Educational Review*, vol. 25, no. 1, pp. 10–19.

Davies, B. (1983), 'The sociology of education', in P. H. Hirst (ed.) *Educational Theory and its Foundation Disciplines*, London, Routledge & Kegan Paul, pp. 100–45.

Deem, R. (1978) *Women and Education*, London, Routledge & Kegan Paul.

Delamont, S. (1980) *Sex Roles and the School*, London, Methuen.

D.E.S. (1965) *The Organization of Secondary Education* (Circular 10/65) London, HMSO.

D.E.S. (1979) *Aspects of Secondary Education in England: A Survey by H. M. Inspector of Schools*, London, HMSO.

Douglas, J. W. B. (1964) *The Home and the School*, London, MacGibbon and Kee.

Douglas, J. W. B., Ross, J. M. and **Simpson, H. R.** (1968) *All Our Future*, London, Peter Davies.

Floud, J. (1954), 'The educational experience of the adult population of England and Wales as at July, 1949', in D. V. Glass, (ed.) *Social Mobility in Britain*, Routledge & Kegan Paul, pp. 98–140.

Floud, J. and **Halsey, A. H.** (1958), 'The sociology of education: a trend report and bibliography', *Current Sociology*, vol. 7, no. 3, pp. 165–235.

Floud, J., Halsey, A. H. and **Martin, F. M.** (1956) *Social Class and Educational Opportunity*, London, Heinemann.

Fogelman, K. (1981) 'Assessing examination attainment in selective and non-selective secondary schools' in I. Plewis *et al.*, *Publishing School Examination Results: A Discussion*, Bedford Way Papers, no. 5, pp. 24–31.

Fogelman, K. (1983) (ed.), *Growing Up in Great Britain*, London, Macmillan.

Fuller, M. (1980), 'Black girls in a London comprehensive school', in R. Deem (ed.) *Schooling for Women's Work*, London, Routledge & Kegan Paul, pp. 52–65.

Glass, D. (1954) (ed.) *Social Mobility in Britain*, London, Routledge & Kegan Paul.

Goodson, I. F. (1982) *School Subjects and Curriculum Change*, London, Croom Helm.

Goodson, I. F. and **Ball, S. J.** (1984) (eds) *Defining the Curriculum*, Lewes, Falmer Press.

Gray, J. (1981), 'Are examination results a suitable measure of school performance?' in I. Plewis *et al.*, *Publishing School Examination Results: a Discussion*, Bedford Way Papers No. 5, pp. 13–23.

Gray, J., McPherson, A. F. and **Raffe, D.** (1983) *Reconstructions of Secondary Education: Theory, Myth and Practice Since the Second World War*, London, Routledge & Kegan Paul.

Hakim, C. (1982) *Secondary Analysis in Social Research*, London, Allen & Unwin.

Halsey, A. H., Heath, A. F. and **Ridge, J. M.** (1980), *Origins and Destinations: Family, Class and Education in Modern Britain*, Oxford, Clarendon Press.

Hammersley, M. and **Woods, P.** (1976) (eds) *The Process of Schooling*, London, Routledge & Kegan Paul.

Harding, J. (1981), 'Sex differences in science examinations' in A. Kelly (ed.) *The Missing Half*, Manchester, Manchester University Press, pp. 192–204.

Hargreaves, D. H. (1967) *Social Relations in a Secondary School*, London, Routledge & Kegan Paul.

Hargreaves, D. H. (1982) *The Challenge for the Comprehensive School*, London, Routledge & Kegan Paul.

Hargreaves, D. H., Hester, S. and **Mellor, F.** (1975) *Deviance in Classrooms*, London, Routledge & Kegan Paul.

Hartnett, A. (1982) (ed.) *The Social Sciences and Educational Studies*, London, Heinemann.

Himmelweit, H. (1954), 'Social status and secondary education since the 1944 Act: some data for London', in D. V. Glass (ed.) *Social Mobility in Britain*, London, Routledge & Kegan Paul, pp. 141–59.

Karabel, J. and **Halsey, A. H.** (1977), 'Educational research: a review and an interpretation' in J. Karabel and A. H. Halsey (eds) *Power and Ideology in Education*, Oxford, Oxford University Press, pp. 1–85.

Keddie, N. (1971), 'Classroom knowledge', in M. F. D. Young (ed.) *Knowledge and Control: New Directions for the Sociology of Education*, London, Collier-Macmillan, pp. 133–60.

Kelly, A. (1981) (ed.) *The Missing Half*, Manchester, Manchester University Press.

Lacey, C. (1970) *Hightown Grammar: The School as a Social System*, Manchester, Manchester University Press.

Layton, D. (1973) *Science for the People*, London, Allen & Unwin.
Main, B. and **Raffe, D.** (1983), 'The transition from "school to work" in 1980/81: a dynamic account', *British Educational Research Journal*, vol. 9, no. 1, pp. 57–70.
Ministry of Education (1954) *Early Learning*, London, HMSO.
Ministry of Education (1959) *15 to 18*, London, HMSO.
Monks, T. G. (1968), *Comprehensive Education in England and Wales: A Survey of Schools and their Organization*, Slough, National Foundation for Educational Research.
Monks, T. G. (1970) *Comprehensive Education in Action*, Slough, National Foundation for Educational Research.
Mortimore, P. and **Byford, D.** (1981) 'Monitoring examination results within a local education authority', in I. Plewis *et al.*, *Publishing School Examination Results: A Discussion*, Bedford Way papers, no. 5, pp. 32–47.
OPCS (1973) *General Household Survey*, London, HMSO.
OPCS (1982) *General Household Survey 1980*, London, HMSO.
OPCS (1983) *General Household Survey 1981*, London, HMSO.
Ottaway, A. K. C. (1960), 'The aims and scope of educational sociology' *Educational Review*, vol. 12, no. 3, pp. 190–9.
Philips, C. (1981), 'Discussion', in I. Plewis *et al.*, *Publishing School Examination Results: A Discussion*, Bedford Way Papers, no. 5, pp. 49–51.
Raffe, D. (1979), 'The "Alternative Route" reconsidered: part-time further education and social mobility in England and Wales', *Sociology*, vol. 13, pp. 47–73.
Rampton Committee (1981) *West Indian Children in Our Schools*, London, HMSO.
Reid, I. (1981) *Social Class Differences in Britain* (2nd edn), London, Grant McIntyre.
Reynolds, D. (1980), 'Review of *Fifteen Thousand Hours*', *British Journal of Sociology of Education*, vol. 1, no. 2, pp. 207–11.
Roberts, H. (1982), 'After Sixteen: What Choice?' in R. G. Burgess (ed.) *Exploring Society*, London, British Sociological Association, pp. 91–113 (2nd edn, Longman, 1986).
Rutter, M. *et al.*, (1979) *Fifteen Thousand Hours*, London, Grant McIntyre.
Salter, B. and **Tapper, T.** (1981) *Education, Politics and the State*, London, Grant McIntyre.
Sharp, R. and **Green, A.** (1975) *Education and Social Control*, London, Routledge & Kegan Paul.
Silver, H. (1973) (ed.) *Equal Opportunity in Education*, London, Methuen.

122   *Robert G. Burgess*

Swann Committee (1985) *Education for All*, London, HMSO.
Tomlinson, S. (1983) *Ethnic Minorities in British Schools*, London, Heinemann.
Turner, G. (1983) *The Social World of the Comprehensive School*, London, Croom Helm.
Weinberg, A. (1969), 'Education', in M. Stacey (ed.) *Comparability in Social Research*, London, Heinemann, pp. 1–31.
Wilkin, M. (1982), 'Educational opportunity and achievement', in I. Reid and E. Wormald (eds) *Sex Differences in Britain*, London, Grant McIntyre, pp. 85–113.
Willis, P. (1977) *Learning to Labour*, London, Saxon House.
Woods, P. (1979) *The Divided School*, London, Routledge & Kegan Paul.
Woods, P. (1980a) (ed.) *Teacher Strategies: Explorations in the Sociology of the School*, London, Croom Helm.
Woods, P. (1980b) (ed.) *Pupil Strategies: Explorations in the Sociology of the School*, London, Croom Helm.
Woods, P. (1983) *Sociology and the School: An Interactionist Viewpoint*, London, Routledge & Kegan Paul.
Woods, P. and **Hammersley, M.** (1977) (eds) *School Experience*, London, Croom Helm.
Young, M. F. D. (1971) (ed.) *Knowledge and Control: New Directions for the Sociology of Education*, London, Collier-Macmillan.

Social class and occupation[1]   7

Catherine Marsh

1 Introduction

The same word, 'class', is used to cover a wide range of concepts. The most ambitious use to which it has been put has been to provide an explanation of broad historical processes; an understanding of differences in class interests has been used to explain wars, the rise of fascism, the success and failure of revolutions. The most robust and coherent theory of class for the explanation of broad social change has been Marxist; it has sought to identify the 'great camps' of opposing classes between whom conflict is inevitable – landlord and serf, bourgeoisie and working class. Classes defined in this way have to be real social groups with the potential for self-identity, organization, expression of collective interest and collective action.

But this is not the only use it has had in social research. It has been used for a wide variety of purposes, most of them much finer-grained than the explanation of broad political and social change. 'Class', as used in sociological explanations of features of industrialized societies, refers to subdivisions of the working class in the terms of Marxist categories just outlined; no sociological class scheme has identified a group that can legitimately be termed 'the bourgeoisie' or 'the ruling class', for example. Arid debates about what class *really* is only occur if we fail to realize that the word is doing service for a wide variety of valid endeavours.

We can distinguish three different sociological uses:

1 Class is viewed as a dependent variable in its own right, as worthy of study and explanation. Students of social stratification have wanted a way of identifying the status of occupations in order to ask what are the determinants of placement in desirable jobs. Sociologists of economic life

have wanted to describe and document trends in the mode of production of societies, and have been interested in such things as the decline of self-employment, the rise of service employment and so on.

2 Class is often used as a control variable in non-experimental research. In the recent debates in Britain about which school type produces the best examination results, for example, it has proved very important to hold constant the 'kind of children' that the school admits in the first place. If we only ever used class as a control variable, inability to specify in theoretical, conceptual terms what it measured would not be so serious.

3 Class is used as an independent variable with explanatory power. It is called upon to show the social bases for individual attitudes or practices, or shared attitudes and ideologies, and even collective practices and collective action. In order for it to have explanatory power, it is important that it be adequately theorized, or circular explanations ensue: if Registrar-General's class is found to correlate with some lifestyle variable, this can only be deemed an explanation if we can be sure that the class schema is not itself just a proxy for lifestyle groupings.

In this chapter, the various schemes that have been used for sociological, as opposed to macro-historical, purposes, will be examined. At the end, some attempt at summary and recommendations will be made, but there is no intention to provide a recommendation of what is *the* best scheme, one scheme that captures most closely *the* major lines of cleavage in society. Before considering the various schemes, however, the process of identifying and coding occupations themselves must be discussed.

2 Occupational classification

Occupational differentiation is strictly non-hierarchical. An occupation is a place in the technical division of labour (Wright 1980) and refers to 'the kind of work done and the nature of the occupation performed' (OPCS 1980: vi). Conceptually it can be distinguished from the social relationships and skills involved in doing it, from the industry in which it is done, from the function which it performs and from the income which derives from it; over the years, social researchers, mainly through refining official schemes for use on the census of population, have learnt to measure these different conceptual dimensions separately.

The earliest censuses merely provided group headings, and coders used their judgment about where to place occupations. The groupings were a hopeless mish-mash, lacking 'fixity of principle or method' (Booth 1886:318): some of the groups were occupational, some were differentiated by skill, some by social standing, and some by a strange animal/vegetable/mineral distinction which grouped butchers and silk operatives and contrasted them with upholsterers and cotton operatives. The decision, taken for the 1911 census, to draw up a list of all the different occupations that people did, represented a major advance. The method used since 1911 has been to list the thousands of *titles* that people used to describe their jobs, and then aggregate them into groups. This does not ensure that the resulting differentiation is based solely on technical factors: the titles of female and manual jobs are much less finely differentiated by the population, for example, for reasons which are probably not merely reflections of job content.[2] Nevertheless, it was a conceptual step forward, and allowed the separate identification of industry, economic activity status and skill.

The hardest distinction to make was that between occupation and employment status; the title 'manager', for example, tells you something about job content, but probably more about relationships with other people. When that distinction was finally made in the scheme drawn up for the 1961 census, the effect was to cut the number of occupational groups from over 500 to over 200. The *Classification of Occupations 1970* (OPCS 1970) shows the 223 occupational unit groups (hereafter OUGs) cross-classified by the seven employment statuses.

Survey interviewers performed quality checks after the 1966 census. There was a discrepancy between the OUG coded from the titles they recorded and the OUG coded from the census form in 10.7 per cent of cases (Gray and Gee 1972); since the survey interviewers collected much more detailed information, the investigators refer to this as the 'mis-classification' rate. While there will always be a residual hard core of vague, unclassifiable jobs, there did seem to be especial difficulty stemming from the use of titles rather than job descriptions; titles are often unclear, over-general or confused with grade titles.

One might have hoped that the new system of occupational classification developed for the 1981 census would improve this. The Department of Employment use an elaborate scheme known as CODOT in their employment exchanges; people applying for jobs are assigned to one of over 5000 occupations purely on the basis of the operations involved in the job. The scheme for the 1981 census, detailed in *Classification of Occupations 1980* (OPCS 1980), was based on CODOT, but only on aggregations of these occupations into 547 occupational groupings (hereafter OGs). Social researchers, who use the 1980 scheme without going through the stage of first coding the detailed occupational category, therefore still rely on the title supplied by the respondent and must match it to the description given for the various OGs. The 1980 occupations are therefore not differentiated by skill and job content alone; indeed, without a detailed work-study, it is probably impossible to identify occupation as a purely technical variable, stripped of its social connotations through disassociation with title. It is doubtful whether the major conceptual breakthrough heralded has in practice been achieved.

What has happened is that a major discontinuity has been introduced which makes comparisons of data coded to the 1970 and 1980 schemes very hard. Despite the official aim of preserving comparability between the two systems (Boston 1980), there are no translation rules.[3] Moreover, recoding 1 per cent of the 1971 census returns indicates that the effect of these changes have been quite large, because about 9 per cent of people would have ended up in different social classes.

There does not appear to have been the technical improvement in coding reliability that was hoped for (Elliott 1982: 48).[4] Researchers who wish to use the 1980 scheme for small-scale projects will also find using the codebook very hard, as it involves two look-up tables, rather than the one required for the 1970 scheme. OPCS and other government departments merely code to an intermediate 'operational code' and then use a computer to combine the information with employment status and perform the look-up.[5] In both the 1970 and 1980 schemes, the cross-tabulation of OUG/OG by employment status makes some combinations illegal; this does not pose problems when employment status is office-coded by experienced coders, but it does when it is supplied by the respondent.

However, despite these difficulties, there is no alternative to the OPCS schemes, and the 1980 version should be used in preference to 1970 because it is both finer and more up-to-date.

The history of difficulties and developments in the British census occupational classification is remarkably similar to that in America, in the scheme developed for the US Census of Population (US Department of Commerce 1981) and the difficulties of making revisions to the scheme while ensuring comparability have also been met

(Subcommittee on Comparability of Occupation Measurement 1982). The US scheme does not, however, systematically differentiate occupation and employment status.

Researchers who wish to make international comparisons would be advised to make sure that full occupational detail is coded, and even at this level, there are problems of comparability, partly because the technical division of labour varies, but also because there are important cultural differences in occupational titles. Attempts to get round these problems of comparability have best been tackled at the occupational level in the creation of the International Standard Classification of Occupation (ILO 1968); it is currently being revised.

3 Reputed prestige or desirability

We shall begin our review of measures based on occupation with the conceptually simple notion of scaling them according to a criterion. In most industrialized and many non-industrialized countries, occupations have been scaled according to their reputed worth as determined by a survey of the general public. We shall first review the construction of an exemplary scale of this kind, and then consider various other American and international scales to illuminate the problem of what exactly the scales measure.

John Goldthorpe and Keith Hope (1974) set out to improve on the Hall-Jones scale used in David Glass' post-war mobility study (Hall and Jones, 1950), to construct a scale for use on the Oxford Mobility Study which would rank jobs in terms of their perceived social desirability. In order to select representative job titles, they first subdivided the jobs listed in Appendix B2 of the 1970 scheme into 125 categories considered to be relatively homogeneous with respect to the 'net extrinsic and intrinsic, material and non-material rewards and deprivations' associated with them (Goldthorpe and Hope 1974:24). They then selected five or ten titles to represent each category, picking 860 titles in all. Since they were only investigating male mobility patterns, they ruled out jobs done exclusively by women.

Goldthorpe and Hope argued that it is better to ask people to rank rather than rate a set of occupations, but this makes the task of covering all the occupations and scoring the replies hard. The authors solved the difficulties in an ingenious way. The respondents were asked first to place twenty *common* occupational titles in rank order of 'social standing', and then to add in twenty occupational titles that were *unique* to that respondent; ties were permitted. The twenty common titles were given standardized scores, and the twenty unique rankings were then interpolated.

The agreement between individuals about the ranking of titles is quite low, as in all exercises of this kind; social consensus about the rank accounts for only 27 per cent of individual variance, while respondent disagreement and respondent inconsistency account for 39 per cent and 25 per cent respectively. However, once the rankings are aggregated across the ten to twenty original raters, respondent disagreement and inconsistency disappear almost completely, and the result is a scale of high reliability: if the whole exercise were conducted again, the resulting scale would correlate .93 with the Hope-Goldthorpe scale. Its *use* in any particular survey would bring some additional intercoder unreliability, of course. The validity coefficient is the correlation of the scale value for an occupation with the true value one would obtain for it if one could assess popular evaluations directly; it is inferred from the intracategory correlation among occupation titles, corrected for attentuation, and is, in this case, .76. Respondent disagreement is higher at the top than the bottom, probably because this scale suffers the problem of having finer subdivisions at the top.

One major advantage of coding to this scale is that it leaves maximum flexibility for further grouping. The authors themselves suggest a 36-point collapsed version of the full 125-point scale, and a discrete class scheme to be discussed below. The scale is also reducible to socio-economic group (SEG) or Registrar-General's social class (RG), since no Hope-Goldthorpe category spans two SEGs or two RGs. The use of the scale presupposes that occupational coding will have been done to the 1970 list, however. A new study would be required satisfactorily to scale 1980 OGs.

Goldthorpe and Hope insist that the scale does not tap prestige, because no observation has been made of how individuals actually confer status upon and accept status from one another: people are making a cognitive not a moral judgment about the general desirability of an occupation, or at least about its reputation; they are saying how much they would like it. Nonetheless, the result correlates highly with other scales of this kind (the authors would argue because most other reputational scales measure social desirability also) but also with more direct measures of social status, in particular the Cambridge scale (discussed in the next section).

It was the scale constructed in 1947 by North and Hatt at the National Opinion Research Center at Chicago (Reiss 1961) which stimulated the most intense debate about the stability and importance of occupational stratification, which provoked an enormous amount of secondary research, and which formed the basis for the NORC scale that is widely-used in the USA today.[6] The scale proved so stable, and correlated so highly with previous studies, that researchers felt that a social fact of tremendous significance had been discovered. The agreement in ordering given by high and low educational groups, males and females, rich and poor, North-east and South, professional and unskilled, old and young, even between those whose stated criteria for evaluation were different, seemed quite striking; the correlations were between .96 and .99 (Reiss 1961: 189).

In 1963, Hodge, Siegel and Rossi replicated this exercise exactly as it had been conducted in 1947; the correlation between the two resulting scales was .99. The authors then repeated the exercise in 1964 on a larger and more representative set of occupations (Hodge, Siegel and Rossi 1967) and Siegel conducted a study in 1965 to cover the remaining 30 per cent of occupations in the 1960 US census list. The results of these three studies were aggregated, the responses standardized, and a scale was produced which is now dated but is still the most widely used in American studies (Siegel 1971).

The very high correlations between scales constructed in different industrialized countries led Inkeles and Rossi in 1956 to hypothesize that they were all measuring a common prestige continuum which resulted from a logic imperative in the process of industrialization itself. However, later studies from non-industrial societies seemed to produce similar scales, and led Hodge, Treiman and Rossi (1967) to advance an even stronger suggestion: since the correlation between GNP and prestige is lower for non industrial than for industrial nations, the 'acquisition of a "modern" system of occupational evaluation would seem to be a necessary precondition for rapid industrialization' (1967: 320). Treiman (1977), in the most recent collection of international prestige studies in which he proposes an international prestige scale, claims that the similarity of orderings stems from the logic of any social organization which involves the division of labour.

There are several flaws in these functionalist arguments. The degree of consensus is systematically overstated (Guppy 1984; Coxon and Jones 1978). Most of the high correlation between scales comes from ranking manual jobs below non-manual jobs, not from agreement about how jobs should be ranked within each sector. Reiss' evidence of structured disagreement in ranking is conveniently forgotten, as are studies like Young and Willmott (1956) which discovered that manual workers in London's East End ranked occupations very differently from Hall and Jones' middle class raters (sometimes even reversing the order completely), and those reported in Lane (1982), which showed that skilled manual jobs are consistently ranked above junior non-manual ones in socialist societies. In international studies, attention has to be restricted to comparable occupations, a biased subset of all occupations; agricultural occupations, for example, are excluded thus making it impossible to test some of the most interesting examples of the precondition hypothesis. In most countries, students are used as the raters.

Moreover, if consensus with 'modern' (i.e. American) values of occupational prestige was intimately linked with the functioning of a 'modern' occupational structure where jobs in a certain imperative co-ordination to one another and requiring certain amounts of education have to be ranked in a particular order and rewarded accordingly, then one would expect the prestige hierarchy to change with the fundamental shifts that have occurred in this occupational structure and in the educational requirements and rewards for particular jobs in the last half century. Ironically, the relative stability of the prestige hierarchy across time militates against this explanation.

Finally, it is important to note that occupational scales derived from the original prestige studies have predominated in stratification research, rather than the prestige scales themselves. Duncan's (1961) scale is probably the most popular. The North–Hatt scores had only been derived for occupations covering half the workforce; Duncan obtained a score for the whole occupational spectrum in the following way. He used information on the income and education of male civilians in the labour force as identified on the 1950 Census of Population to predict the North–Hatt ratings for all occupations covered in the original 1947 survey (regressing the proportion of 'excellent' or 'good' ratings in those occupations against standardized proportions with above median incomes and against age-standardized proportions of high-school graduates in each occupation). To devise a score on an index of socio-economic status for jobs not included in the survey, he used the regression coefficients as weights to predict a value on the basis of the known income and education distribution of each occupation.

This scale and a similarly-constructed Canadian scale (Blishen 1958) are usually called scales of socio-economic status, but their derivation in this manner from prestige studies makes their conceptual independence of prestige uncertain. (For a debate in the North American literature on the relative merits of prestige and socio-economic scales, see Powers 1982.)

4 Associational measures

Status is communicated in relationships of equality or deference between people. Reputational prestige studies only measure it indirectly, if at all. One way to study it directly might be to examine the patterns of association between people, their choice of friends or marriage partners, on the assumption that people pick as friends and partners people whose status they perceive as equal to their own.[7]

These patterns can be used to scale occupations on a status continuum, but occupational identifiers are not intrinsically required; residential identifiers or even names could be used.

Stewart, Prandy and Blackburn (1980) based their Cambridge scale on occupational friendship choices. The data was collected from a rather restricted sample of people; male white-collar workers who lived within a 60 miles radius of Cambridge. The respondents gave the occupations of four friends; those friends could therefore be blue-collar workers, but the occupations selected by this means were naturally not a cross-section of all blue-collar jobs.

The authors then selected those occupations that contained reasonable numbers of either respondents or friends of respondents, and examined the patterns of friendship networks that they revealed. They calculated a measure of dissimilarity between each pair of occupations by summing the positive percentage differences between the friendship choices for that pair. The coefficients were then read into a multi-dimensional scaling (MDS) package, a data reduction technique designed to account for patterns in the dissimilarities on as few dimensions as possible. Only one large and interpretable dimension emerged. The scale, however, only covered one third of all OUGs. So, closing their ears to Duncan's strictures against such a procedure (Duncan 1961), they used their judgment to interpolate the other two thirds.[8] This scale is currently being developed on a wider range of occupations using the 1980 list, subdividing some of the OGs where this seems necessary. When it becomes available, as well as offering the Cambridge scale values, it will offer the finest occupation coding scheme available for survey use, and will be collapsible to earlier OPCS schemes.

One of the main advantages of this principle of scaling occupations is that it is expandable to any specialized needs in a more detailed survey where more precise status hierarchies are required; researchers only need to collect information about friendship patterns in order to reconstitute their own scale. This can be done as part of the main data-gathering exercise and does not require a separate survey.

The authors are not happy about calling it a scale of social status; it orders occupations whose incumbents are likely to associate, rather than ordering occupations whose incumbents give or receive deference. They stress that the scale measures the market *outcomes* of different jobs, the style of life associated with them, rather than any dimension which *constitutes* the social structure and creates different market capacities in different sections of the population. It correlates highly with Hope–Goldthorpe (.88) but there are also patterned differences between the scales. The Cambridge scale shows a complete division between foremen and all white collar workers, for example, whereas these categories overlap in Hope–Goldthorpe, a result which is consistent with the former being a scale of status and the latter a scale of social desirability of the jobs. The scale, however, correlates even more highly with other occupational scales constructed in the traditional reputational way: .93 with Treiman's standard international scale (Treiman 1977) and .95 with an Australian scale developed at ANU (Broom *et al.* 1977). Social desirability, association and social status are, in short, empirically close if conceptually distinct.

Critics of scaling procedures of this kind argue that the undimensionality and high degree of agreement that the resulting scales evince is an artefact of the data collection procedures. Coxon and Jones (1978) used techniques such as asking respondents to sort three occupations into two similar occupations and one different one, and to explain the principles they used to do this; by this means they showed that one could produce evidence of many different cognitive dimensions which respondents use if the nature of the task they were given was changed.

5 Groups differentiated by lifestyle

We now come to groupings of occupations formed by *a priori* judgment. A common criterion for grouping is lifestyle pattern. One such measure, the Registrar-General's schema (RG), is the most widely-used measure of social class (OPCS 1980); to assign a person correctly to a social class one needs to know their detailed occupation and their current employment status.[9] Stevenson, the architect of RG, positively defended basing the scheme on occupation: ranking people by income would produce such obviously bizarre results as a publican ranking above a clergyman, whereas what needed to be identified was 'culture or the lack of it' (1928:207).

The skeleton of Stevenson's scheme, revised for the 1921 Census, was the separation of three ordered groups – the upper and middle class, skilled workmen and unskilled labourers; intermediate classes II and IV were inserted to cover the grey areas. The scheme has never been radically revised since then. In 1931 clerks suffered downward mobility as a group from class II to class III. In 1961 the concept of employment status was distinguished from that of occupation, and classes had to be derived from the cross-tabulation of the two. In 1971 the distinction between manual and non-manual occupations was made more systematic and class III was subdivided. The damage done to the ordinality of the scale was not assessed, nor did the female preponderance within class IIIN gave cause for alarm.

The reliability of RG when applied to survey data has been estimated by Elliott (1982), who found 87 per cent agreement among coders (91 per cent among expert coders). The reliability of RG as used by the Registrar of Births and the Census office has been estimated by Lette and Fox (1977) using data from the official records of a 1 per cent sample of the population; the class of men who registered the birth of a child before the end of 1971 was compared with their class as recorded at the Census in April 1971.[10] Only 81 per cent of people stayed in the same class during that short period, but there was little movement across the manual/non-manual boundary, and the majority only moved one class. The reliability of class V seemed worse than the others, with only 5 per cent remaining in this class.

Different validity claims have been made for RG. Conceived as a measure of culture, the validity of the scheme was originally established not conceptually but by pointing to the sharp gradients it produced in adult and infant mortality. In 1961 and 1971, it was claimed that it measured 'social standing in the community', and in 1981 it was claimed that the classes group 'people with similar levels of occupational skill'.[11] Its interpretation as a measure of social standing in the community has been questioned by Bland (1979), who showed the marked overlap between the social classes in terms of the Hope–Goldthorpe score of their constituent occupations. He calculated that the jobs of 33 per cent of the male workforce would have to be recoded in order to produce a monotonically ordered scheme based on social standing, and that class IIIN would disappear in the process; classes II and IIIN both overlap with class I at the top and class V at the bottom.

Fertility analysts in the 1940s felt that RG was an insufficiently fine classification scheme for demographic research. Professor Glass worked in conjunction with researchers at the GRO to develop an unranked set of socio-economic groups (SEGs). The scheme, like RG, requires prior coding of OG and employment status (OPCS 1980). This measure was tried first in the 1951 census, and then revised for the 1961 census into a nineteen category system grouping 'people whose social, cultural and recreational standards are similar' (CSO 1975:30). There is no evidence that any checks were performed to validate the discreteness of the categories in these respects, although a study by Wood (1981/2) did show however that they do not measure income differences very effectively.

In some ways SEG is retrograde conceptually; it reintroduces industry into the system, having separate categories for farm-workers and members of the armed forces, and its distinction between occupation and employment status is less clear than RG's. Nonetheless, its finer subdivisions have made it popular.[12] The seventeen SEGs, when cross-classified with the six RGs, produce thirty-seven socio-economic classes; this fine subdivision is, however, rarely used in social research.[13]

British market researchers have developed their own method of grading individuals into six ordered classes, A, B, C1, C2, D and E, the upper middle, middle, lower middle, skilled working, semi-skilled and unskilled working classes and 'those at the lowest levels of subsistence' respectively.[14] Sociologists who have contracted field-work to a commercial company sometimes also use this method (e.g. Runciman 1966).[15]

There are no definitive coding instructions for this scheme. It is most fully codified for the National Readership Survey, which guides advertisers on target markets; it claims to be based solely on occupation (Monk 1978), but the interviewers' manual for the NRS, in describing the classes, cues interviewers to use housing and income information as guidelines. When it is used on other surveys, by other companies, the only guide to the coding rules in use is often the house training manual.

The popularity of the ABC scheme is based on the fact that it is most widely used as a method of *field coding* social class. Most commercial companies in fact set their quota samples on the basis of social grade, so the interviewer *has* to be able to class the head of household on the doorstep; this practice has been widely criticized as leading to concentration on class stereotypes (Joint Industry Working Party 1981; Bermingham 1981).

Doorstep coding of something as complicated as social class is a risky procedure; it is impossible to maintain either quality control or

strict comparability across time and organization. While some experiments at OPCS suggest that field coding of Registrar-General's
social class could be taught to interviewers, and might even prompt
them to collect better and more relevant occupational detail (Green
1981), the evidence for this is still slender, and comes only from a
fieldforce which is incomparably well-supervised.

The ABC scheme is not reliable. The end product is sensitive to the
particular fieldwork company collecting the data, and the proportions of individuals assigned to each class are worryingly erratic over
time (Joint Industry Working Party 1981) and between surveys
(Bermingham 1981). Validity claims for it are based on its correlation
with a wide range of consumer durables (Monk 1978); income
performs as well as it when bivariate relationships alone are considered (Joint Industry Working Party 1981) but social grade does
have residual explanatory power when income is factored out (Lunn
1965). In view of its unreliability, however, its validity for social
research purposes in general should be doubted.

If lifestyle or consumption patterns are thought to be of importance
in a particular field of study, perhaps income and wealth data should
be collected directly; they are relatively neglected in much research,
probably more because of exaggerated fears about the difficulty of
collecting information about them than because of strong convictions
like Stevenson's that mere money is unimportant.

6 Market and work situation

David Lockwood (1957) discussed social class in terms which many
sociologists have subsequently found useful. He did not accept that
purchasing power in the market was the only important source of
social divisions, since one could not in that way explain the social
position of the impecunious clerk. Features of the work an individual
did also had a bearing; the black-coated worker clearly enjoyed a
different work situation to his blue-overalled colleague.

These two components of market and work situation have been
viewed as the core dimensions of class by many sociologists, and John
Goldthorpe and his colleagues have elaborated a class schema explicitly built on this idea, first for work on social mobility and more
recently for use on the 1983 British Election Study. There are several
versions of the scheme, but all share the goal of constructing classes
whose incumbents share both similar economic prospects and similar
amounts of autonomy and authority. In order to achieve this goal,

heavier and more systematic use is made of employment status and the form of the labour contract than in other groupings based on occupation.

The first version of the scheme was formed by grouping collapsed Hope–Goldthorpe categories, since these are relatively finely differentiated in both occupational and employment contract terms;[16] the new version developed for the 1983 British Election Survey is a look-up procedure from the cross-tabulation of OG and employment status. The class categories, which are unranked,[17] are shown in the table below.

Notice the subdivision of class III into personal service workers and other routine non-manual workers; this should make the scheme particularly suitable for classifying women's occupations. There is evidence to suggest that this scheme is the best of all existing measures at predicting work-related dependent variables (Marsh 1983); Dale, Arber and Gilbert (1985) found it only worked best for men, but this was using the older version before class III was split.

Figure 1   Versions of the Goldthorpe class scheme

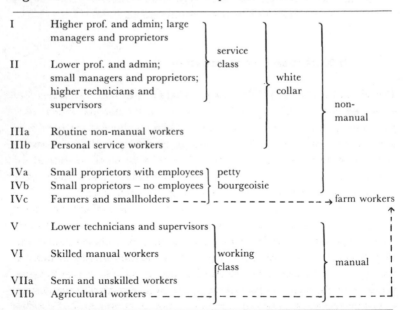

Source: Erikson, Goldthorpe and Portocarero 1979; Goldthorpe 1983a

7 Authority and autonomy

Marx's opposing camps of bourgeoisie and working class are not differentiated by occupation but by the ownership/non-ownership of capital. In most capitalist countries, the effective ownership of capital is in such a few hands, and those who are forced to sell their labour power to the corporations and institutions of modern capitalism are in such an overwhelming majority, that the usefulness of Marxist class categories might appear small.

In recent years, however, sociologists have attempted to adopt some of Marx's insights about how the ownership of capital gives the bourgeoisie power over people and things to develop class schemas which move away from divisions in the technical division of labour towards the division of power, authority and control at the workplace. These schemas have then been applied to some of the traditional concerns of sociologists with inequality, social stratification and political and work attitudes. Robinson and Kelley made an explicitly revisionist attempt to adapt Marxist class to the critique of Dahrendorf and others who argued that authority can gain independence of ownership and become the more important factor in class formation. Erik Olin Wright and his colleagues developed a scheme which concentrates on authority and autonomy *at work*, and so argue that no such revision has taken place. Claims that a 'capitalist class' can be identified in this way are highly problematic but, rather than engage in essentialist debates about what a unitary concept of class is 'really' about, it is preferable to take the two proposed schemas as hypotheses concerning the role of social relations at work in structuring people's social experiences and beliefs.

Researchers from Yale and the Australian National University have collaborated on a project covering the USA and Britain (Robinson and Kelley 1979). The central claim in this research is that there are two different dimensions of class – control and authority. The control dimension is operationalized as whether or not one has a supervisor. This dimension is claimed to derive from Marx on the basis of a dubious assertion that 'those who have no supervisor control the means of production while those who are not supervised do not' (p. 44). The incumbents of occupations which are not supervised on performance are deemed as members of the capitalist class, a decision that is particularly weak for women; female capitalists include restaurant, bar and cafeteria managers, cooks and registered nurses! The authority dimension is measured by the existence and number of levels of subordinates: if a person supervises anyone, they are deemed to be in a position of authority.

These operationalizations are best understood as locating individuals in a hierarchy of supervision at work. There are no theoretical grounds for the authors' contention that they constitute a bringing together of Marx's and Dahrendorf's theories; membership of Robinson and Kelley's 'capitalist class' increases income expectations by only $4,000 for men and actually decreases them for women. Nor can we accept the conclusion that the two dimensions of authority and control are 'empirically as well as conceptually distinct' (p. 46); the low correlation between them merely proves that there are some people who have supervisors who themselves supervise, a possibility that the questionnaire itself acknowledged.

Position in the hierarchy of supervision is nevertheless shown to be an important determinant of the income and subjective class position of men in their sample; it increases multiple R^2 by 50 per cent over and above education and occupational prestige. It is less successful for women, indicating difficulties in asking good questions about supervision hierarchies where women are concerned. It is also of small predictive value in explaining political attitudes, although stronger in the UK than in the USA.

The second research project is that associated with the American Marxist, Erik Olin Wright, who has taken great pains to distinguish occupation from class, not just theoretically but also in his empirical research. Wright argues that, although there are always two basic opposing classes in every mode of production, some contradictory locations between the two poles can be found; managers, for example, may control labour and physical capital, but have no control over money capital. Moreover, remnants of older modes of production linger on, and thus complications are introduced by groups such as small owners who work on their own account, especially if they employ a few others, and employees such as professionals who have never surrendered their autonomy for their wage contract.

Reanalysing data from the Survey of Working Conditions collected at Michigan in 1969, Wright argued that Marxist class categories are important predictors of such traditional sociological concerns as income differentials and income returns to education (Wright and Perrone 1977; Wright 1978b). He is now engaged in a large comparative study in which purpose-built survey data is being collected (Wright 1982). The aim of this project is to document and compare class structure in different countries, and to look at the outcomes of class in social and political terms. The distinctions between the various class and contradictory class locations can be much more carefully drawn in purpose-built surveys.

Capitalists are defined as large employers and the petty bourgeoisie as small employers. Managers and supervisors are defined as people who supervise (in the earlier work) or who take an active part in decision-making and in the authority chain of command (a five-category variable in the later work). Semi-autonomous employees are those who are not supervised (earlier) or who have real autonomy in how they work (later). Workers make up the rest – people who do not employ, and who lack authority and autonomy. The working class makes up half the class structure, and contains more women and blacks than other classes.

It is too early to evaluate this schema fully. The dimension of autonomy is defined very subjectively, and leads to high reported autonomy rates for some groups such as teachers and sales personnel. Moreover, it is doubtful if it is very far removed from the idea of skill level, used to differentiate occupational groups in the more traditional schemes. The most important contribution, reinforcing and elaborating Robinson and Kelley's conclusion, is that authority relations at work are important and should be examined directly and carefully.

There are two ironies in the empirical sociology based on these Marxisant schemas. One is that the greatest change that has taken place in the social relations of production since the nineteenth century capitalism that Marx wrote of, namely the extension of public ownership and state employment, is ignored in the empirical class definitions.[18] The other is that they tend to inflate the size of the 'capitalist class' to the point of absurdity: the concept is robbed of its critical power and attention is deflected from the one segment of the population who fit all the criteria for a social class as a real social group with self-identity, organization and the power to act in its collective interest.

8 Problems and alternatives

Classifications based on occupation have been by far the most common in Britain, but by no means universal (Morgan 1983); two especially critical questions have been raised about them:

1 Since the majority of people at one point in time have no job, to whose occupational group should they be assigned?
2 Since any given individual tends to have many jobs over a lifetime, which job should be selected?

The standard solution to the first problem is to group individuals into households (units with common catering arrangements) and classify the entire household by means of the occupation of the 'head' or the 'chief wage earner'. This sweeps the problem under the carpet for most people, but is not, on the face of it, very satisfactory, since it is much more common to find working household members in different social classes from the head than in the same (Garnsey 1978).

The problem has received most attention as it affects the social class of women (Britten and Heath 1983; Elias 1981; Garnsey 1978; Fox and Goldblatt 1982; Goldthorpe 1983b; Murgatroyd 1982; Oakley and Oakley 1979). The schemes considered in this chapter have been developed with men's occupations in mind, and are not well-suited to grouping women's jobs anyway; some argue that the head of household solution has merely prevented the necessary work required to develop a scheme suitable for women (see Dale, Arber and Gilbert 1983 for important steps in this direction). But the debate has raised the important question of the appropriate unit of analysis in different subject areas – the individual, the family, the household, the benefit unit . . . ? The debate so far has been insufficiently informed by empirical data, and we are left with fragmentary results which suggest that a woman's own occupation is the better predictor of who she will marry (Haskey 1983) and of her fertility (Britten and Heath 1981) but that her husband's is the better predictor of her mortality (Fox and Goldblatt 1982). There is a need to study neglected problems, such as the clustering of occupations or unemployment experience which occur commonly within households and the distribution of rewards within the household.

The second difficulty for occupational schemes relates to the time dimension and the importance of understanding the related concepts of career and lifecycle. Job changing is a regular and patterned phenomenon; around 13 per cent of employed people surveyed in the GHS in the late 1970s changed their jobs each year (although this proportion has declined as the recession has deepened), and 40 per cent in the Oxford Mobility Study were found to have changed social class since their first job (Goldthorpe 1980: Table 5.1). Some jobs, like research fellowships, are held exclusively by people at particular stages of their careers and lifecycles, while others, like clerks, have different significance for different incumbents: they are springboards for careers when they are held by young men, but are dead-end jobs when they are held by older women.

Both of these problems are particularly acute for the unemployed. Like women, they may be assigned to the class of another household member, but increasingly there are households where no one works. If they are old, they may be assigned to the class of their last, or, preferably, last *major* job, but this does not solve the problem for the increasing numbers of young people who have never worked. Rather than try to force the unemployed into a classification scheme based on somebody's job, it may be necessary to argue, as some have argued about women (Llewellyn 1981, for example), that occupation is less relevant for them, and turn instead to other classifications such as level of educational attainment.

Alternative measures have also been suggested which would apply to whole households, and thus solve the first problem. One that is fairly frequently used (it is collected on the Census, for example), is car-ownership, but it is still greatly influenced by the lifecycle stage of the household, and is a better indicator of wealth for men than for women, who may not drive for cultural as well as for financial reasons.

Another popular household-level indicator that works effectively in Britain is housing tenure. Nearly all households can be classified into owner-occupied, privately rented and local authority rented and, like car-ownership, the information is easily collected. This measure has been assessed and compared with occupational social class in discriminating mortality differentials by Fox and Goldblatt (1982): it proved to be the most powerful discriminator of mortality in the study, and, in the case of employed men, did not require any additional explanatory power from occupational social class (1982: 210).[19] Its power in predicting fertility, both in terms of birth timing and family size, has also been investigated (Murphy and Sullivan 1983); in general it has more gross discriminatory power than RG, but both have independent contributions to make in the explanation. It has a further advantage of tenure over social class in that its three subgroups are all substantial in size, making differentials between owner-occupiers and council-house tenants therefore of greater social consequence than those between classes I and V.[20] But it, too, is linked to lifecycle, and is not so impressive at older ages where mortality rates are influenced by health-related mobility.

Research Services Limited (1981) have developed a measure which deals with the second problem, explicitly incorporating an individual's place in the life cycle (whether a dependent, adult but pre-family, adult in family, later life) with social class (white v. blue collar only) and income (better-off v. worse-off). The resulting measure, called SAGACITY, has twelve groups, and is mainly used for market research and media planning. In short, whereas other class measures sometimes implicitly confuse occupation and lifecycle,

SAGACITY does so explicitly.

Many members of the public consider 'where you live' to be an important dimension of class (Reid 1977:27). In the market research world, a classification of local areas into eleven different social types has become popular in recent years; called ACORN, it was developed by cluster analysis of small area statistics of economic, lifestyle and demographic variables from the 1971 Census (Webber and Craig 1975; Webber 1979; Webber 1981). Commerical researchers use it to identify precise locations for specialized target markets; it has great potential in the design of efficient first stage samples (Blyth 1982), and could also be used to provide a residential classification system for social research where an ecological unit larger than the household was held to be important. It cannot satisfactorily be used as a *substitute* for household or individual measures, since there is so much heterogeneity within the areas identified. Nor does it, of course, circumvent the difficulties discussed above, since geographical mobility is as common as job mobility.

Finally, we should mention the attempt to solve the problem of 'single indicator' measures by creating composite indices. The Social Index developed for the Bristol Cohort Study (Osborn and Morris 1979), for example, combines RG with educational, local area and housing measures into a composite score. The result is an index which can be given no concrete interpretation.

The two problems raised at the beginning of the section cannot be overcome by conceptual *fiat*. The solution is not to develop class schemes based on patterned trajectories through the occupational structure, or which include lifecycle or residential elements within them; it is surely preferable to obtain separate measures of age, lifecycle, residence and so on, and so study the interaction between them and occupation.

9 Conclusions and recommendations

General recommendations are contrary to the spirit of this chapter, which has argued that different measures have been used for and appear to perform best at different tasks. Where technical problems associated with each measure are known, these have been indicated, and some idea has been given of the kind of uses to which each has been put. But it has not been possible systematically to compare the reliability, validity and stability of the measures, let alone demonstrate that each is actually *best* for the purposes to which it has been put. The spirit of these conclusions, therefore, is to encourage the kind of research that would help, cumulatively, to an understanding of some of these difficult questions, by making experimentation with and comparison between different schemes more easy.

Occupational measures of class are not about to be replaced. There is no decline in interest in occupation and employment status as a dependent variable of interest, nor is there any evidence for concluding that measures based on these are superfluous as explanatory variables. Despite fashionable discussions about the reduced impact of occupational class on voting behaviour, it is still one of the most powerful discriminators; despite findings that housing tenure has as powerful an effect on mortality as occupational class, the latter still has an important independent effect for some groups.

It would be unfortunate if the social research community swung away from untheorized occupational class measures and plumped instead for something else like income or tenure. There are signs, for example, that the market research community, disillusioned with the ABC method, are looking to market classifications, geographical classifications or socio-psychological classifications instead; there is, however, a big difference between despairing over a poor occupational measure and proving that they are all irrelevant.

So, researchers should ensure they collect sufficient detail to create a suitable occupational measure. *For this, there is no alternative to asking detailed questions about the nature of the respondent's job and then office-coding OG and employment status.* Do not be tempted to take short-cuts by field-coding, nor coding directly from the details given on the schedule to one of the social class schemes. The expense in time and money will be amply repaid by having maximum flexibility at the stage of data analysis to experiment with class schemes based on different rationales; these will be easy to create automatically through look-up computer routines. And the data will be in a form suitable for all sorts of secondary analysis.

Those who want a measure of social status/lifestyle, or for whom an interval scale is particularly important may find that the new version of the Cambridge scale is the most useful. Those who require a variable whose explicit focus is on differences in the work situation will probably find that some version of Goldthorpe's class scheme is most suited to their needs. But so long as OG and employment status have been coded, none of the Registrar-General's schemes are ruled out; researchers could easily check their results against a variety of official data sources, for example.

More problematic is the issue of whose occupation to code. We clearly can no longer remain satisfied with the once-prevalent idea that all that mattered was the class of the head of household; the recent focus on the problems of classifying women will have served a useful purpose if it encourages routine collection of respondent's own occupational details as well. But one would need to be very sure of one's ground before deciding to reject the head of household concept completely; once again, what is needed to clinch the argument is empirical evidence about the relative importance of the situation of different members of the household for different dependent variables. Moreover, if one is aiming for a class measure which identifies real social groups, as opposed to structural social variables, then it will be very important to obtain information about the occupations of people who live together, or who are close friends.

Perhaps most problematic of all is the incorporation of a time perspective into class coding. The assumption of most survey analysis is that it is the respondent's *current* situation that is the most critical; underlying this is an implicit model that the current situation reflects some aspect of their recent experience, and this experience is of important explanatory power. Yet, once this is made explicit, it is seen to be a rather deficient theory; sociology has for years tried to show up links between direct experiences (at work, of inequality etc.) and to link these with dependent variables such as political attitudes, and found repeatedly that the model requires fleshing out with other important prior cultural variables and also with an understanding of the respondents' orientations to the future before satisfactory explanatory power is achieved. If this is an important consideration in a particular research project, details of previous jobs may be indispensable; they are particularly important in studying the old and the unemployed.

None of the above should be read as implying that occupational measures provide the only or even the most important classifications. There are very good reasons why a series of variables have become standard on the facesheet of surveys – income, education, housing tenure, sex, marital status and age (or combined into a measure of life-cycle); researchers have been caught out too frequently by prematurely assuming that the effect of one of these variables could be ruled out. If our understanding of the construct validity of social class is to progress, we need to have much more understanding of the independence of these various facesheet variables from one another. Some of these variables have been suggested as alternatives for occupational measures. The safest conclusion is to collect them in addition, rather than in preference to, occupational measures.

Notes

1 My thanks are due to Sara Arber, Nick Bateson, Bill Blyth, Martin Bulmer, Bob Burgess, John Fox, John Goldthorpe, Neil Guppy, Donald Monk, Kate Purcell and Roger Thomas for their helpful comments on earlier drafts of this paper.

2 The 1970 occupational classification, which contains 223 separate occupational categories, groups 53% of women in five of its categories, and 24% of them in one alone – OUG 139, clerical and secretarial (Dale, Gilbert and Arber 1983). There also tends to be a negative correlation between size of occupational group and the prestige accorded to it in the various international studies.

3 According to the official description of the two schemes of 1970 and 1980, such comparability was completely impossible, since the conceptual basis of the class schemes erected on the occupational classification was supposedly radically altered. See section 5.

4 The coding reliability of OGs seems similar to that found for OUGs in 1966. Elliott (1982), in a smaller and somewhat different coder variance experiment, found 78% agreement where Gray and Gee found 10.7% 'misclassified'; he also showed the importance of quality control and coding experience in achieving high reliability.

5 Help may be sought by such researchers from the ESRC Data Archive at Essex. A very useful reverse coding document for the 1970 scheme is deposited there, which enables a coder to see what other occupations go into the various groups before deciding if it is appropriate. Researchers in different departments in British universities are currently producing programs to cope with the difficulties of the 1980 scheme, and these will find their way to Essex in due time.

6 The method of construction of the North–Hatt scale was similar to that outlined in the Hope–Goldthorpe scale, except that occupations were rated, not ranked, on a five-point scale from 'excellent' to 'poor'. The ninety occupations covered were not selected to be representative of the occupational structure but primarily to provide continuity with previous studies, so two thirds of them were white-collar.

7 Note, however, that such an assumption, when systematically built into a classification system, would make the empirical study of status of marriage or friendship partner circular.

8 Goldthorpe (1981/2) has replicated the scaling procedures just discussed on the Oxford Mobility Study data. Respondents gave the occupational details of the three individuals (or couples) with whom they spent most of their time. Using the collapsed version of the Hope–Goldthorpe scale, Goldthorpe performed MDS on the matrix of friendship choices, rotating the solution to obtain maximum correlation with the Hope–Goldthorpe scale. The first dimension of the solution was accepted as a scale of social status: the scale correlates .75 (Kendall's tau) with the Hope–Goldthorpe scale. It produces a very simple layer-cake picture of society; professionals come at the top, followed by managers, administrators and proprietors, then technicians, the self-employed and higher grade service workers, and finally all manual workers and their supervisors.

9 Note that, although this scheme was devised in the Registrar-General's office, many of the official and registration uses to which it is put do not collect details on employment status, so correct class coding is made impossible. See Haskey (1983) for a discussion of this problem on marriage licences.

10 Some of the changes represented real occupational movement, but the largest part reflect error in the coding process. The precise amount which comes from occupational change will be estimable in the future by seeing how much smaller the 'no change' percentage becomes as time elapses.

11 The class category descriptors did not change, however, between 1971 and 1981, and the 1981 schema is probably very similar to the 1971 one (Bland 1982).

12 It is also often collapsed into a six-category version which resembles RG but is not the same as it. This collapsed SEG has become widely known through its use on the General Household Survey and the Labour Force Survey, and the published reports of these surveys provide evidence of its discriminatory power in relation to a wide range of income, housing, health and lifestyle variables.

13 For an exception, used to examine women's social position, see Murgatroyd (1982).

14 The scheme was devised by Research Services Limited after the Second World War. It became known as the National Readership Survey (NRS) scheme because RSL became the NRS contractors, and even as the IPA scheme because the Institute of Practitioners in Advertising fund the NRS.

15 The scale is frequently collapsed into a four-point scale, AB, C1, C2 and DE; Kahan *et al.* (1966), however, argue that C1 should be subdivided further for discriminating on newspaper readership and subjective social class, and Bermingham (1981) argues that collapsing Ds and Es confuses occupational and lifestyle issues illegitimately.

16 The scale value of the category was *not* used however, to determine in which class a category should be placed.

17 See Marsh (1983) for a demonstration that the scheme works better as a ranked variable than any explicitly ordinal measures.

18 Wright (1978a; 1983), however, discusses the importance of the state and public ownership for class formation at length in his theoretical work. As material from the comparative project is published, some empirical insights on the importance of this variable may be expected to emerge.

19 The authors are careful, however, to point out the dangers in interpreting social class gradients prematurely in a prospective study.

20 In his analysis for the Royal Commission on the Legal Services, Wood (1981/2) discovered unsurprisingly that tenure was much more effective than RG in predicting usage of solicitors' services.

References

Bermingham, J. P. (1981) 'Have you been 'DE'-classified recently?' in 'Reclassifying People: What's New in 1981?' Proceedings of Admap Conference, The London Press Centre, October.

Bland, R. (1979) 'Measuring "social class" ', *Sociology* 13(2) May: 283–91.

Bland, R. (1982) 'History and properties of the OPCS "social class" scale', paper given to the Edinburgh Survey Methodology Group Survey Methods Seminar, Edinburgh, December.

Blishen, B. (1958) 'The construction and use of an occupational class scale', *Canadian Journal of Economics and Political Science* Vol. 24: 519–31.

Blyth, W. (1982) 'Preclassifying consumers', in proceedings of ESOMAR seminar, Classifying Consumers – A Need to Rethink, Brugge, Belgium, June: 67–74.

Booth, C. (1886) 'Occupations of the people of the United Kingdom 1801–1881', *Journal of the Royal Statistical Society*, series A, June: 314–444.

Boston, G. (1980) 'Classification of occupations', *Population Trends*, Vol. 20: 9–11.

Britten, N. and **Heath, A.** (1983) 'Women, men and social class', in E. Gamarnikow *et al.* (eds) *Gender, Class and Work*, London: Macmillan.

Broom, L., Duncan-Jones, P., Lancaster-Jones, F. and **McDonnell, P.** (1977) Investigating Social Mobility, Departmental Monograph No. 1, Department of Sociology, Research School of the Social Sciences, Australian National University, Canberra.

Central Statistical Office (1975) *Social Trends* No. 6, edited by E. J. Thompson, London: HMSO.

Coxon, A. P. M. and **Jones, C. L.** (1978) *The Images of Occupational Prestige: a study in Social Cognition*, London: Macmillan.

Dale, A., Gilbert, G.N. and **Arber, S.** (1985) Alternative Approaches to the Measurement of Social Class for Women and Families, University of Surrey, Department of Sociology; report submitted to the Equal Opportunities Commission, October.

Duncan, O.D. (1961) 'A socio-economic index for all occupations' in A. J. Reiss *et al.* (1961).

Elias, D. P. B. (1981) 'The MRG/EOC Occupational Classification', University of Warwick: Manpower Research Group paper MRG DP 131, September.

Elliot, D. (1982) 'A study of variation in occupation and social class coding – summary of results', *Survey Methodology Bulletin* 14, May: 48–9.

Erikson, R., Goldthorpe, J. H. and **Portocarero, L.** (1979) 'Intergenerational class mobility in three Western European societies: England, France and Sweden', *British Journal of Sociology* 30, December.

Fox, A. J. and **Goldblatt, P. O.** (1982) 'Longitudinal Study; Socio-demographic Mortality Differentials: a first report on mortality in 1971–1975 according to 1971 Census characteristics based on data collected in the OPCS Longitudinal Study', Series LS No. 1, London: HMSO.

Garnsey, E. (1978) 'Women's work and theories of social stratification', *Sociology* 12(2) May: 223–44.

Goldthorpe, J. H. (1980) *Social Mobility and Class Structure in Modern Britain*, Oxford: Clarendon Press.

Goldthorpe, J. H. (1981–2) 'Social standing, class and status', paper presented to the Social and Community Planning Research seminar on social class, London, November 1981; reported in

SCPR Survey Methods Newsletter, Winter.
Goldthorpe, J. H. (1983a) 'Revised class schema, 1983, based on OPCS Classification of Occupations 1980', Nuffield College, Oxford: mimeo.
Goldthorpe, J. H. (1983b) 'Women and class analysis: in defence of the conventional view', *Sociology* 17 (4) November.
Goldthorpe, J. H. and **Hope, K.** (1974) *The Social Grading of Occupations: a New Approach and Scale*, Oxford: Clarendon Press.
Gray, P. and **Gee, F. A.** (1972) 'A Quality Check on the 1966 Ten Percent Sample Census of England and Wales', London: HMSO.
Green, H. (1981) 'Interviewer coding of occupation and industry on the women and employment survey', *Survey Methodology Bulletin*, 13, October: 14–29.
Guppy, L. N. (1984) 'Dissensus or consensus: a cross-national comparison of occupational prestige scales', *Canadian Journal of Sociology* 9 (1): 69–83.
Hall, J. and **Jones, D. C.** (1950) 'Social grading of occupations', *British Journal of Sociology* 1 (1): 31–51.
Haskey, J. (1983) 'Social class patterns of marriage', *Population Trends* No. 34, Winter.
Hodge, R. W., Siegel, P. M. and **Rossi, P. H.** (1967) 'Occupational prestige in the United States 1925–1963' in R. Bendix and S. M. Lipset (eds) *Class, Status and Power*, 2nd edn, London: Routledge & Kegan Paul: 322–34.
Hodge, R. W., Treiman, D. and **Rossi, P. H.** (1967) 'A comparative study of occupational prestige' in R. Bendix and S. M. Lipset (eds) *Class, Status and Power*, 2nd edn, London: Routledge & Kegan Paul: 309–21.
Inkeles, A. and **Rossi, P. H.** (1956) 'National comparisons of occupational prestige', *American Journal of Sociology*, January: 329–39.
International Labour Office (1968) *The International Standard Classification of Occupations*, revised edn, Geneva: ILO.
Joint Industry Working Party (1981) *An Evaluation of Social Grade Validity*, London: The Market Research Society, 15 Belgrave Square, SW1X 8PF.
Kahan, M., Butler, D. and **Stokes, D.** (1966) 'On the analytical division of social class', *British Journal of Sociology*, 17: 122–32.
Lane, D. (1982) *The End of Social Inequality*, London: Allen & Unwin.
Leete, R. and **Fox, J.** (1977) 'Registrar-General's social classes: origins and uses', *Population Trends* 8: 1–7.
Llewellyn, C. (1981) 'Occupational mobility and the comparative

150   *Catherine Marsh*

method' in H. Roberts (ed.) *Doing Feminist Research*, London: Routledge & Kegan Paul.

Lockwood, D. (1957) *The Blackcoated Worker*, London: Allen & Unwin.

Lunn, J. A. (1965) 'Social grade', *Commentary*, July.

Marsh, C. (1983) 'Occupationally-based measures of social class', in J. Ritchie (ed.) *The Measurement of Social Class*, London, SRA.

Monk, D. (1978) *Social Grading on the National Readership Survey*, 4th edn (revised), Joint Industry Committee for National Readership Surveys, 44 Belgrave Square, London SW1X 8QS.

Morgan, M. (1983) 'Measuring social inequality: occupational classifications and their alternatives', *Community Medicine* 5: 116–24.

Murgatroyd, L. (1982) 'Gender and occupational stratification', *Sociological Review* 30 (4): 574–602.

Murphy, M. J. and **Sullivan, O.** (1983) 'Housing Tenure and Fertility in Post-war Britain', Centre for Population Studies Research Paper no. 83–2, January.

Oakley, A. and **Oakley, R.** (1979) 'Sexism in official statistics' in J. Irvine, I. Miles and J. Evans (eds) *Demystifying Social Statistics*, London: Pluto Press: 172–89.

Office of Population Censuses and Surveys (1970) Classification of Occupations 1970, London: HMSO.

Office of Population Censuses and Surveys (1980) Classification of Occupations 1980, London: HMSO.

Osborn, A. F. and **Morris, T. C.** (1979) 'The rationale for a composite index of social class and its evaluation', *British Journal of Sociology* Vol 30: 39–60.

Powers, M. (ed.) (1982) *Measures of Socioeconomic Status: Current Issues*, Boulder, Colorado, Westview Press.

Reid, I. (1977) *Social Class Differences in Britain: a Sourcebook*, London: Open Books.

Reiss, A. J. Jr. with **O. D. Duncan, P. K. Hatt** and **C. C. North** (1961) *Occupations and Social Status*, New York: The Free Press of Glencoe.

Research Services Limited (1981) 'SAGACITY: a Tool for More Effective Market Analysis and Media Planning,' Research Services Limited, Station House, Harrow Road, Stonebridge Park, Wembley, Middlesex.

Robinson, R. V. and **Kelley, J.** (1979) 'Class as conceived by Marx and Dahrendorf: effects on income inequality and politics in the United States and Great Britain', *American Sociological Review* 44, February: 38–58.

Runciman, W. G. (1966) *Relative Deprivation and Social Justice*, London: Routledge & Kegan Paul.

Siegel, P. M. (1971) Prestige in the American Occupational Structure, PhD Dissertation, Chicago, Illinois, March.

Stevenson, T. H. C. (1928) 'The vital statistics of wealth and poverty', *Journal of the Royal Statistical Society*, Part II: 207–30.

Stewart, A., Prandy, K. and **Blackburn, R. M.** (1980) *Social Stratification and Occupations*, London: Macmillan.

Subcommittee on Comparability of Occupation Measurement (1982) 'Report to the SSRC Advisory and Planning Committee on Social Indicators and the US Bureau of the Census', Washington DC: Social Science Research Council.

Treiman, D. J. (1977) *Occupational Prestige in Comparative Perspective*, New York; Academic Press.

United States Department of Commerce (1981) '1980 Census of Population; Occupational Classification System: Detailed Occupational Categories,' Washington DC: Bureau of the Census, September.

Webber, R. J. (1979) 'Census Enumeration Districts: a Socio-economic Classification,' OPCS Occasional Paper No. 14.

Webber, R. J. (1981) 'ACORN as an attitudinal discriminator' in 'Reclassifying People: What's New in 1981?', proceedings of Admap Conference, London Press Centre, October.

Webber, R. J. and **Craig, J.** (1975) 'A Socio-economic Classification of Local Authority Areas', Studies on Medical and Population Subjects No. 35, London: HMSO.

Wood, D. (1981–2) 'Social class differentials', paper presented to the Social and Community Planning Research seminar on social class, London, November 1981; reported in SCPR Survey. Methods Newsletter, Winter: 6–7.

Wright, E. O. (1978a) *Class, Crisis and the State*, London: New Left Books.

Wright, E. O. (1978b) 'Race, class and income inequality', *American Journal of Sociology* 83 (6).

Wright, E. O. (1980) 'Class and occupation', *Theory and Society*, 9: 177–214.

Wright, E. O. (1982) 'The comparative project on class structure and class consciousness: an overview', Comparative Project on Class Structure and Class Consciousness Working Paper No. 1, Department of Sociology, University of Wisconsin, Madison, Wisconsin 53706.

Wright, E. O. (1983) 'Capitalism's futures', *Socialist Review* No. 68, vol. 13 No. 2, March–April: 77–126.

Wright, E. O. and **Perrone, L.** (1977) 'Marxist class categories and income inequality', *American Sociological Review* 42 (1): 32–55.

Young, M. and **Willmott, P.** (1956) 'Social grading by manual workers', *British Journal of Sociology* 7.

Work, employment and unemployment 8

Kate Purcell

Introduction

In order to explore changing research priorities and methodological
issues for sociologists and others engaged in social research it is
necessary to relate contemporary patterns of employment and unemployment in the context of social and economic change to theoretical
debates within sociology and society. Throughout the last decade our
experience of employment and pace of social and economic change,
particularly the relative ratios of employed and unemployed persons,
have changed to such an extent that in a volume such as this, it now no
longer makes sense to have a chapter on work or employment which
posits employment as a universal experience. The social meanings of
employment and unemployment and their sociological implications
change as their relative ratios change.

In October 1983 in the UK alone, well over three million people
were registered as unemployed: 13 per cent of the workforce according to official definition, of whom 1,261,400 were under twenty-five
and represented approximately 35 per cent of their age group and 38
per cent of the total registered unemployed (DE Gazette, November
1983: SS 34). These statistics significantly underestimate the extent of
unemployment, as will be discussed in detail later, and most economic forecasters predict a progressive increase in long-term unemployment (which is generally defined as unemployment lasting for
twelve months or more), since the likely number of jobs created will
be outstripped by the continuous decline in numbers of existing jobs
and by growth of the workforce (London Business School Centre for
Economic Forecasting, 1983).

Sociologists who have studied industry and technology are
amongst the least surprised by these developments. Twenty years ago
Blauner wrote: 'With technological and population trends ever

threatening to increase the already high levels of unemployment, the most serious and immediate social problem of our industrial economy is clearly not the nature of work but the very existence of sufficient jobs' (1964:viii). Such a formulation implies that employment *per se* is a 'good thing', from the point of view of both society as a whole and the individual, which is ironic, since Blauner (and indeed the majority of sociologists who have carried out research amongst manual workers in industry) emphasizes the degradation and lack of fulfilment inherent in such employment, particularly the very jobs which are most vulnerable to automation, technological change and market decline. This paradox emphasizes the complexity of the issues involved because the economic and ideological implications of employment permeate all social experience in contemporary western societies, where prestige (Eisenstadt, 1968: 70) is largely determined by participation and productivity in the labour process.

The most influential early sociologists and social scientists explicitly identified work and employment as central to an understanding of industrial societies, both for understanding social action and in explaining social change. In particular, Marx, Weber, Freud, Hobhouse and Durkheim explored the relationship between the organization of employment and production, social stability, disorder and conflict, and the centrality of work in the development of individual identity and social integration. The study of employment patterns and orientations to work and work organizations continues to be a major concern of sociologists in their analyses of the structure and process of societies as well as in specific projects within industrial, organizational and occupational sociology, because there is a very real sense in which a society *is* its division of labour, reproduced daily and inter-generationally in the structures and processes of its economic and social interdependencies.

Work

Work and employment are often taken to be virtually synonymous but it seems particularly important to distinguish between them in contemporary labour markets in the light of theoretical concern to re-evaluate the relationship between public and private worlds (Stacey and Price,1981) and between the formal and informal economy (Pahl, 1980). Employment inherently posits a contractual *relationship* between employee and employer and provides the mechanism whereby production and consumption are related. 'Work' does not necessarily involve this exchange, implying merely productive *activity*, whether it be the expenditure of physical energy or mental endeavour. In the context of contemporary capitalist society, the word 'work' has a number of other connotations, which derive from identification with employment. Employment involves the sale and purchase of labour power as a commodity in a market, resulting in the direction of activity during 'working hours' by persons who have acquired the right to do so by virtue of the labour contract. Researchers using occupation as a key variable in social investigation need to be aware of the ideological context in which people experience and define their activities. All sorts of activities are carried out around and related to employment which are not in themselves considered part of work, and all sorts of activities outside employment are experienced as work by the actors concerned although they may not have a market value as labour. It is not simply that such activities may become an increasingly important source of identification and experience for individuals where work becomes more routinized or scarce. Moorhouse's (1984) work on the work ethic amongst hot red enthusiasts draws attention to the fact that it may be generally misleading to make assumptions that people's occupations are either their own main source of identity and an indication of their skills, or a meaningful way to classify them socially.

The informal economy

Outside the formal sector of the economy, there has always been some provision of goods and services within the community, but Pahl has argued that such transactions are a considerable and growing sector. He explored Gershuny's hypothesis that the informal economy appears to be supplanting its formal equivalent in post-industrial society with consumption of material goods merely a means towards private production and provision of services within the home and community (Gershuny, 1978; Gershuny and Pahl, 1980). His initial optimism that such cases indicate a trend towards *re*skilling within the informal economy and the home have been considerably modified in the light of labour market and community fieldwork in the Isle of Sheppey (Pahl and Wallace, 1984; Pahl, 1984) where, in line with observations by Henry (1982) it was clear that successful manipulation of the informal economy was most accessible to those with a secure base in the formal section. The unemployed are doubly disadvantaged insofar as their lack of jobs means lack of money and credit to provide the initial investment in tools, materials and publicity usually necessary for informal ventures and they lack the social and professional networks, equipment and facilities which enable those in employment to supplement their formal economy incomes.

Paid and unpaid work

In relation to the debate about the boundaries of work and employment, feminist scholars have also argued that domestic work, childcare and reproduction should properly be recognized as work and a vital component of social productivity. The Domestic Labour Debate within Marxism has explored the theoretical relationships between domestic work and capitalism at great length. (See Kaluzynska, 1980, for a summary and full references.) Empirical research demonstrates unequivocally that most women, whether or not they are also in employment, expend considerably more time, energy and effort in the home than men (Oakley, 1974; Newlands, 1980). Housework and childcare are interestingly ambiguous categories in the folk understanding of work. Whilst few would deny them the label of work (and they do have a market value when performed outside the family) their job content is subsumed within the affective relationships of wife and mother, in which roles they are encompassed, so that they are denied the status of 'real' work (Purcell, 1978). Because such work is initially undertaken 'for love' and not for money, there is an assumption that the Protestant Ethic element is (and ought to be) suspended by intrinsic delight in duty (Murcott, 1983; Sokoloff, 1982) although the labour involved is experienced by many women as low status, unwaged work defined by economic dependency (Oakley, *op. cit.*).

In addition, being a wife and mother often involves work outside the home or work in the home related to the *husband's* employment. The hours and arrangements of most jobs are assigned on the assumption that child rearing and domestic work are carried out elsewhere by others, during working hours at least. In the words of Delphy 'a normal day's work is that of a person who does not have to do his own domestic work' (1976: 161). However, many occupations also explicitly incorporate wives, making assumptions about their availability and willingness to contribute to their husband's workload and his ability to play his role, as has recently been discussed by Finch (1983). The ironic obverse of this is that employers who discriminate against women and are unwilling to promote them frequently give the reason that women are less likely to be willing to be geographically mobile (Llewellyn, 1981; Hunt, 1975) and it is assumed that *their* partners would be unwilling to uproot themselves to follow the wife's career, which illustrates the way in which implicit notions about gender and the sexual division of labour permeate job specifications, recruitment and promotion and thus reflexively reinforce established patterns of employment and women's dependency. State tax and welfare provisions similarly make assumptions about women's dependence and availability. Both within the family and in the community, care of the sick, disabled, young and elderly is very largely undertaken by women and is unequivocally unpaid work (Finch and Groves, 1980).

Employment

Economic activity in the UK: sources

The main sources available to social scientists who wish to investigate or utilize employment as a key variable are official statistics compiled by government departments. Labour statistics have been compiled in Britain since the late nineteenth century but the quantity and range of available information has increased greatly in the last decade, due to the political necessity of conforming to EEC norms, an increasing administrative need for more systematic information and the growing sophistication of information retrieval systems. The most significant change has been a qualitative one, with a shift in emphasis and resources from data based on administrative records, such as the Department of Employment (DE) official employment statistics, towards the development of special surveys designed specifically to provide statistical material for secondary analysis, such as the General Household Survey (GHS) (Hakim and Hawes, 1982: 16–17). Given that the provision of data for research is merely a by-product of administrative records, the former have to be used with caution due to the frequent and irregular classificatory changes introduced by successive governments. For example, categories of people included as 'economically active' have periodically changed, so that longitudinal analysis is fraught with difficulty. The additional problem of ensuring standard classification of data compiled on a national scale is compounded by wide variation of labour market conditions amongst different areas, leading to different expectations and utilization of the official services. A detailed list of the published statistics is compiled by the Central Statistical Office (CSO, 1982).

The DE publishes figures of employment, unemployment, vacancies notified to Job Centres, industrial disputes, earnings, wage rates, hours of work and labour costs in the *Department of Employment Gazette*, which gives the most up-to-date statistics available. The Central Statistical Office (CSO) publishes labour statistics regularly in the *Monthly Digest of Statistics* and the *Annual Abstract of Statistics*. In addition, detailed analyses and comparisons are published annually in *Social Trends*, the *Census of Employment* and the *New Earnings Survey*. Historical trends are documented in *British Labour Statistics Historical Abstract* and the now discontinued *British Labour Statistics Year Book*, which has been superseded by biennal *Labour Force Surveys* (LFS), compiled to enable comparison and aggregation with similar data for other countries of the European Community. These all suffer from the drawback that they are largely confined to registered employment and unemployment, and unregistered and 'hidden' equivalents are generally agreed to be considerable. The concept of 'economic activity' reflects concern with employment and productive activity which enters directly into the national accounts but from the point of view of sociological analysis, knowledge of the informal economy is crucial to an understanding of the dynamics of local labour markets and people's attitudes and experience regarding employment and unemployment. The *General Household Survey* and decennial *Census of Population* data give some indication of the extent of unregistered employment and unemployment but are likely to underestimate considerably the extent of casual, irregular and insubstantial employment. For example, a mail order catalogue agent, childminder or cleaner may consider herself to be primarily a housewife and therefore be categorized as economically inactive, or may consider that, although such work is an essential component of her identity and experience, it is not what the survey or census is investigating. There is also known to be considerable undeclared employment in the home and the community, the extent of which is almost impossible to estimate, hidden for fear of fiscal reprisals. Questions about 'second jobs' and 'subsidiary jobs' are asked of the GHS sample, eliciting the response that nearly 7% of those surveyed had a second or subsidiary job, but again this is considered to be an underestimate (CSO, 1983: 82–6). Sheila Allen's research on homeworkers in North Yorkshire exposes an important dimension of the extensive underestimation of women's employment. She cites one example of a woman who supported herself and her two children by working fifty-five hours per week at two part-time jobs and homeworking, who was also a childminder. Allen concludes: 'She is not an ordinary worker in any dominant ideological construction of workers, but she typifies the working pattern of many women' (1983: 659).

The labour force

The DE uses four separate measures of employment in different contexts and it is important to be clear about which is most useful to specific secondary users. First, they use 'Employees', referring to all employees insured under the National Insurance Acts; second, they use 'Employees in Employment' which refers to the above category minus the registered unemployed; third, they use 'Civil Employed' referring to employees in employment plus employers and the self-employed; and fourth, they use 'Working Population', which consists of the third category plus the armed forces (who are excluded from the other defintions).

The term 'labour force' is normally used to describe those who are *economically active*, taken to be employees in work, self-employed in work and those registered as unemployed, although it is sometimes used loosely to refer to the entire population of working age, including 'economically inactive' categories such as full-time students, house-wives and people unable to work because of chronic illness or permanent disability. The DE statistics define the economically active as self-employed employees and those seeking work through Job Centres who are assessed to be 'capable and available for work, whether they are entitled to employment benefit or not'. There is some evidence that the definition of 'capability' for work is a subjective and variable judgment and the categories considered 'available' have been defined differently at different times (Hakim and Hawes, ibid.: 20). For DE statistics, employment status is classified by the civil servants who administer the register.

The Census form provides categories of employment status but requires the people filling it in to classify themselves and the members of their household. The Census defines the economically active as those in a full-time or part-time job at any time in the week preceding enumeration, those waiting to take up a job already accepted, those seeking work and those prevented by temporary sickness from seeking work. The economically inactive are the permanently sick or disabled, housewives and those wholly retired from employment, at school or in full-time education. The infrequency of the Census limits its utility for social scientists since it provides a series of snapshots of the population rather than continuous data, but it covers the whole of Great Britain, offers considerably greater disaggregation than any other source, is more comprehensive and does permit comparison with preceding censuses, which are the longest established sources of such data. It provides the only comprehensive data on *occupational* employment and is thus particularly illuminating for those who wish to study changes in occupational distribution and the changing patterns of employment within the labour force (Hyman and Price, 1979: 227).

An annual *Census of Employment* was initiated in 1971, whereby the DE carried out a postal survey of 'pay points' – establishments of enterprises which administer the pay and income tax of employees. Every third year a full census was to be carried out and in the intervening years, only those pay points with more than three employees. Following public expenditure cuts, the census has been carried out less frequently since 1978 and data collected will increasingly be supplemented by sample surveys.

The LFS is published biennially. The LFS is larger than the GHS, sampling 105,000 households, but its reliability is marred by the fact that 'one responsible adult' is required to give data for all members of the household. It has the advantage of providing data comparable to statistics collected for other EEC countries. The GHS covers only 15,000 households but is a continuous multi-purpose survey, with all adult members of each household interviewed weekly throughout the year, covering a wide range of data. It has been carried out continuously since 1971 and so can be used for time series analysis. Both these surveys have a response rate of well over 80 per cent but even more than in most surveys perhaps, the non-respondents are unlikely to be randomly distributed throughout the labour market and may be the most interesting group in terms of exploring the boundaries of the formal and informal economies.

Various *ad hoc* surveys have investigated particular issues such as women's labour force participation, job training and labour mobility. An increasing proportion of government data sets are now deposited in the Economic and Social Research Council (ESRC) Data Archive at Essex University to encourage secondary analysis by social scientists (Hakim, 1982).

Distribution of the workforce

Both employment and unemployment are differentially distributed amongst the economically-active population, between sexes, according to race, age, region and amongst different industries and occupations, reflecting both tradition and change in the division of labour. Manufacturing industry has developed as a result of the dialectical relationship between geographical and demographic factors and the current and emergent patterns of employment and unemployment reflect these historical antecedents (Massey and Meegan, 1982).

The politics and geography of employment and unemployment are of crucial importance in understanding both labour statistics and the experience of communities. A discussion of the current data will throw some light on the possibilities and pitfalls for researchers. In essence, the proportions of employers self-employed with employees, own account/self-employed without employees, and employees have changed considerably throughout this century (Brown, 1978: 68) with the former two categories declining relative to the third. This, allied to a large expansion in public sector employment: 30 per cent of the employed labour force in 1982, including 7½ per cent in public corporations (Morrison, 1983), has profound implications for the division and dependence of labour. The job classification emerging from such work restructuring tends to obscure rather than illuminate differences and similarities in work experience. Employees are classified according to industry and according to occupation. Brown's (1978) useful and comprehensive work explores the changing industrial distribution of the labour force since 1841, when 23.1 per cent of the economically-active labour force was still employed in agriculture, forestry and fishing. Table 1 gives an indication of the extent to which patterns of employment have changed in this century.

Table 1 Distribution of employees according to industry, as percentages of all industries and services*

INDUSTRY	YEAR		
	1901 %	1971 %	1981 %
Total Labour Force (millions)	15.4**	24.9	29.6
Agriculture, forestry and fishing	8.7	1.6	1.6
Mining and quarrying	5.9	1.8	1.5
Manufacturing (including Gas, Electricity and Water)	32.9	40.0	30.1
Construction	8.0	5.7	5.3
Services	42.1	50.9	61.4

* Excluding HM Forces
** Excluding Women in Agriculture
Source: Brown 1978, Table 2.4, pp. 66–7 and *Annual Abstract of Statistics*, 1983, 113–16, Table 6.2.

These figures are misleading insofar as they are not strictly comparable due to classificatory changes, as discussed, and they minimize the extent of change in patterns of employment. For example, in 1901 14.3 per cent of employees were engaged in private domestic service, an enormously diminished category of employment not currently listed separately in the statistics. Many of the functions fulfilled by domestic servants are now carried out on a larger scale by employees listed under 'miscellaneous services', which includes laundries, hairdressing, entertainment and a wide variety of other services. In addition, the aggregate figures conceal important variation amongst different sectors of the work force within industries, as Brown explains (ibid: 65). In manufacturing, industries such as textiles and clothing have employed a decreasing proportion of the population throughout most of the century whereas until recently 'metal manufacture, machinery, implements, vehicles and precious metals, etc.' has employed an increasing proportion of the labour force. The location and scale of employment has typically undergone considerable change, which has implications for the distribution of the labour force, employees' experience of work and industrial relations. The degree of concentration of British industry is greater than in either Europe or the USA, with very large companies employing an increasing proportion of the workforce (Prais, 1976: 164) and this trend towards larger units is also substantially true of white collar and professional employment, which are growing proportions of the labour force, reflecting both the expansion of the service sector and the decline in manufacturing.

The sociological and methodological difficulties associated with the classification of occupations has been discussed by Bechhofer (1969) and by Marsh in this volume, but sociological attempts to formulate occupational classifications continue to be widely used in analyses of class and social mobility. Those who wish to classify or identify populations or samples according to employment status or job status need to consider their reasons for using the variables and to be suspicious of established labour force categories and occupational classifications. It needs to be remembered that such definitions are ultimately cultural constructs which reify custom and practice (or selective versions of it) and any classification is bound to be to some extent arbitrary. There has been a great deal of theoretical and empirical work undertaken recently in an attempt to analyse and reformulate concepts such as 'level of skill' which obscure differences and similarities amongst employees, and to evaluate the extent to which levels of skill are affected by technological change, as will be discussed below. Perhaps the most graphic illustration of how employment statistics require disaggregation and sceptical analysis is a consideration of women's work and employment.

The sexual division of labour

The most enduring division between workers, whether employed or not, is the sexual division of labour. Virtually all societies observed by sociologists and anthropologists have had distinct sexual divisions of labour, although the tasks carried out by each sex have varied considerably, to such an extent that it is difficult to argue for universal characteristics and aptitudes for women and men. Nevertheless, the cultural pattern in the UK currently is that, despite Equal Pay and Sex Discrimination legislation to promote equal opportunities, the labour market is characterized by occupational segregation by sex. The extent of such segregation has been comprehensively documented by Hakim (1979) and the limitations of Equal Opportunities legislation in relation to such occupational segregation has been explained by Bruegel (1983).

Table 2 shows the distribution of employees throughout the labour force, and the very different distribution of women and men. The disaggregation clearly demonstrates the industrial concentration of female employees and indeed, underestimates their occupational concentration, since most of the females listed in 'male dominated' industries such as agriculture, mining and construction are likely to be workers providing lower grade clerical and technical services within the industry in question.

Female employees are *horizontally* segregated from males in so far as most women work in jobs where there are no comparable male employees. Furthermore, even within industries where women are employed in large numbers, there is *vertical* segregation with women concentrated in the low-paid, low-skilled grades and men generally higher-paid and credited with the possession of more skills and qualifications. This concentration appears to have increased over time (Westergaard and Resler, 1976: 103) and in manual work, the trend is towards greater job segregation, with men increasingly over-represented in skilled work and women constituting an increasing proportion of those classified as semi- and unskilled workers.

However, the relative value of men's and women's work as indicated by pay scales and differences in job statuses is an excellent example of the way in which subjective cultural evaluations are aggregated in the evolution of custom and practice to create systematic

Table 2　UK employees in employment: by industry: by sex: 1981

Industry	Sex Males *thousands*	%	Females *thousands*	%
Agriculture, forestry & fishing	270	2.2	89	1.0
Mining and quarrying	316	2.6	16	0.2
Manufacturing				
Food, drink & tobacco	385	3.1 (8.9)	247	2.8 (14.5)
Chemicals, coal & allied products	320	2.6 (7.4)	113	1.3 (6.6)
Metal manufacture	290	2.4 (6.7)	36	0.4 (2.1)
Engineering & allied industries	2,171	17.7 (50.1)	568	6.4 (33.2)
Textiles, leather & clothing	291	2.4 (6.7)	417	4.7 (24.4)
Rest of manufacturing	873	7.1 (20.2)	329	3.7 (19.2)
Total manufacturing	4,330	35.3 (100.0)	1,709	19.1 (100.0)
Construction	1,023	8.3	109	1.2
Gas, electricity & water	272	2.2	68	0.8
Services				
Transport & communication	1,164	9.5	276	3.1
Distributive trades	1,180	9.6	1,455	16.3
Insurance, banking, finance	577	4.7	656	7.3
Professional & scientific services	1,161	9.4	2,533	28.4
Miscellaneous services	1,017	8.3	1,397	15.6
Public administration	954	7.8	625	7.0
Total services	6,053	49.6	6,942	78.3
All industries & services	12,264	100.0	8,934	100.0

Source: *Social Trends* 13, 1983, p. 54, Table 4.5
(Figures in brackets show the percentage distribution of employees in employment in manufacturing)

differences which have the appearance of inevitability. As Routh (1980) has observed, the entire workforce does not compete for work and relative reward within the same labour market except in the most abstract of senses; individuals generally define their occupational skills, the range within which they expect to be paid and the region in which they are prepared to seek employment within narrow limits and they do not tend to make comparisons with employees outside these boundaries. Thus, women segregated in 'women's jobs' do not compare their earnings with those of males in similar jobs but with the earnings they could achieve in other 'women's jobs' locally. Similarly, they rarely challenge why allegedly 'women's skills' like manual dexterity should be evaluated less highly than 'men's skills' such as physical strength (Pollert, 1981: 62–9, Phillips and Taylor, 1980, Cockburn, 1983:47, Friedman and Meredeen, 1980: 129–32). When carrying out research of employees, it is important to remember that such concepts as level of skill reflect traditional values and social categories as well as, and sometimes instead of, objective skill differentials.

Unemployment

Unemployment is of interest to sociologists both in terms of how it reflects and affects social organization, interaction and integration generally, and in terms of its significance to the individuals and communities most directly involved. It relates 'the personal troubles of milieu' to 'the public issue of social structure' (Mills, 1959: 8–9). Like employment, unemployment is unequally distributed among the labour force, throughout regions, amongst occupations and industries, between women and men and according to age.

Statistical sources for unemployment are similar to those for employment and whilst in many ways extremely detailed and extensive, suffer from the same drawbacks: they deal largely with *registered* unemployment and take no account of job-hunting independent of the services of job centres or careers offices. Unregistered unemployment is estimated to be considerable; up to half as much again in the case of married women workers who, in periods of high unemployment or situations where jobs are scarce, have been shown to be less likely to register for employment if they have no confidence in the agencies' ability to find work for them (McNabb, 1977). In addition, research indicates that unemployed people most often ultimately find jobs by informal mechanisms, most often through friends and relatives, and there is considerable evidence to suggest that employers find it easy to fill vacancies without the mediation of government agencies (Sinfield, 1981: 45–6).

Changing patterns of unemployment

In any free society where people have at least some element of choice of where they work, what they do and by whom they are employed, a certain level of unemployment is regarded as inevitable, even in times of full employment when there is no shortage of demand for labour. 'Frictional' unemployment reflects seasonal variations in demand for particular categories of employees, a lack of fit between demand and supply of labour at any given time or place and short-term voluntary or enforced gaps in employment between jobs. It is also generally accepted that some proportion of the population is unemployable, through disability or what Beveridge somewhat enigmatically referred to as 'defects of character' (Beveridge, 1912: 137). The size of this proportion is difficult to define and subject to elastic interpretation according to unemployment levels and political perspectives, as will be discussed later. There is no convincing evidence that frictional unemployment increases relatively in periods of high unemployment (Showler, 1981: 46) so we have to look for structural explanations.

Unemployment can be measured in terms of stocks and flows and is subject to seasonal variation, so that the Department of Employment gives both actual and seasonally-adjusted figures in order to be able to estimate long-term trends as accurately as possible. Flow rates vary throughout the workforce according to the variables discussed earlier, but in most occupations and regions the inflow rate into unemployment has increased dramatically in recent years, whereas the outflow rate has remained stable or fallen. A study of the unemployed flow indicates those categories of employees most vulnerable to unemployment and particularly subject to long-term unemployment (Stern, 1983) but the current increasing asymmetry between inflow and outflow rates vividly illustrates the changing structure of employment.

Government manpower schemes have been developed to encourage employers to retain workers, to create new jobs and more significantly, to provide temporary work experience for young people (Middlemass, 1981: 142–4). The essential objectives of such schemes has been to raise the demand for labour, to reduce the supply of labour or to keep youths off the unemployment register (Metcalf and Richardson, 1982: 26) and they have a temporary effect on unemployment statistics (Social Trends 1983) but their impact has been argued to have a negative effect on long-term trends. There is some evidence that employers have used the cheap temporary labour promoted by the schemes rather than create real jobs with long term prospects and by concentrating on the marketability of the workers, such measures reinforce the tendency to look to the qualities of *supply* of labour to explain unemployment rather than at the shortfall in *demand* for it (Hill, 1981).

This highlights the political significance of unemployment and the importance of scrutinizing statistics very carefully. Others have traced the political and economic interpretations of unemployment and the fiscal and monetary policies implemented by successive governments (Marsden, 1982: 239–50, Peston, 1981: 26–37) but it is worth noting here that perceptions of the acceptable level of unemployment and the meaning of full employment appeared to involve a rate of less than 2 per cent unemployment of whom 35 per cent were assumed to be unemployable or 'work shy', to a previously inconceivable unemployment rate of 13.3 per cent in March 1983 which appears to be very widely accepted as inevitable and as containing a high proportion of 'work shy' people: labelling which Deacon (1981) refers to as 'scroungerphobia'. After detailed consideration of unemployment rates, political pronouncements, media presentation and survey findings, he concludes that 'unemployability' is a function of the tightness of the labour market and research findings consistently emphasize that, contrary to the tenets of 'scroungerphobia', the majority of the unemployed experience a considerable decline in living standards. A household consisting of husband, non-working wife and two children is likely to receive 30–50 per cent of its normal income during periods of unemployment of the wage earner (Tomlinson, 1983: 36) and there is a strong correlation between unemployment and poverty (Townsend, 1979: 589–617).

It is clearly the case that unemployment will affect different people in different ways depending on their economic circumstances, alternative sources of self-esteem and activity (Hartley, 1980a, Pahl, 1982) and the values and expectations of their subculture and reference groups concerning work and employment. As the scale of unemployment increases and unemployment becomes a more frequent experience for a larger proportion of the population, attitudes and perspectives are likely to change. It has been observed that unemployment ceases to bear stigma in cases of high unemployment where young people have come to *expect* to be on the dole and the release from school into unemployment may be seen as welcome freedom to those who conform to peer group rather than dominant value systems (Willis, 1977; Seabrook, 1982). The influential unemployment studies of the 1930s (Bakke, 1933; Eisenberg and Lazarsfeld, 1938; Jahoda, Lazarsfeld and Zeisel, 1972, and the Pilgrim Trust, 1938) documented the psychological effects of unemployment on the individual and upon communities and until recently, their findings that people go through a predictable series of responses, ranging from initial shock, energetic attempts to find alternative employment, pessimism engendered by repeated failure and ultimately, fatalism and resignation, were taken as axiomatic. But the types of response and the duration of such stages will clearly depend upon previous experience and expectations, as Sinfield and others have observed (Sinfield, 1981: 35–41). School leavers in Strabane in Northern Ireland, where the unemployment rate has consistently been high and is currently 40.1 per cent of the workforce, are likely to define unemployment differently to their peers in Alton in the south-east of England where the rate is currently 4.4 per cent (DE *Gazette*, November 1983, ibid.). Hartley and Fryer (1983) argue that psychological 'orthodoxy' in discussing the personal effects of unemployment has obscured the diversity of responses which can be identified in response to the very different experiences of different people and has proved to be an obstacle to investigation of alternative structures of meaning. Jahoda exemplifies the orthodox approach when she argues that employment is an essential category of experience because it fulfils 'more or less deep-seated needs in most people, who strive to make some sense out of their existence. They need to structure their day; they need wider social experiences; they need to partake in collective purposes (and they want the products that result from collective action); they need to know where they stand in society in comparison to others in order to clarify their personal identity; and they need regular activities' (1982: 83–4). These aspects of experience are undoubtedly crucial, but to argue that they are provided *mainly* by employment is to underestimate both the significance of other means of fulfilment and the countervailing negative experiences of much employment, which might outweigh or diminish these positive aspects. Nonetheless, given the way that the social, reward and status systems of society operate, it is undoubtedly the case that most people experience the need for work activity integrated into the social mainstream, and interpret that as a need for employment, independent of financial needs (Westwood, 1984:100). The alternatives available to and perceived by most people are limited by economic constraints and the cumulative restrictions imposed by socialization and life experiences (Jacobs, 1982; Seabrook, 1982).

The trend for sociologists to undertake local labour market studies which incorporate changes in the structure and organization of employment and document changing patterns of employment and unemployment, in addition to specific studies of work places and industry, is likely to provide more insight into how and why particular people become unemployed, what options are available to them and how they and their communities are affected by unemployment. Most of the work on individual reactions to redundancy and unemployment so far has concentrated on psychological and financial stress with little reference to political attitudes and wider loyalties: a gap which the current sociological studies are designed to fill.[1]

Future research objectives and considerations

Government policies designed to reduce inflation and bolster the value of sterling, population growth, the structural decline of manufacturing industry (Massey and Meegan, 1982), the increasing introduction of new technology which cuts down on the need for labour in both manufacturing and service occupations (Sinfield, 1981: 133–46), employers' attempts to control labour costs in the face of increasing world market competition (Peston, 1981: 32–3), the exporting of work to Third World countries where labour costs are lower (Fröbel, Heinrichs and Kraye, 1980) and the effects of world recession generally (Sorrentino, 1981) all contribute to the present high unemployment levels in the UK. Whether or not the current recession is followed by lower levels of inflation, increased output and greater prosperity, it is unlikely that there will be a fundamental decrease in unemployment levels. High levels of unemployment have significant impacts both on the employed and unemployed. Those directly affected experience impoverishment, marginalization, loss of full participation in 'political citizenship' (Tomlinson, 1983: 38), likely downward job mobility and an increased likelihood of recurrent unemployment (Norris, 1978) quite apart from a diverse range of physical and psychological effects. Blackburn and Mann (1979) in their study of a local labour market in Britain, have shown how the external labour market in the community is becoming more fluid. They identified occupational segregation on the basis of sex and race in line with the findings of Hakim (*op.cit.*) and the dual labour market theorist but found, somewhat surprisingly, that the divisions between skilled, semi-skilled and unskilled men were less rigid than has often been assumed. Evidence of studies from the unemployed suggests that interchangeability and most particularly, downward occupational mobility of manual workers, is becoming more frequent as the labour market becomes looser and the competition for scarce employment opportunities becomes more fierce. In survey work, how should we classify skilled workers who, having been made redundant, are currently employed in unskilled jobs? The insolubility of questions such as these reveals that, in the past, data on occupations has been used as an indicator of the characteristics of the occupational structure, position in the occupational structure, occupational history and future 'chances' in the labour market. The legitimacy of such usage depends on there being full employment at each skill level and upon labour market chances positively correlating with the occupational hierarchy. Since neither condition now holds, neither level of skill nor future labour market chances can be inferred from current occupation. The empirical significance of this is that employment history may become a more significant variable for understanding the dynamics of workplace behaviour and industrial relations, and the operational definition of class concepts becomes increasingly more problematic.

For many of those who remain employed, the 'frontiers of control' (Goodrich, 1975) are pushed back as labour market power is reduced in the face of employers' compulsion to cut costs (Purcell and Sisson, 1983). Workers' bargaining strength is diminished and they are more susceptible to intensification (Massey and Meegan, ibid.: 31–61) where greater productivity and increased effort are demanded without the need for any incentive other than avoidance of the dole queue. Underemployment, subemployment and temporary employment are all experienced by an increasing proportion of the workforce. The promotion of equal opportunities for women and members of ethnic minorities is unlikely to be given high priority by employers where there is oversupply of white male workers (Chiplin and Sloane, 1982: 20–1) and evidence suggests that the high and rising levels of unemployment are stopping many people from pursuing sex discrimination and equal pay cases (EOC, 1982). The fear of unemployment may actually *reduce* frictional unemployment in so far as 'job stagnation' occurs. There is some evidence that workers stay in jobs they would like to leave because of lack of alternatives (Sinfield, 1981:130). At the recruitment end of employment, educational and formal skill qualifications are being used as criteria for appointment to jobs where such attributes are at best irrelevant. The effect on the community is of general impoverishment and a growing sense of insecurity amongst many of those who remain in employment (Purcell, 1982: 60). The cumulative effect of mass unemployment is to polarize those who have relatively secure jobs, income and access to affluent consumption patterns and those who have no job or are unskilled, badly paid and vulnerable to unemployment. The political implications have not been lost on successive governments and high levels of unemployment were undoubtedly a contributory variable to the inner-city riots in 1981 (Scarman, 1981). School leavers and graduates are increasingly likely to face unemployment with no immediate prospect of stable employment. Whether or not such trends indicate 'the work society running out of work' (Dahrendorf, 1980) it is a crucial task for sociologists to document changing patterns and changing relationships between work, employment and unemployment and it is impossible to consider any but the smallest, most tightly-defined aspect of any of these without considering the wider implications. Research on the impact of unemployment merges uncomfortably with work on deskilling in employment and dual and segmented labour markets to depict increasing inequalities and growing polarization within the labour market, in which a diminishing sector of the population participates. Redistribution of work, changing definitions of employment activities and a re-evaluation of the criteria upon which production and the provision of services are to be organized could overturn this pessimistic forecast. A great deal of research needs to be done to document the positive and negative responses of individuals and communities to unemployment and work restructuring, the ideological pressures which are brought to bear by various interest groups and the measures introduced to manage the social reorganization which is inevitably involved, whether the optimistic or pessimistic view of future trends prevails. Perhaps the main task confronting sociologists of work is a reconceptualization of categories and boundaries which we use in our research, paying particular attention to the significance of variables such as age, ethnic identity and gender and attempting to develop an analytic framework which incorporates work according to the broadest possible definition, going well beyond the official statistics.

Note

Pahl and Wallace at the University of Kent have completed a study of the local labour market and economic activity outside the formal sector in the Isle of Sheppey. Harris, Lee and Morris, University College Swansea, are studying the interface between domestic organization and the labour market behaviour and experience of a sample of redundant steelworkers. Westergaard, Walker and Noble of Sheffield University are studying the labour market experience of redundant workers and Bell and McKee of the University of Aston are carrying out research on the effects of unemployment on families. Martin and Wallace of Trinity College, Oxford, have carried out a survey of redundant women workers. Since 1980, the ESRC has sponsored a series of workshops on local labour markets currently convened by Professor Bryan Roberts of Manchester University.

References

Allen, S. (1983), 'Production and reproduction in the lives of women homeworkers' in *Sociological Review*, vol. 31, no. 4, New Series, pp.649–65.

Bakke, E.W. (1933), *The Unemployed Man*, London, Nisbet.

Bechhofer, F. (1968), 'Occupations' in M. Stacey (ed.) *Comparability in Social Research*, London, Heinemann.

Beveridge, W. (1912), *Unemployment: A Problem of Industry*, London, Longmans, Green.

Blackburn, R.M. and **Mann, M.** (1979), *The Working Class in the Labour Market*, London, Macmillan.

Blauner, R. (1964), *Alienation and Freedom*, Chicago, The University of Chicago Press.

Brown, R.K. (1978), 'Work', in P. Abrams (ed.) *Work, Urbanism and Inequality*, London, Weidenfeld & Nicolson. An updated version of this paper appeared in P. Abrams and R.K. Brown (eds) *UK Society: Work, Urbanism and Inequality*, London, Weidenfeld & Nicolson, 1984.

Bruegel, I. (1983), 'Women's Employment, Legislation and the Labour Market', in J. Lewis (ed.) *Women's Welfare, Women's Rights*, London, Croom Helm.

Central Statistical Office (1982), *Guide to Official Statistics*, no. 4, HMSO.

Central Statistical Office (1983) *Regional Trends*.

Central Statistical Office (1983a) *Annual Abstract of Statistics*, no. 119, London, HMSO.

Central Statistical Office (1983b), *Social Trends*, 13, London, HMSO.

Chiplin, B. and **Sloane, P.J.** (1982), *Tackling Discrimination in the Workplace*, Cambridge, Cambridge University Press.

Cockburn, C. (1983), *Brothers: Male Dominance and Technological Change*, London, Pluto Press.

Dahrendorf, R. (1980), 'Is the Work Society running out of Work?', *Omega*, vol. 8, no. 3.

Deacon, A. (1981), 'Unemployment and Politics in Britain Since 1945' in B. Showler and A. Sinfield (eds) *The Workless State*, Oxford, Martin Robertson.

Delphy, C. (1976), 'Continuities and Discontinuities in Marriage and Divorce', in D.L. Barker and S. Allen (eds) *Sexual Divisions and Society: Process and Change*, London, Tavistock.

Department of Employment, *Gazette*, vol. 91, no. 11, November 1983.

Department of Employment (1971) *British Labour Statistics Historical Abstract 1886-1968*, London, HMSO.

Department of Employment (1972), *Classification of Occupations and Directory of Occupational Titles*, London, HMSO.

Department of Employment (1978) *British Labour Statistics Year Book 1976*, London, HMSO.

Department of Employment *Labour Force Surveys*, London, HMSO (published annually).

Department of Employment *Monthly Digest of Statistics*, London, HMSO (published annually).

Department of Employment *New Earnings Survey*, London, HMSO (published annually).

Eisenberg, P. and **Lazarsfeld, P.F.** (1938), 'The Psychological Effects of Unemployment', *Psychological Bulletin*, pp.358–90.

Eisenstadt, S.N. (1968), 'Prestige participation and strata formation' in J.A. Jackson (ed.) *Social Stratification*, Cambridge, Cambridge University Press.

Equal Opportunities Commission (1982), *Seventh Annual Report*, London, HMSO.

Finch, J. (1983) *Married to the Job*, London, Allen & Unwin.

Finch, J. and **Groves, D.** (1980), 'Community Care and the Family: a case for equal opportunities?' *Journal of Social Policy*, 9 (4) October 1980.

Friedman, H. and **Meredeen, S.** (1980), *The Dynamics of Industrial Conflict – Lessons from Ford*, London, Croom Helm.

Fröbel, F., Heinrichs, J. and **Kraye, O.** (1980), *The New International Divison of Labour*, Cambridge, Cambridge University Press.

Gershuny, J. (1978), *After Industrial Society*, London, Macmillan.

Gershuny, J. and **Pahl, R.E** (1980), 'Britain in the decade of the three economies', *New Society*, 3 January, pp.7–9.

Goodrich, C. (1975), *The Frontier of Control*, London, Pluto Press.

Hakim, C. (1979), *Occupational Segregation*, D.E. Research Paper no. 9, London, HMSO.

Hakim, C. (1982), *Secondary Analysis in Sociological Research*, London, Allen & Unwin.

Hakim, C. and **Hawes, W.R.** (1982), 'The Labour Force', in *Labour and Income*, Milton Keynes, Open University Press. Part of course D291 *Statistical Sources*.

Hartley, J.F. (1980a) 'The Impact of unemployment upon the self-esteem of managers', *Journal of Occupational Psychology*, vol. 53, pp. 147–55.

Hartley, J.F. (1980b), 'Psychological approaches to unemployment', in *Bulletin of the Psychological Society*, 33, pp.412–14.

Hartley, J.F. and **Fryer, D.** (1984), 'The Psychology of unemployment: a critical appraisal', in G. Stephenson and J. Davis, (eds) *Progress in Applied Social Psychology*, vol. 2, Wiley.

Henry, S. (1982), 'The Working Unemployed: perspectives on the informal economy and unemployment', *Sociological Review*, New Series, vol. 30, pp.460–77.

Hill, M. (1981), 'Unemployment and Government Manpower Policy' in B. Showler and A. Sinfield (eds) *The Workless State*, Oxford, Martin Robertson.

Hunt, A. (1975), *Management Attitudes and Practices Towards Women at Work*, London, HMSO.

Hyman, R. and **Price, R.** (1979), 'Labour Statistics' in J. Irvine, I. Miles and J. Evans (eds) *Demystifing Social Statistics*, London, Pluto Press.

Jacobs, P. (1966), 'Unemployment as a way of life', in A.M. Ross (ed.), *Employment Policy and the Labour Market*, Berkeley and Los Angeles, University of California Press.

Jahoda, M. (1982), *Employment and Unemployment – A Social Psychological Analysis*, Cambridge, Cambridge University Press.

Jahoda, M., Lazarsfeld, P.F. and **Zeisel, H.** (1972), *Marienthal: The Sociography of an Unemployed Community*, London, Tavistock.

Kaluzynska, E. (1980), 'Wiping the floor with Theory – a survey of writings on Housework', *Feminist Review* 6, pp.27–54.

Llewellyn, C. (1981), 'Occupational mobility and the use of the comparative method', in H. Roberts (ed.) *Doing Feminist Research*, London, Routledge & Kegan Paul.

London Business School Centre for Economic Forecasting (1983), *Economic Outlook 1982–86*, vol. 7, no. 5, February.

Marsden, D. (1982), *Workless*, London, Croom Helm.

Massey, D. and **Meegan, R.** (1982), *The Anatomy of Job Loss*, London, Methuen.

McNabb, R. (1977), 'The Labour Force Participation of Married Women', *Manchester School of Economic and Social Studies*, no. 3.

Metcalf, D. and **Richardson, R.** (1982), 'Unemployment', in A.R. Prest and D.J. Coppock, *The UK Economy* (9th edition), London, Weidenfeld & Nicolson.

Middlemass, K. (1981), 'Unemployment: the Past and Future of a Political Problem', in B. Crick (ed.) *Unemployment*, London, Methuen.

Mills, C.W. (1959), *The Sociological Imagination*, New York, Oxford University Press.

Moorhouse, H.F. (1984) 'The Work Ethic and Hot Rods'. Paper given at the British Sociological Association conference on Work, Employment and Unemployment at Bradford University, April 1984.

Morrison, H. (1983), 'Employment in the public and private sectors 1976 to 1982', CSO *Economic Trends*, no. 352, pp.82–9, London, HMSO.

Murcott, A. (1983), *The Sociology of Food and Eating*, Farnborough, Gower.

Newlands, K. (1980), *Women, Men and the Division of Labour*, Worldwatch Paper no. 37, Worldwatch Institute, Washington, D.C.

Norris, G.M. (1978), 'Unemployment, Subemployment and Personal Characteristics (A) The Inadequacies of Traditional Approaches to Unemployment (B) Job Separation and Work Histories: the Alternative Approach', *Sociological Review*, New Series, vol. 26, pp.89–108, 327–47.

Oakley, A. (1974), *The Sociology of Housework*, Oxford, Martin Robertson.

Office of Population Censuses and Surveys (1983a), *Census 1981, National Report on Great Britain*, Part 1, London, HMSO.

Office of Population Censuses and Surveys (1983b) *General Household Survey, 1981*, London, HMSO.

Pahl, R.E. (1980), 'Employment, work and the domestic division of labour', *International Journal of Urban and Regional Research*, vol. 4, no. 1.

Pahl, R.E. (1982), 'Family, community and unemployment', *New Society*, 21 January.

Pahl, R.E. (1984), *Divisions of Labour*, Oxford, Basil Blackwell.

Pahl, R.E. and **Wallace, C.** (1984), 'Household work strategies in economic recession' in M. Redclift and E. Mignione (eds) *Beyond Employment*, Oxford, Blackwell.

Peston, M. (1981), 'Economic Aspects of Unemployment' in
B. Crick (ed.), *Unemployment*, London, Methuen.
Phillips, A. and **Taylor, B.** (1980), 'Sex and Skill: Notes Towards a
Feminist Economics', *Feminist Review* 6, pp.79–88.
The Pilgrim Trust (1938), *Men Without Work*, Cambridge,
Cambridge University Press.
Pollert, A. (1981), *Girls, Wives, Factory Lives*, London, Macmillan.
Prais, S.J. (1976), *The Evolution of Giant Firms in Britain*, Cambridge,
Cambridge University Press.
Purcell, J. and **Sisson, K.** (1983), 'Strategies and Practice in the
Management of Industrial Relations' in G.S. Bain (ed.) *Industrial
Relations in Britain*, Oxford, Basil Blackwell.
Purcell, K. (1978), 'Working Women, Women's Work and the
Occupational Sociology of Being A Woman', *Women's Studies
International Quarterly*, vol. 1, no. 2, pp.153–63.
Purcell, K. (1982), 'Female Manual Workers, Fatalism and the
Reinforcement of Inequalities', in D. Robbins et al (eds)
Rethinking Social Inequality, Farnborough, Gower.
Routh, G. (1980), *Occupation and Pay in Great Britain 1906–79*,
London, Macmillan.
Scarman, Lord L.G. (1981), *The Brixton Disorders*, London, HMSO.
Seabrook, J. (1982), *Unemployment*, London, Quartet Books.
Showler, B. (1981), 'Political Economy and Unemployment' in B.
Showler and A. Sinfield (eds) *The Workless State*, Oxford, Martin
Robertson.
Showler, B. and **Sinfield, A.** (1981) (eds) *The Workless State*,
Oxford, Martin Robertson.
Sinfield, A. (1981), *What Unemployment Means*, Oxford, Martin
Robertson.
Sokoloff, N.J. (1982), *Between Money and Love*, New York, Praeger.
Sorrentino, C. (1981), 'Unemployment in International
Perspective' in B. Showler and A. Sinfield (eds) *The Workless State*,
Oxford, Martin Robertson.
Stacey, M. and **Price, M.** (1981), *Women, Power and Politics*, London,
Tavistock.
Stern, J. (1983), 'Who becomes unemployed? Unemployment
Inflow Rates in GB for 1978', in D.E. *Gazette*, vol. 91, no. 1,
pp.21–3.
Tomlinson, J. (1983), 'Does Mass Unemployment Matter?' in
National Westminster Bank Quarterly Review, February.
Townsend, P. (1979), *Poverty in the United Kingdom*,
Harmondsworth, Penguin.

Westergaard, J. and **Resler, H.** (1976), *Class in a Capitalist Society*, Harmondsworth, Pelican.

Westwood, S. (1984), *All Day Every Day*, London, Pluto.

Willis, P. (1977), *Learning to Labour*, London, Saxon House.

Leisure 9

Stanley Parker

It is only comparatively recently that leisure has come to be accepted as a legitimate subject for sociological study. There is no single explanation of why leisure should have been admitted so late into the sociological field. Perhaps it is a combination of the low priority given to leisure activities and experiences in a still work-oriented society, a feeling that leisure and its alliterative companion pleasure cannot be a serious subject for study, and the highly personal and subjective nature of the beast.

However, there *are* such things as leisure institutions, leisure organizations, leisure providers and consumers – and there *are* manifestations of leisure behaviour that can be classified, counted, and perhaps even theorized about. There are books written by sociologists on leisure (Dumazedier, 1974; Kaplan, 1975; Parker, 1976; Roberts, 1981, to name but a few), several American journals (*Journal of Leisure Research, Leisure Sciences, Society and Leisure*) and a more recent British journal (*Leisure Studies*) on the subject. In North America there are something like two thousand 'leisure programs' at various universities and colleges, and in Britain, Australia and elsewhere courses in recreation and leisure studies have been set up or are in the process of being set up.

Changes are taking place in modern industrial societies which tend to enhance the role of leisure, both in the lives of individuals and in the structure of their institutions. Increased unemployment, although it is by no means to be equated with leisure, raises the question of whether the gap left by the 'collapse of work' (Jenkins and Sherman, 1979) can be at least partly filled by leisure (see the chapter by Kate Purcell in this volume). Earlier and longer retirement raises similar problems (see the chapter by Janet Finch in this volume). And significant questions of politics and of social control lie behind some of the attempts to provide recreation (a rather more respectable word than leisure) activities for groups in the population who are seen to be deprived or who act in anti-social or allegedly self-destructive ways.

Against that background this chapter successively reviews basic concepts and indicators of leisure, relevant methods of data collection and analysis, the various types of research question posed as part of the sociological study of leisure, the issue of data comparability, and finally the developing links between leisure theory and research.

Basic concepts and indicators

Under this heading there is a great deal to cover: various definitions and conceptual approaches to leisure and related topics, types of leisure activity, behaviour and experience, and indicators of leisure. A thorough review of definitions could alone take up the whole chapter, so the references will be selective rather than exhaustive.

Elsewhere (Parker, 1983) I have suggested that definitions of leisure tend to fall into three main groups: residual, normative and mixed. *Residual* definitions take the twenty-four hours in the day and subtract from them periods which are not leisure: working, sleeping, eating, attending to physiological needs, and so on. Examples of this kind of definition are given by Giddens (1964) and Gross (1961). *Normative* definitions insist that leisure is essentially not a period of time but a quality of activity or experience; unavoidably this type of definition involves value judgments about what attributes of the activity or experience we think are worthy of being called leisure (Pieper, 1952; Touraine, 1974). *Mixed* definitions seek in effect to combine the other two, starting with a residual or time element and accompanying this by a normative statement about what leisure ought to be (Dumazedier, 1960; Gist and Fava, 1964).

Murphy (1974) distinguishes six views of leisure: as a state of being, discretionary time, denoting lifestyle, anti-utilitarian activity, non-work activity, and arising from a holistic view of life. Some definitions of leisure are complex and others relatively simple. Kaplan (1975) believes that leisure

> consists of relatively self-determined activity-experience that falls into one's economically free-time roles, that is seen as leisure by participants, that is psychologically pleasant in anticipation and recollection, that potentially covers the whole range of commitment and intensity, that contains characteristic norms and constraints, and that provides

opportunities for recreation, personal growth and service to others.

But Roberts (1981) prefers simplicity and argues that, although Kaplan's definition may convey certain qualities of leisure experience, it is unnecessarily elaborate and therefore confusing. No researcher has ever found it practical to work from so elaborate a definition. Also, whether leisure is psychologically pleasant and results in personal growth and service to others are, according to Roberts, better regarded as hypotheses requiring investigation than issues to be resolved by definition.

Bacon (1972) conceives of leisure as a complex, multi-dimensional concept and he criticizes approaches which study it as an isolated and residual sphere of unobligated behaviour. For Ennis (1968) leisure is not contained in any single institutional area but can be expressed in any of them, and Kelly (1982) tends to agree with this.

Until a few years ago most approaches to leisure were in terms either of free time, activity or 'state of mind'. More recently a number of researchers have written of the *experience* of leisure (Mannell, 1980; Harper, 1981; Kelly, 1983). The appropriate way of finding out about time and activity is empirical research; the understanding of a state of mind requires a psychological or philosophical approach. With experience, however, the appropriate method is said to be phenomenology, the study of the necessary factors which make a thing what it is. As Harper (1981) puts it, *what* leisure is, is a phenomenological question; *whether* and to what extent it is is an empirical question.

Of the concepts allied to leisure, *recreation* is probably the closest, although for some scholars the two concepts have radically different emphases. Most definitions of recreation refer explicitly or consequentially to leisure. Thus for Bucher and Bucher (1974) 'recreation is concerned with various types of activities in which human beings engage during their leisure hours' (i.e. adopting a residual or time definition of leisure to enable recreation to constitute an activity dimension). Carlson (1972) takes a similar view. Some observers compare recreation with leisure to the detriment of the former. Thus Cheek and Burch (1976) see leisure behaviour as tending to be self-contained, aperiodic and enjoyable, and recreation behaviour as routinized enjoyment undertaken for rational reasons as a means to some other end and not just for personal enjoyment. McCormack (1971) makes a similar point: 'Recreation is a system of social control, and like all systems of social control it is to some degree manipulative, coercive and indoctrinating. Leisure is not.'

Sport is one form of recreation, and has been defined as 'a human activity that involves specific administrative organization and a historical background of rules which define the objective and limit the pattern of human behaviour; it involves competition and/or challenge and a definite outcome primarily determined by physical skill' (Singer, 1976). This is both ambiguous and arguable (what is a 'definite outcome'?). Some useful texts on the sociology of sport (e.g. Dunning, 1971) manage to avoid the problem of definition altogether, while others (e.g. Snyder and Spreitzer, 1978) discuss some of the relatively few definitions that have been offered.

Although participant sport accounts for only a small proportion of the general population's leisure experiences, it has attracted a considerable amount of attention from sociologists, and sport research has been developed far more than research into other leisure areas. Sport sociology, in both Britain and North America, has a large enough literature and has accumulated research which may be seen to constitute a sub-discipline of sociology itself rather than of the sociology of leisure. Of the many texts on particular aspects of the sociology of sport I shall mention only two: Oglesby (ed. 1978) has brought together twelve contributions to the discussion of sports feminism, and Holt (1981), in his study of sport in France, includes a welcome analysis of what it does for the spectator as well as the participant. The British Sports Council (in conjunction with the Social Science Research Council) has provided funds over a five-year period for fundamental research into a wide range of leisure activities, resulting in the publication of a number of 'state of the art' reviews, including work and leisure, leisure for women, adolescents, the over 50s and ethnic groups, leisure expenditure, and the commercial sector.

The concept of *play* is also related to leisure. According to Brightbill (1963), play is the free, pleasurable, immediate, and natural expression of animals, particularly the young. Huizinga's (1970) classic study of play in different cultures confirms these universal features, adds those of disinterestedness, the creation of rules and of the play-community which continues after the game is over. Among several scholars of play, Ellis (1971) is notable for having assembled fifteen theories seeking to explain why people play.

If there is one concept that often has a better press than that of leisure it is *culture*. Williams (1965) is probably not alone in preferring to write of culture and in finding 'a hollowness about leisure as a concept, as if it were only time to be filled'. Touraine (1974) refers, perhaps over-simply, to 'the distinction between active and passive leisure activities or, if one prefers, between elite and mass culture'. The more penetrating critiques of passive and alienated leisure in capitalist society emanate from a cultural analysis of consumerist and commodified leisure, in contrast with the more humanly productive forms that leisure could take in a more socialist society (Fromm, 1956).

Finally there are the somewhat similar concepts of *free time* and *spare time*. Of the two, free time may be seen as the more potentially developmental: it implies a freedom *to* do something as well as to escape from constraints. Free time is best regarded as one dimension of leisure, others including activity and experience. Spare time implies a lack of commitment or knowing what to do, a situation of having 'time on my hands' (Paddick, 1982). It can, however, be filled by leisure or recreation, sport or play or cultural activities – and then it is no longer spare.

Turning now to types of leisure, there are various ways of classifying these. Perhaps the commonest way is by type of activity. Although there is no agreed list of general leisure activities, the following are some of the more frequently cited: arts, countryside recreation, entertainment, informal recreation, hobbies, outdoor recreation, sport, tourism. The British General Household Survey 1977 (1979) lists leisure activities under the headings of active outdoor sports, active indoor sports and games, spectator sports, outings, countryside activities, sightseeing, entertainment and cultural pursuits, social activities, betting and gambling and home-based activities.

Types of leisure may also be classified temporally, the shorter periods making some forms of leisure activity difficult if not impossible to engage in. Thus there is the possibility of leisure during the working day, at the end of the day, at weekends, during holiday or vacation times, and at the end of the working life (retirement). The first and last of these time periods have received some research attention: Brown *et al.* (1973) has studied 'leisure in work' and Roberts (1983) 'playing at work', while most textbooks on retirement have something to say about leisure.

The final question to be raised in this section is: what are the indicators of leisure? This is an exceptionally difficult question. But some answer to it is necessary if we are to proceed to the next stage of accumulating data about leisure. Apart from the sophisticated and sociologically challenging concerns with the quality of leisure (as part of life) experiences, there are three main indicators of leisure that have been used as a basis for research: numbers or frequencies of leisure activities, expenditure of time, and expenditure of money.

Data collection and analysis

The largest amount of data on leisure has been collected in the form of statistics on participation rates in various forms of pre-defined leisure activity. These participation rates can be either in the form of numbers of people taking part over specified periods or frequencies of participation, also over specified periods. The statistics are usually collected from large samples and each sampled person is asked only a small number of fairly simple questions. Typical of this kind of data collection is the British General Household Survey, in which about 23,000 adults have been interviewed each year (to be cut to about 20,000). In 1973, 1977 and 1980 questions were asked about leisure and, in addition to being presented in the official reports for those years, the results have been further analysed by Birch (1976) and Veal (1979).

The first British national surveys dealing entirely with leisure were carried out in the mid-1960s (British Travel Association/University of Keele, 1967, 1969; Sillitoe, 1969). Although both surveys were mainly concerned with getting data about participation in sport and outdoor recreation for planning purposes, they also collected some data on other kinds of leisure participation. These and subsequent national or large-scale participation surveys have been critically reviewed by Duffield and Long (1979).

The usual method of collecting data about time devoted to leisure is by time budget survey or diary records. It is possible to ask people questions just about the time they spend on leisure, but it has generally been found more satisfactory to ask for an account of *all* expenditure of time during normal waking hours, albeit with an emphasis on certain kinds of activity and an implicit ignoring or superficial mention of others. Thus the British Broadcasting Corporation (1965, 1978) have carried out large-scale time budget surveys, paying particular attention to media consumption. Academic and institutional researchers (e.g. Young and Willmott, 1973) have carried out time budget studies on a smaller scale, and have been able to analyse their findings more fully, though perhaps with less statistical accuracy.

Research on expenditure of money on leisure has been carried out by both official and commercial bodies. The British surveys of Family Expenditure and National Income and Expenditure (both annual reports) give expenditure data under specific headings, some of which are clearly leisure (e.g. 'miscellaneous recreational goods') while others are partly leisure in a proportion impossible to determine (e.g. 'travel', 'books'). Ryan (1976) has attempted to evaluate 'the leisure pound' from a commercial provider standpoint.

Another kind of leisure data concerns the number of, or expenditure on, facilities provided for leisure. For example, some years ago the various regional Sports Councils made 'initial appraisals' of such capital-intensive facilities as swimming pools, indoor sports centres and golf courses. For researchers wishing to study participation in particular forms of sport, the various governing bodies usually have some basic data about numbers of clubs and numbers of members, but these data are not always published. Lewes and Parker (1975) give information about these and other data sources, and critically review the adequacy of the information they provide.

So far we have mentioned sample surveys, diary records, official and organizational statistics as sources of data on leisure. Although reasonably reliable statistically, these methods of data collection and analysis may not be valid as measures of leisure. To note two points of criticism: surveys of what people do in their 'leisure' time notoriously underestimate time spent in informal leisure, as more penetrating case-study research has revealed (Deem, 1982). And Chase and Godbey (1983) have shown that self-reported rates of participation in such activities as swimming and tennis tend to be seriously exaggerated when compared with actual records of attendances.

Two other methods of leisure data collection deserve mention: historical records and observation, whether participant or non-participant. (Historical records will be dealt with in the next section on comparable data.) Observation is important if we want to understand what people actually do, which may sometimes be different from what they say they do. For example, one may need to go to a leisure centre to observe that where the people are and what they prefer to do is often not to use the expensive sports facilities but to enjoy a cup of tea in the canteen and to socialize. Participant observation is especially useful in delineating the dimensions of a leisure context such as the pub (Smith, 1981), bingo (Dixey, 1982) or gambling (Newman, 1973).

Research questions

Seeley (1963) has made an important distinction between sociography (data assembling and ordering) and sociology (causal analysis). The previous section dealt largely with sociographical questions as necessary precursors to sociological analysis. Here we shall be concerned with the issues and problems to which sociologists have so far addressed themselves or may be expected to do so in the future. Some of the writers noted are not sociologists: their inclusion is, I believe, justified because they have raised sociological questions or multi-disciplinary questions which include a sociological aspect.

Below I have selected, from a much larger possible number, eleven questions for brief discussion. The list is mixed, as may be expected in an area of study still in its infancy. Not all of the questions are of equal sociological importance; purists may say that some are not socio-logical at all. The list would have been somewhat different ten years ago, and will probably be different again in ten years' time. Another reviewer would no doubt present a different list: hopefully he or she would include at least some of the same or similar questions to mine.

The first question is the role of *sport* in society. I have already referred to the substantial amount of social science research that has been devoted to this subject, quite apart from the applied research in such areas as physiology and biomechanics. The sports lobby is a powerful one, and it gains much of its influence from the functional role that competitive and organized sport plays in our society. This role has increasingly come to be questioned by radical and Marxist critics (Hargreaves, 1975; Brohm, 1978). They argue that there is substantial evidence that sport operates as a means of social control, notably in the teaching of school sports. Sport is inherently competi-tive, and is therefore an effective mode of socialization into the competitive mores of contemporary society. In industry, manage-ment (at least lower levels) has become actively engaged in organiz-ing and facilitating games on the shop floor, particularly where they revolve around output (Burawoy, 1978). In view of these and other considerations Edwards' (1973) conclusion that 'sport is both politic-al in character and basically conservative' seems well justified. The ramifications of sport extend into the controversial questions of amateur versus professional, the ongoing commercialization of sports such as cricket and athletics, internationalism and racism in sporting organizations. All deserve further study by social scientists.

A second and related question broadens out from the first: that of the *politics* of leisure. Not only is the provision of leisure facilities and opportunities – certainly in the public sector – to a large extent a matter for political decision at local or central government level but, as Kaplan (1975) asks, should not unpaid time devoted to political activity be entered into the ledger of leisure? An issue posed by Meisel (1978) as a task for political science may also be seen as an issue for sociology: to illuminate and document the manner in which political problems, issues and processes are influenced by the way people occupy their leisure time. Van Moorst (1982) disagrees with those who argue that leisure is gaining increasing autonomy from the influence of other institutions, and he maintains that the usage of time in any society is primarily a function of the existing mode of production. Wilson (1980) has made a useful analysis of the political functions of leisure.

A third question concerns what might be called the *hidden agenda* of leisure experience. It has become too easy to think of leisure as simply activities of one kind or another, or as so much free time to be filled. The temptation to think in this way is increased when we realize that activities and expenditures of time and money can be counted (despite some marginal complications discussed above) in a way that leisure experiences cannot. Nevertheless, we must not imagine that we have given a true account of leisure if we have categorized and measured people's leisure activities and expenditures. Roberts (1981) is right to point out that with leisure it is not so much a matter of *what* we do as *who* we do it with. Glyptis and Chambers (1982) have noted that more than half of all leisure is spent at home, although surveys often underrate this. Leisure research has become too dominated by the needs of planners and providers – it is not that we need less of this type of research, but from a social science standpoint we certainly need to recognize the importance for most people of informal types of leisure. Those need not be without implications for planning and policy, but what has been done has reflected an over-concern with activities at the expense of experiences.

Fourth, we may question why the *arts* have been so neglected in leisure studies. Part of the explanation is that, unlike many sports scholars who are willing to relate their concerns to those of leisure, arts scholars tend to see artistic products as 'works' rather than as playthings. There is also the close link between arts and culture and, as we have seen, culture is an even wider concept than leisure, threatening to subsume 'leisure studies' under 'cultural studies'. But, as compared with sports, the arts not only in part reinforce conventional values (Goodlad, 1971) but also function as powerful media of social criticism via the cinema, theatre and television. There is, to put it crudely, a dominant, consensus culture and a subordinated, radical culture. Publications such as the occasional papers of the Birmingham University Centre for Contemporary Cultural Studies are helping to increase our knowledge of the sociology of the arts as part of leisure, but there is still much more to be done. In terms of institutionally sponsored research, the Sports Council has made the running and the Arts Council limps some way behind.

A fifth research question is that of the relationship between *work and leisure*. This continues to fascinate a number of us in the leisure studies community (see Staines, 1980, for a review of the literature), although it may be said to have gone through three main phases. The first was to concentrate on the study of leisure in relationship to work, seeing leisure, as Bacon (1972) puts it, as a concept whose most characteristic determinant is work. There followed a reaction to this in the form of an insistence that leisure should be studied in its own right, since for many and perhaps increasing numbers of people leisure is the main thing in their lives and is quite independent of any work they may do (Dumazedier, 1974, is a leading exponent of this approach). It seems that we are now well into a third and synthesizing stage of returning to studies of leisure in relation to work but with a fuller recognition that other spheres of life and social structure – politics, community life, education, religion – enter into the equation of sociological understanding.

The sixth and seventh questions emanate from what has been happening to work in our society. The study of the consequences for leisure of *unemployment* (and of retirement, below) has recently attracted research attention. With the dramatic rise in unemployment in the last few years, more people have lives which fulfil one condition of leisure: they have the time which they formerly spent in paid work. But often they do not have the money to cope with such large blocks of 'leisure', nor in most cases have they prepared themselves for it. Furthermore, their status as 'unemployed' is not validated by society. As Smith and Simpkins (1980) shows, the unemployed, far from being envied as a new 'leisure class', are subject to societal disapproval and suffer discriminatory labels such as 'cheat' and 'scrounger'. Although recent reports on the unemployed such as those by Seabrook (1982) and Roberts *et al.* (1982) go some way towards deepening our understanding of what it is like to be unemployed in a still work-oriented society, they need to be followed up by more imaginative 'action research' projects directed towards doing something positive about this large-scale human tragedy.

Those who have been forced into an early and unwanted *retirement* constitute another minority who on the face of it have lives of leisure. For the comparatively small number of people (mostly men) who are retired early from their employment in good health and with a reasonable occupational pension, this can indeed be a period of enjoyable leisure, in which old interests can be developed or new ones taken up (McGoldrick, 1983). But many retirees – and particularly those who retire early through ill health and without an occupational pension – the reality is deprivation rather than leisure (Parker, 1982). With growing numbers of people facing earlier retirement, more needs to be done to prepare them for the drastic change in their pattern of living, and research should be mounted to monitor the effectiveness with which the problems of adjustment to retirement are being tackled.

The next two research questions concern the problematic leisure of two further groups in society: youth and women. The leisure of *young people* has not been neglected in the literature: the incidence of juvenile anti-social and 'deviant' behaviour has made sure that explanations of such behaviour have been sought and remedies advocated (Smith, 1973; Marsland, 1982). The question of whether unemployed youth feel deprived or excluded from the mainstream of society has been taken up in different ways. Roberts *et al.* (1982) argue that young people today have a habit of drifting in and out of the labour market, perhaps working in the 'black economy', and that many of them prefer to take breaks from employment, particularly if the jobs available are unsatisfying. Corrigan (1979; 1982) chronicles the apparently lazy leisure style of unemployed male youths hanging around on street corners: 'Contained within the whole experience of doing nothing is a wide selection of important activities which contain some form of interest, some form of excitement. . . it is only outside of (the) major alienated experiences of work or school in a capitalist society that working class people have the time and energy to organise, educate and find out about their world. . . '

The topic of *women* and leisure has grown apace with the whole area of women's studies. A decade ago women might have been divided into feminists and traditionalists. Today one major division is between militant feminists and moderate feminists. The recent literature on leisure reflects this. Deem (1982) argued that women's enjoyment and use of free time is constrained by domestic labour, job attitudes, behaviour and working hours of male partners, child care, lack of independent income and absence of transport. In the same issue of *Leisure Studies*, Gregory (1982) countered, although in moderation of Deem's case rather than in opposition to it, that the home-based mother of young children may regard as work the labour of bringing them up, but her developing family relationships mean that leisure and work may be going on simultaneously. McIntosh (1981) and Talbot (1979) are also worth reading on the subject of women and leisure.

Tenth, the relationship between *education* and leisure raises some important research and policy issues. Education *for* leisure is appropriate at all stages of life, but particularly for young people – who need some guidance about choosing from the plethora of ways of spending time and money – and for those about to retire, hopefully to leisure but if not probably to boredom or frustration. Education *as* leisure has been comparatively neglected, although Jary's (1973) study of the substantial leisure component in evening classes could be replicated and extended with advantage. Gebhardt's (1975) suggestion that 'leisure should become the sphere for the development of skill and competence in the art of living' is both a normative point of view and a provocative research proposal.

Finally, what of the *future* of leisure? Sociology is not to be confused with futurology, but the two have something in common: a concern with understanding the general directions that society is taking. With regard to time available for leisure the trend data must be interpreted with care. An average reduction of four hours a week working time per decade over the last century or so does not necessarily mean that working time will disappear altogether around the year 2084. Perhaps more instructive are the various scenarios of work and leisure that have been put forward, since they alert us to the developmental possibilities within our present society. Thus Martin and Mason (1982) have proposed four scenarios based on a combination of two polarized values of economic growth and two types of social attitudes to work and leisure. With high economic growth and a continuation of conventional values there will be 'conventional success'; with low economic growth and a continuation of conventional values there will be 'frustration'; low economic growth and transformed (more leisure-oriented) values will produce (or require?) 'self restraint'; and high economic growth with transformed values will result in 'transformed growth'.

Comparable data

In this section we shall look briefly at comparable leisure data in three respects: various historical periods, multi-national surveys, and international comparisons based on separate national inquiries.

If one takes 'data' to mean facts and figures about participation rates in various forms of leisure activity, physical resources devoted to leisure purposes, etc, then such data applying to different periods of history are not possible to obtain, except for very recent periods. Because of the comparative recency of many of today's most popular or most capital-intensive forms of leisure (television, leisure centres, and suchlike) historical comparisons would in any case be largely inappropriate.

There are, however, questions of historical comparability which it *is* legitimate to address, and the recent spate of books on the history of leisure over the last century or two (Bailey, 1978; Cunningham, 1980; Philips, 1978; Walvin, 1980) have mostly included some treatment of these. Because sample surveys of the general population's activities and attitudes are a relatively recent invention, historians deal in another kind of data. They do not see the category of leisure as self-evident or achievable by the process of abstract definition (Critcher, 1980). Rather, leisure is to be regarded as a social construction; the idea of leisure is seen as inextricably bound up with the revolution of industrial capitalism. What now can seem to be a static sphere of life – free time – appears to the historian as the end product of a struggle over both the amount of free time and the permitted uses of it (Burns, 1973). These two considerations – leisure as social construction and leisure as struggle – condition the possibilities of comparison between any two or more historical periods.

The second question is of multi-national surveys (i.e., those carried out in different countries using the same or closely similar research instrument) and need not detain us long because there has been only one. The multi-national time budget project (Szalai, 1972) obtained data from twelve countries (not including Britain) about the amount of free time that people in various domestic, age and socio-economic categories claimed to have. As a method of inquiry, time budgets suffer from memory problems of informants and often low response rates. The Research Commission of the World Leisure and Recreation Association has on its agenda the mounting of further multi-national research projects on more sociological aspects of leisure, though difficulties of sponsorship and of getting international agreement on specific questions for research are formidable.

Finally, there are a small number of publications reporting surveys or other data which, though not designed to be closely comparable, do lend themselves to comparison within limits. Comparison between leisure in the west and in the Soviet *bloc* has engaged the attention of several writers, including Riordan (1982) and Rogers (1974). Ibrahim (1982) and Ibrahim and Asker (1984) have contributed two interesting articles on leisure and Islam and on leisure in Egypt, the latter containing data on sports and leisure facilities that are not too difficult to compare with other national data.

Links between theory and research

In this final section we consider various sociological theories in relation to the study of leisure and to its influence on or by other life spheres and social institutions; theories relevant to particular types of leisure; and the status of 'leisure' sociology in relation to other sociologies and to general sociology.

Partly because of its comparative infancy, the sociology of leisure has not developed a great deal of theory, although there are certainly general theories of social structure and change which have been applied to the area of leisure. Thus a structural-functional approach has been used to show that leisure has certain Parsonian-type functions for the social group or for society itself (Gross, 1961). Much of the literature on the sociology of leisure and community life in Britain in the 1950s and 1960s – and even into the 1970s – was characterized by a commitment to the values of liberal and social democracy, and to the reformism which was expressed in the mixed economy and the welfare state (Young and Willmott, 1957; Stacey, 1960). In the last two decades, a variety of Marxist perspectives have come more to the fore, usually not dealing primarily with leisure phenomena, but nevertheless with clear implications for their study: Williams (1965) and Corrigan (1979) are examples.

In a recent review of sociological contributions to the study of leisure, Parry (1983) suggests that the stronger (largely Marxist) linkage of sociology with economics, in alliance with the new feminism and the growth in unemployment, has refocused attention on unwaged labour – particularly of women – and on dependency. This has redressed the balance away from the preoccupations of industrial sociology (by definition concerned with those in work) towards a consideration of the 'leisure' of the unwaged, including women, unemployed youth, the retired and the redundant. Theorizing and research about informal economic activity and community action (Gershuny, 1978) is one response to this change in economic climate. An interesting and researchable claim has been made by Lane (1978) that the leisure ideology is 'left' and the market ideology is 'right': 'In the labour market ideology man realizes himself through his productivity, and that is the measure of his worth. For the leisure ideology, man is measured by his self-reflexive sense of pleasure and growth.' We live, it seems, not just in a mixed economy but also among mixed ideologies.

Turning now to theories (or at least theoretical propositions) relevant to particular types of leisure, we can see that these have been applied in a variety of behavioural and institutional settings. I shall discuss briefly sport, games, arts, tourism, and the 'harried leisure class' – again, the list and the examples are selective.

Research supporting the claim that competitive sport is functional for capitalist society has already been referred to. This theme has recently been elaborated by Lipsky (1981): 'It is quite clear that the sports team meshes with the goals of administrative capitalism. It is no accident that as American society became more complex and bureaucratic, the more corporate games of football and basketball rose to popularity.' Haywood (1976) has reviewed this and other theories relevant to the functions of games and sport.

Theories of games have sought to classify them in meaningful ways and to explain cross-cultural differences revealed by research (ideally the twin processes of research to test theory and theory to explain research results go hand in hand). Caillois (1962) has delineated four 'fundamental categories' of games: *agon* signifying competition, with a winner emerging (football, chess); *alea* or games of chance (roulette, a lottery); *mimicry* involving illusion and make-believe (theatre, carnival); and *ilinx*, rapidly whirling or falling movement (acrobatics, tobogganing). Rogers (1982) has produced a critical commentary on this formulation. Other researchers have put forward socialization or 'conflict-enculturation' hypotheses to account for cross-cultural variations in play (Child and Child, 1973; Roberts and Sutton-Smith, 1962).

Theory-and-research in the arts has not received much attention. Wolff (1981) has critically examined theories about the ideological nature of art, presenting an account of the relationship between social structure, ideology and the arts. Harker (1980) explains the development of post-war popular music in terms of the structure of the industry that produced it. Frith (1978) has written a sociology of rock. Tourism has quite a substantial literature. Because of the concerns of national and commercial providers and promoters, psychological research into the motivations and satisfactions of tourists has received more attention than sociological research. Newman's (1973) analysis of holidays and social class is, however, noteworthy, as are MacCannell's (1976) hypotheses about why various forms of sightseeing 'draw the tourist into a relationship with the modern social totality'.

The final theory to be considered here is not really about any particular type of leisure behaviour but concerns one prominent feature of an allegedly growing minority of the population in modern industrial society. Linder (1970) has written of 'the harried leisure class', and his analysis is as follows. A dwindling scarcity of goods entails an increasing scarcity of time. There is much evidence that people in advanced industrial societies (and particularly in the United States) live under the tyranny of the clock. The benefits of capital-intensive methods of production have led to huge increases in output per head of goods, but this has not been matched in the spheres of self and personal property maintenance. The more goods and gadgets people have, the more time will have to be spent buying and maintaining them. Some part of what would otherwise be spent as leisure time is thus devoted to do-it-yourself work.

The quality of leisure, too, is affected by the need to save time. A corollary of 'time famine' is 'anti-leisure'; 'activity which is undertaken compulsively, as a means to an end, from a perception of necessity, with a high degree of externally imposed constraint, with considerable anxiety, with a high degree of time consciousness and a minimum of personal autonomy'(Godbey, 1975). Although this is not a picture of life characteristic of the majority of the population in the United States today, and far less in Britain, it applies to a significant and perhaps growing minority. The incidence, forms and correlates of anti-leisure are well worth monitoring.

The third and final question under the heading of links between theory and research concerns the present status of 'leisure sociology' within general sociology. Many of the roots of leisure sociology lie within the field of industrial sociology and the sociology of occupations, but there are other approaches which feed into leisure sociology besides work, occupations and industry. Parry (1983) has pointed out the contributions that community studies have made to our understanding of leisure behaviour and institutions. Curran and Tunstall (1973) have suggested that other sub-fields in social science can contribute to the sociology of leisure, including those of social stratification, family and kinship, youth and age, and education, knowledge and culture.

Conclusion

On a narrow view of leisure as simply 'what people do in their spare time', it is arguably not a key variable in sociological understanding. The case for treating it as a key variable rests principally upon appreciating that it is the interaction of leisure with other social processes which qualifies it for sociological research and theorizing. We may argue about whether leisure is determined by work or work by leisure, and we may carry out research to support one or other emphasis. People are educated *for* leisure, but in some ways education can *be* leisure. Similar considerations apply to the family, religion, and so on. It is not so much that leisure sociologists look at one isolated bit of life and society called 'leisure'. Rather, they look at the whole of life and society through the lens of leisure.

References

Bacon, A.W. (1972), 'Leisure and research: a critical review of the main concepts', *Society and Leisure*, no. 2, pp. 83–92.

Bailey, P. (1978), *Leisure and Class in Victorian England*, London, Routledge & Kegan Paul.

Birch, F. (1976), 'Leisure patterns in Britain', *Population Trends*, Spring, pp.18–23.

Brightbill, C.K. (1963), *The Challenge of Leisure*, New York, Prentice-Hall.

British Broadcasting Corporation (1965), *The People's Activities*, London.

British Broadcasting Corporation (1978), *The People's Activities and Use of Time*, London.

British Travel Association/University of Keele (1967, 1969), *Pilot National Recreational Survey*, London.

Brohm, J. -M. (1978), *Sport – A Prison of Measured Time*, London, Ink Links.

Brown, R., Brannen, P., Cousins, J. and **Samphier, M.** (1973), 'Leisure in work', in M.A. Smith *et al.* (eds), *Leisure and Society in Britain*, London, Allen Lane, pp. 97–100.

Bucher, C.A. and **Bucher, R.D.** (1974), *Recreation for Today's Society*, Englewood Cliffs, N.J., Prentice-Hall.

Burawoy, M. (1978), 'Toward a Marxist theory of the labor process: Braverman and beyond', *Politics and Society*, vol. 8, no.3.

Burns, T. (1973), 'Leisure in industrial society', in M.A. Smith *et al.* (eds), *Leisure and Society in Britain*, London, Allen Lane, pp. 40–55.

Caillois, R. (1962), *Man, Play and Games*, London, Thames.

Carlson, R.E. (1972), *Recreation in American Life*, Belmont, Wadsworth.

Chase, D.R. and **Godbey, G.** (1983), 'A research note on the accuracy of self-reported participation rates', *Leisure Studies*, vol.2, May, pp.231–6.

Cheek, N.H. and **Burch, W.R.** (1976), *The Social Organization of Leisure in Human Society*, New York, Harper.

Child, E. and **Child, J.** (1973), 'Children and leisure', in M.A. Smith *et al.* (eds), *Leisure and Society in Britain*, London, Allen Lane, pp. 135–47.

Corrigan, P. (1979) *Schooling the Smash Street Kids*, London, Macmillan.

Corrigan, P. (1982), 'The trouble with being unemployed is that you never get a day off', in A.J. Veal *et al.* (eds), *Work and Leisure: Unemployment, Technology and Lifestyles in the 1980s*, London, Leisure Studies Association, pp. 50–5.

Critcher, C. (1980), 'The politics of leisure – social control and social development', in *Prospects for Leisure and Work*, London, Leisure Studies Association.

Cunningham, H. (1980), *Leisure in the Industrial Revolution*, London, Croom Helm.

Curran, J. and **Tunstall, J.** (1973), 'Mass media and leisure', in M.A. Smith *et al.* (eds), *Leisure and Society in Britain*, London, Allen Lane, pp. 199–213.

Deem, R. (1982), 'Women, leisure and inequality', *Leisure Studies*, vol. 1, Jan., pp. 29–46.

Dixey, R. (1982), *Women, Leisure and Bingo*, Leeds, Trinity and All Saints College.

Duffield, B. and **Long, J.** (1979), *Large-scale Participation Surveys: Lessons for the Future*, Cheltenham, Countryside Commission.

Dumazedier, J. (1960), 'Current problems of the sociology of leisure', *International Social Science Journal*, no.4, pp. 522–31.

Dumazedier, J. (1974), *Sociology of Leisure*, Amsterdam, Elsevier.

Dunning, E. (ed.) (1971), *The Sociology of Sport*, London, Cass.

Edwards, H. (1973), *Sociology of Sport*, Homewood, Ill., Dorsey Press.

Ellis, M. (1971), *Why People Play*, Englewood Cliffs, N.J., Prentice-Hall.

Ennis, P. H. (1968), 'The definition and measurement of leisure', in E.B. Sheldon and W.E. Moore (eds), *Indicators of Social Change*, New York, Russell Sage, pp. 525–72.

Frith, S. (1978), *Sociology of Rock*, London, Constable.

Fromm, E. (1956), *The Sane Society*, London, Routledge & Kegan Paul.

Gebhardt, P. (1975), 'Education for leisure', in Department of Tourism and Recreation, *Leisure – A New Perspective*, Canberra, Australian Government Publishing Service.

General Household Survey, 1977, London, HMSO, 1979.

Gershuny, J. (1978), *After Industrial Society? The Emerging Self-service Economy*, London, Macmillan.

Giddens, A. (1964), 'Notes on the concept of play and leisure', *Sociological Review*, March, pp. 73–89.

Gist, N.P. and **Fava, S.F.** (1964), *Urban Society*, New York, Crowell.

Glyptis, S. and **Chambers, D.** (1982), 'No place like home', *Leisure Studies*, vol.1, September, pp. 247–62.

Godbey, G. (1975), 'Anti-leisure and public recreation policy', in S. Parker *et al.* (eds), *Sport and Leisure in Contemporary Society*, London, Leisure Studies Association.

Goodlad, J.S.R. (1971), *Sociology of Popular Drama*, London, Heinemann.

Gregory, S. (1982), 'Women among others: another view', *Leisure Studies*, vol. 1, January, pp. 47–52.

Gross, E. (1961), 'A functional approach to leisure analysis', *Social Problems*, Summer.

Hargreaves, J. (1975), 'The political economy of mass sport', in S. Parker *et al.* (eds), *Sport and Leisure in Contemporary Society*, London, Leisure Studies Association.

Harker, D. (1980), *One for the Money: Politics and Popular Song*, London, Hutchinson.

Harper, W. (1981), 'The experience of leisure', *Leisure Sciences*, vol.4, no.2.

Haywood, L.J (1976), 'The functions of games and sport – a review of theories', *Research Papers in Physical Education*, vol.3, no.2.

Holt, R. (1981), *Sport and Society in Modern France*, London, Macmillan.

Huizinga, J. (1970) *Homo Ludens*, London, Routledge & Kegan Paul.

Ibrahim, H. (1982), 'Leisure and Islam', *Leisure Studies*, vol. 1, May, pp. 197–210.

Ibrahim, H. and **Asker, N.F.** (1984), 'Ideology, politics and sport in Egypt', *Leisure Studies*, vol. 3, January, pp. 97–106.

Jary, D. (1973), 'Evenings at the ivory tower', in M.A. Smith *et al.* (eds), *Leisure and Society in Britain*, London, Allen Lane, pp. 263–77.

Jenkins, C. and **Sherman, B.** (1979) *The Collapse of Work*, London, Methuen.

Kaplan, M. (1975), *Leisure: Theory and Policy*, New York, Wiley.

Kelly, J. (1982), *Leisure*, New York, Wiley.

Kelly, J. (1983), *Leisure Identities and Interaction*, London, Allen & Unwin.

Lane, R.E. (1978), 'The regulation of experience: leisure in a market society', *Social Science Information*, vol.17, no.2, pp.147–84.

Lewes, F.M.M. and **Parker, S.** (1975), *Leisure*, vol.IV, no.7, in W.F. Maunder (ed.), *Reviews of UK Statistical Sources*, London, Heinemann.

Linder, S.B. (1970), *The Harried Leisure Class*, London, Columbia University Press.

Lipsky, R. (1981), *How We Play the Game*, Boston, Beacon Press.

MacCannell, D. (1976), *The Tourist: A New Theory of the Leisure Class*, London, Macmillan.

McCormack, T. (1971), 'Politics and leisure', *International Journal of Comparative Sociology*, September, pp. 169–81.

McGoldrick, A. (1983), 'Company early retirement schemes and private pension scheme options', *Leisure Studies*, vol.2, May, pp.187–202.

McIntosh, S. (1981), 'Leisure Studies and Women', in A. Tomlinson (ed.), *Leisure and Social Control*, Brighton Polytechnic.

Mannell, R.C. (1980), 'Social psychological techniques and strategies for studying leisure experiences', in S. Iso-Ahola (ed.), *Social Psychological Perspectives on Leisure and Recreation*, Springfield, Ill., Thomas.

Marsland, D. (1982), 'It's my life: young people and leisure', *Leisure Studies*, vol.1, September, pp.305–22.

Martin, W. and **Mason, S.** (1982), *Leisure and Work: the Choices for 1991 and 2001*, Sudbury, Suffolk, Leisure Consultants.

Meisel, J. (1978), 'Leisure, politics and political science', *Social Science Information*, vol. 17, no.2, pp.185–229.

Murphy, J.E. (1974), *Concepts of Leisure*, Englewood Cliffs, N.J., Prentice-Hall.

Newman, B. (1973), 'Holidays and social class', in M.A. Smith *et al.* (eds), *Leisure and Society in Britain*, London, Allen Lane, pp. 230–40.

Newman, O. (1973), *Gambling: Hazard or Reward*, London, Athlone Press.

Oglesby, C. (ed.) (1978), *Women and Sport: From Myth to Reality*, Philadelphia, Lea and Febiger.

Paddick, R. (1982), 'Time on my hands: hands off my time', *Leisure Studies*, vol.1, September, pp.355–64.

Parker, S. (1976), *The Sociology of Leisure*, London, Allen & Unwin.

Parker, S. (1982), *Work and Retirement*, London, Allen & Unwin.

Parker, S. (1983), *Leisure and Work*, London, Allen & Unwin.

Parry, N.C.A. (1983), 'Sociological contributions to the study of leisure', *Leisure Studies*, vol.2, January, pp.57–82.

Philips, J. (1978), *Victorians at Home and Away*, London, Croom Helm.

Pieper, J. (1952), *Leisure the Basis of Culture*, London, Faber.

Riordan, J. (1982), 'Leisure: the state and the individual in the USSR', *Leisure Studies*, vol.1, January, pp.65–80.

Roberts, J. (1983), 'Playing at work', *Leisure Studies*, vol.2, May, pp.217–30.

Roberts, J.M. and **Sutton-Smith, S.B.** (1962), 'Child training and game involvement', *Ethnology*, vol.1.

Roberts, K. (1981), *Leisure*, 2nd edn, London, Longman.

Roberts, K., Noble, M. and **Duggan, G.** (1982) 'Youth employment: an old problem or a new life-style?', *Leisure Studies*, vol.1, May, pp.171–81.

Rogers, M. (1982), 'Caillois' classification of games', *Leisure Studies*, vol.1, May, pp.225–32.

Rogers, R. (1974), 'Normative aspects of leisure time behaviour in the Soviet Union', *Sociology and Social Research*, July.

Ryan, M. (1976), 'The use of forecasting to reduce risk in leisure investment', in J. Haworth and S. Parker (eds), *Forecasting Leisure Futures*, Leisure Studies Association.

Seabrook, J. (1982), *Unemployment*, London, Quartet Books.

Seeley, J. (1963), 'Social science? Some probative problems', in M. Stein and A. Vidich (eds), *Sociology on Trial*, Englewood Cliffs, N.J., Prentice-Hall.

Sillitoe, K.K. (1969), *Planning for Leisure*, London, HMSO.

Singer, R.N. (1976), *Physical Education Foundations*, New York, Holt, Rinehart & Winston.

Smith, C.S. (1973), 'Adolescence', in M.A. Smith *et al.* (eds), *Leisure and Society in Britain*, London, Allen Lane.

Smith, M.A. (1981), *The Pub and the Publican*, University of Salford, Centre for Leisure Studies.

Smith, M.A. and **Simpkins, A.F.** (1980), *Unemployment and Leisure*, University of Salford, Centre for Leisure Studies.

Snyder, E.E. and **Spreitzer, E.** (1978), *Social Aspects of Sport*, Englewood Cliffs, N.J., Prentice-Hall.

Stacey, M. (1960), *Tradition and Change: A Study of Banbury*, London, Oxford University Press.

Staines, G.L. (1980), 'Spillover versus compensation: a review of the literature on the relationship between work and nonwork', *Human Relations*, vol.33, no.2, pp.111–30.

Szalai, A. (ed.) (1972), *The Use of Time*, The Hague, Mouton.

Talbot, M. (1979), *Women and Leisure*, London, Sports Council.

Touraine, A. (1974), *Post-Industrial Society*, London, Wildwood House.

Van Moorst, H. (1982), 'Leisure and social theory', *Leisure Studies*, vol.1, May, pp.157–70.

Veal, A.J. (1979), *Sport and Recreation in England and Wales: An Analysis of Adult Participation Patterns in 1977*, University of Birmingham, Centre for Urban and Regional Studies.

Walvin, J. (1980), 'Leisure in modern British society', in S. Glyptis (ed.), *Prospects for Leisure and Work*, London, Leisure Studies Association.

Williams, R. (1965), *The Long Revolution*, Harmondsworth, Penguin.

Wilson, J. (1980), 'Sociology of leisure', *Annual Review of Sociology*, vol.6.

Wolff, J. (1981), *The Social Production of Art*, London, Macmillan.

Young, M. and **Willmott, P.** (1957), *Family and Kinship in East London*, London, Routledge & Kegan Paul.

Young, M. and **Willmott, P.** (1973), *The Symmetrical Family*, London, Routledge & Kegan Paul.

Politics 10

David Jary

The 'key variables' which are the concern of this chapter are those politics variables most commonly used in survey research. In the Social and Economic Archive Centre's ranking list of the most used standard variables politics variables came a 'bad fourteenth' (Stacey, 1969). Politics variables lack the all-round significance or the degree of stability found associated with the most used standard variables. Although in the 1950s and 1960s an individual's party affiliation was a relatively stable phenomenon, this has not been so recently. While certain 'politics' variables, especially 'party affiliation', sometimes figure as 'face sheet' or background variables, a majority of the variables discussed in the present chapter are likely to be of greater significance to the researcher with a more specific interest in politics.

Three categories of politics variables will be examined:

i) 'party affiliation' variables,
ii) indicators of political participation and political attitudes,
iii) class and status variables in relation to politics.

Obviously the focus in this chapter excludes from consideration many politics variables with claims as 'key variables' in other contexts. This said, however, survey analysis need not be seen as the preserve of any particular epistemological school ('empiricism'). In recent years an increasing range of theoretical perspectives has been brought to bear within survey investigation of politics – a recognition that surveys, whatever their limitations, provide the surest way of getting at overall parameters of political opinion and behaviour.

1 Research contexts and theoretical perspectives in politics research

In order to set the discussion of particular variables in a general context, the primary research contexts and the theoretical perspectives in which politics 'key variables' have emerged will first be identified.

(a) *Research contexts*

(1) *Nationwide electoral surveys*
The best known studies are those carried out by the University of Michigan's Survey Research Centre (Campbell *et al.*, 1954, 1960). The most significant British surveys of this type were undertaken by Butler and Stokes (1969) at Nuffield College and continued at Essex University by Alt, Crewe and Sarlvik. Nationwide surveys are also regularly conducted by commercial opinion polling organizations. Whatever the wider reservations about many surveys carried out by polling organizations, these organizations have made a significant contribution to the operationalization and comparability of politics variables.

(2) *Constituency studies*
Compared with studies of the first type, the advantage of studies of this second type is that they can employ a range of research methods in addition to the sample survey and enable a more detailed exploration of the embeddedness of individual politics in group membership and social networks. Most seminal of studies in this category are Lazarsfeld *et al.* (1944), Berelson *et al.* (1954), at Columbia, and in Britain, Benney, Gray and Pear (1956).

(3) *Cross-national studies*
A focus largely on Britain and America in the present chapter means that studies of this type will concern us relatively little. Although there are difficulties in translating questions across cultures, cross-national studies can highlight distinctive national patterns of political affiliation and help to establish concepts and indicators with universal application, e.g., Gallie's (1979) use of 'Eurobarometer' data and Almond and Verba's (1963) five nation comparative study of political attitudes.

(4) *Focused studies*

Most significant of studies in this category are those concerned to investigate particular types of voter or the political implications of particular class orientations and class locations (e.g., McKenzie and Silver, 1968, Goldthorpe and Lockwood, 1963, Newby, 1977). Focused studies have been undertaken partly to obtain greater specification of variables and relationships arising in more global studies, But, especially recently, these have also involved research – including neo-Marxian research – challenging many of the central theoretical and methodological assumptions of previous research (e.g., Moorhouse and Chamberlain, 1974).

(b) *Theoretical perspectives*

Whatever the criticisms of survey research in some areas of sociology, research into politics is not an area in which the outstanding problem has been a lack of relation between research and theory. Nor can it be claimed that a degree of cumulative growth in both theory and research variables has not been achieved. Lazarsfeld, for instance, was a leading pioneer of theoretically directed multivariate tabular analysis and an advocate of 'middle-range' theory.

(1) *Main theoretical perspectives in the initial study of 'politics'*

Three main perspectives stand out in the earliest survey analysis of party affiliation and electoral behaviour:

> i) *Social psychological approaches.* Here politics is seen as the outcome of individual attitudinal or personality dimensions – the approach of numerous attitude scalers, and also central to the initial perspective of the Michigan school.

> ii) *The political predispositions approach* – analysis of basic socio-economic dimensions, e.g., Lazarsfeld *et al.* (1944), in which socio-economic status, religion and rural-urban location are found the significant predisposing factors influencing political affiliation. Age and generation, sex and gender, ethnic grouping, and regional location are further basic socio-economic dimensions of general importance.

> iii) *Political behaviour as the outcome of group membership.* In the pioneering work of the Columbia school explanations in these terms are complementary to those of the second type, indicating the processes by which basic socio-economic fac-

tors exert their influence (e.g., group pressure and 'opinion leadership') and also explaining deviations from 'expected' patterns (e.g., 'cross-pressures'). A crucial 'discovery' both of the Columbia and Michigan researchers was the stability of 'party affiliation' for most voters and the tendency of voters to return to a persistent affiliation even if temporarily drawn away. This gives rise to the key concept of 'party identification': a voter's 'enduring psychological link with a political party' (Budge *et al.*, 1976). Far from the 'abstracted empiricism' sometimes suggested (Mills, 1959), a 'middle range' theory of the interpersonal and media influences acting on individual politics can be said to have resulted from the initial study of voting behaviour. Moreover, a strongly stated macroscopic theory also followed in the wake of this theory: with 'stable liberal democracy' dependent upon 'a domesticated class conflict' – 'conflict within consensus' – as its central basis of political and party cleavage (Berelson *et al.*, 1954, Lipset, 1960).

(2) *The Butler-Stokes model of British electoral behaviour*
Although located within the 'orthodox' conceptual and theoretical perspective so far outlined, the research of Butler and Stokes (1969) deserves special mention, as an important synthesis, for its significant use of multivariate cross-tabulations, and above all for its particular model of British electoral behaviour. Its distinctive model of the British electorate is of cumulative historical leftward shift in generational patterns of 'party identification' in which the individual party identification of younger generations is related to occupational class and is also influenced in its initial momentum by 'parental party identification'. Voters especially tend to inherit their parental party identification where this has been 'strong' and also shared by both parents and is for main parties. However, with increased volatility of party identification ('erosion of partisanship'), this general model of electoral behaviour is today being reappraised from within the predominant tradition in politics research (Crewe, 1974).

(3) *Neo-Marxian and Critical Theoretic approaches*
Alternatives to the 'orthodox' tradition in politics research exist in neo-Marxian and Critical Theory. The importance of these approaches has increased in recent years, not least with the declining economic effectiveness in western societies and with suggested 'crisis in legitimacy' (Habermas, 1976). At the most general level there exist overall methodological-cum-theoretical challenges to the central

perspectives guiding orthodox research, e.g., to behaviouralism, plural elitism and generally rigid structural-functional assumptions about societal and political alternatives (see Bachrach, 1969). Thus, objections can be levelled against *any* politics variables which may be framed and interpreted merely in terms of 'subjective' orientations and overt relations, and fail to take into account the possibility of 'mobilisation of bias' and of underlying and arguably more objective processes and 'real' interests. This said, however, an increasing recognition among neo-Marxian sociologists of the 'relative auton-omy' and 'heterogeneity' of politics has brought a reaction against simply discounting the independent importance of 'empirical' atti-tudes. For example, although class may continue to be seen as primarily a matter of economic location, interests may also be acknowledged as mediated by power and authority relations, as well as by individual and group consciousness. This being so, issues arising within Marxism, and between Marxism and contending theories (e.g., questions about class location, about 'political strategy'), become theoretical and in part empirical issues requiring research, *including* survey research, and there are clear signs of a new willingness of neo-Marxian and dissenting theorists and researchers to provide this. No longer can it be considered justified simply to impute interests or to discount 'subjective' data as mere 'appearance', but nor can such data be seen as alone decisive in the way sometimes previously assumed.

(4) *Habermas's account of modern society*

As an alternative to orthodox models, the Critical Theory of Haber-mas (1976) is especially of interest in the context of the present chapter given its attempted synthesis of aspects of structural-functional and neo-Marxian traditions. For Habermas, modern soci-ety – 'advanced capitalism' – is characterized by continued economic and class contradictions, and by a new politicization of administrative decisions as a result of increasing state interventions made necessary by these economic contradictions, as well as by the new contradic-tions which these political interventions in turn introduce. A tenden-cy to 'legitimacy crisis' occurs under these circumstances, and espe-cially in a situation in which previous bases of legitimacy (e.g., declining 'subject orientation') are not being renewed and where new patterns of child socialization and formal education, and new areas of employment (e.g., welfare professions) acting as 'foreign bodies' within capitalism, tend to produce a more critical political culture challenging capitalist values. The outcome of this, in Habermas's view, could be either increasing radicalism or a new repression, and this is a view broadly shared by other theorists (e.g., Wright, 1978, Jessop, 1980). Theoretical perspectives such as these, alongside more orthodox theories, must today provide the framework in which politics variables receive their formulation and interpretation.

(5) *Neo-Weberian approaches*

A final approach to the study of 'politics' which must be mentioned – amongst the most important – is the neo-Weberian approach. In many ways this can be seen as a 'bridge' between orthodox and Marxian approaches, exploring the questions raised by both while accepting the central positions of neither. Of particular importance is the emphasis on power and authority and market position as parallel alternative bases of class interests and class conflict (e.g., Dahrendorf, 1959). Under these circumstances, the general exploration of empirical attitudes and political consciousness becomes especially paramount, as seen for example in the work of Goldthorpe and Lockwood and the related 'actionalism' of Willener or Touraine (see Davis, 1979).

II Key variables

(a) *Party affiliation variables*

Party affiliation variables will be discussed first for several reasons. Party affiliation is the main dependent variable in electoral research and is widely relevant in politics research. It is also the politics variable most likely to find use as a background variable, of interest in its own right and also useful as a broader if somewhat uncertain indicator of wider attitudes and behaviour. As well as this, the use and interpretation of other politics variables often requires a prior identification of party affiliation. What will also emerge is that standard formulations of party affiliation variables are well established and that adequate levels of validity and reliability can be expected from their use, at least in their basic forms. Three categories of party affiliation variables will be discussed: 'voting intention', 'recalled vote', and 'party identification'.

(1) *Voting intention*

The Gallup organization's standard question for voting intention is:

'If there was a general election tomorrow, which party would you support?' NOP's basic question, and that also employed by Butler and Stokes (1969) differs in asking more directly: '. . . How would you vote?' Where the date of a general election is known, questions also refer directly to this.

Two features of 'voting intention' as a variable explain its widespread use as a general indicator of party affiliation in addition to its obvious use in the forecasting of elections: it is easily elicited using simple, relatively unambiguous and broadly standardized questions and its use as a party affiliation variable also enables researchers to relate their own data to the wealth of voting intention data assembled both by opinion pollsters and sociologists. The failure of public opinion polls to always successfully predict elections need raise few doubts concerning the broad validity and reliability of 'voting intention' as an operational variable: while 'normal sampling error'can pose problems in the forecasting of close run elections, the same degree of precision is not essential for most sociological research purposes. Further reassurance concerning the overall validity of 'voting intention' as an operational variable also exists in research indicating the comparability of responses to conventionally administered questionnaires with those gained under conditions designed to simulate the secrecy of the official ballot (Teer and Spence, 1973). Whatever its convenience as a party affiliation variable, however, the relative ephemerality of 'voting intention' – and its hypothetical character outside the immediate period of an election – will nevertheless be seen as a disadvantage for some research purposes, where a researcher is interested in more underlying patterns of party affiliation. It is here that 'recalled vote' and 'party identification' can be turned to.

(2) *Recalled vote*

Like 'voting intention', 'recalled vote' is easily employed and can be regarded as a broadly valid and reliable operational variable when used with reference to an immediately previous election. However, when used to inquire into voting over a series of elections validity and reliability are more suspect.

Compared with 'voting intention', the obvious attraction of 'recalled vote' is its more direct reference to actual behaviour. It also avoids the extremes of volatility associated with 'voting intention' outside the immediate context of an election. Questions employed to elicit recalled vote are usually designed with the intention of combating the reluctance of some respondents to disclose non-voting. Butler and

Stokes, for instance, initially establish voting or non-voting with the following questions: 'We find many people around the country who have good reasons for not voting. How about you? Did you vote in the General Election this year or did something prevent you from voting?' Only after such a tentative approach are questions about the direction of vote introduced. For voting over a series of elections questions are usually phrased to assist accurate recall, for example: 'How did you vote in 1959, when Macmillan led the Conservatives and Gaitskell the Labour Party, and Grimond the Liberals? Evidence on the validity and reliability of data collected on voting and non-voting is not unequivocal but is broadly reassuring, at least in so far as a single and recent election is concerned. NOP post-election surveys, for example, indicate an acceptably close correspondence between recalled vote and actual voting (Teer and Spence, 1973), while Campbell *et al.* (1960) assess the likely magnitude of false reports as 3 per cent, but acknowledge that larger errors than this may have been cancelled out in their aggregate distributions. In general research indicates that recalled vote is always likely to exceed actual voting (Mughan, 1974). For 'party preference' itself, Campbell *et al.* (1960) record a slight tendency (around 3 per cent) for over reporting of voting for the winning side, and errors of this magnitude, although not always in the same direction, are suggested by other researchers (Butler and Stokes, 1969, Teer and Spence, 1973). The panel design of Butler and Stokes's study permits analysis of validity and reliability for longer periods of recall and over multiple elections. For example, of 508 respondents interviewed in 1966 and reporting a Labour vote in that year, only 441 reported a Labour vote for that year when interviewed in 1970. Over longer periods and for multiple elections (especially if local elections are included) validity and reliabilities are likely to fall dramatically. Parry and Crossley (1950) estimate only one in three respondents as correctly reporting their voting behaviour in six named elections.

(3) *Party identification*
Butler and Stokes establish 'party identification' with the question: 'Generally speaking, do you usually think of yourself as Conservative, Labour or Liberal?' Where respondents answer 'None' or 'Don't know', a follow-up question is asked: 'Do you generally think of yourself as a little closer to one of the parties than the others?'

The central importance of 'party identification' as a variable in politics research was noted earlier. Its major justification is its greater likelihood of association with stable social and political orientations,

although there is some indication that in Britain compared with
America 'party identification' does tend to be strongly influenced by
current party preference (Butler and Stokes, 1969).

Attempts have also been made to capture 'strength of party
identification', e.g., the degree of commitment to party affiliation or
its personal salience. Here simple self-rating scales (e.g., 'very
strong', 'strong', 'not very strong') are typically employed. That these
procedures possess some validity is shown by an association found
between 'strength of party affiliation', stability of party identification,
and levels of political participation such as turnout (Crewe *et al.*,
1977). Crewe (1974) has also suggested the advantage of distinguishing between 'positive' and merely 'negative' identifiers, where the
latter's party affiliation is a consequence merely of lack of alternatives. Thus there is also to be noted an increased likelihood of
detachment from stable party identification in circumstances where
an extended range of party options becomes available, such as the
appearance of the SDP-Liberal Alliance. Whether or not in the long
run there occurs a major transformation in the pattern of support for
main parties, in the short-run the presence of the SDP is a source of
extra problems in the operationalization and interpretation of party
affiliation variables. Questions must also arise concerning the continued adequacy of the Butler-Stokes general model of generational
shift and broad stability of party identification in present circumstances. However, while scepticism is in order regarding the specific
adequacy of the Butler-Stokes model, the continued significance of
'party identification' in more general terms – which can include
'negative' and fluid identifiers – need not be in doubt (Mughan, 1979,
Budge *et al.*, 1976). Moreover, 'party identification' remains for many
an enduring feature of political attitudes and behaviour. In the 1983
General Election, for example, although the vote for Labour fell
dramatically, 38 per cent of the electorate continued to present
themselves as 'Labour identifiers' (Crewe, 1983).

Conclusions on party affiliation variables

In conclusion, there are a number of caveats which must be noted
where party affiliation variables are used as proxy indicators of wider
political and social attitudes and behaviour. Undoubtedly, it is the
case that individual 'party identification' acts to some extent as an
'economising' device, filtering as well as stabilizing an individual's
monitoring of the social and political environment. However, it must
be stressed that relatively little can be safely assumed about the detail

of the attitudes and behaviour likely to be associated with party identification, given that;

>   i) the extent of left–right conceptualization of politics or consistent commitment to general values is highly variable between individuals, as well as between groups and classes and

>   ii) significant dimensions of political attitudes (e.g., attitudes on law and order issues) to some extent cross-cut left–right orientation on economic issues. This being so, party affiliation variables will ideally be used as general indicators of wider social and political attitudes only along with other variables.

(b) *Political participation and political attitudes*

Given the considerable weight of interpretation often placed upon political participation variables, many of the operational indicators in use must be seen as disappointing. Major differences of focus and interpretation exist between researchers, reflecting different overall characterizations of the political system.

(1) *Participation in party politics*

A convenient and generally uncontroversial basic assumption here is that individual participation is hierarchically structured, in a double sense: i) participation in party politics can be conceptualized as 'ordinal', with participation at higher levels (e.g. campaign or party worker) implying participation at lower levels such as voting (Milbrath, 1965), ii) levels of participation are higher with higher socioeconomic status.

(2) *Organizational membership*

More controversial is the assumption that organizational membership of all kinds 'brings out latent political predispositions and encourages participation in party politics' (Berelson *et al.*, 1954). Thus, individual membership of voluntary associations has sometimes simply been aggregated in assessing political significant participation (see Pickvance in this volume for a fuller discussion). However, a criticism here is that this obviously ignores the differential political significance possessed by organizations. Furthermore, insufficient in general is known about the political impact of organizations, especially at the local level (e.g., Newton, 1974), to enable any simple alternative rule of thumb.

One organizational membership with political significance in its own right, however, is *trades union membership.* Individual membership is also associated with Labour 'party affiliation' – the outcome of a tendency both for trades union membership to encourage Labour party preference and for Labour supporters to seek trades union membership (Butler and Stokes, 1969). Both the 'unionateness' or otherwise of trades union membership and the degree of 'unionateness' of particular unions (i.e. the extent of affiliation with the labour movement) are also considered significant variables by researchers (Prandy *et al.*, 1974).

(3) *Informal political participation and general orientation to politics*
The following indicators can be noted as typical of those in widespread use:

> i) indicators of political 'inputs' such as writing to politicians – e.g., Almond and Verba (1963).

> ii) 'measurement' of levels of political interest or knowledge of politics – usually simple self-rating scales or questions assessing the ability to name political leaders or local MPs (e.g., Abrams, 1960b). Although a considerable weight of interpretation may be placed on indicators of this kind, instruments are relatively *ad hoc* in formulation and must be seen as controversial especially in wider interpretation. A significant case in point is the Columbia researchers' identification as 'opinion leaders' (and as 'gatekeepers' in the 'two-step flow of mass communications') all respondents who answer positively to one or both of the following questions: Have you tried to convince anyone of your political ideas recently? Has anyone asked you for your advice on a political question recently? Subsequently appraisal has raised serious doubts about the weight of interpretation placed on these indicators (Hamilton, 1971).

(4) *Support for 'democracy', and individual feelings of political 'efficacy', 'satisfaction', etc.*
Examples of scales of the first type are Stouffer's (1955) 'Political Tolerance Scale' and Prothro and Grigg's (1960) 'Attitudes towards Democratic Principles Scale'. Typical of the many simpler scales of the second type is Budge's (1971) 'efficacy scale', which seeks to measure respondents' 'feelings whether they can get things done through politics if they wish'. In Almond's terms, 'efficacy' concerns

orientations to 'inputs' to the political system, whereas 'trust' operationalizes orientation to 'outputs'. Scales and more informal measures of both these types have been a major source of 'evidence' in those claims for the fundamental 'legitimacy' and 'effectiveness' of Anglo-American 'democracy' with which behavioural and structural-functional forms of political sociology have been especially associated.

It is widely agreed that the more elaborate scales have been relatively ineffective (Robinson *et al.*, 1968). The researcher is likely to find that little is gained by using these in preference to more *ad hoc* indicators. However, it is problems of interpretation which are most in evidence in connection with variables of this general type. These problems are evident when relatively minor differences in question wording or emphasis are found to produce markedly different responses. In a wider way, variables confidently interpreted as an indication of support for democracy or system legitimacy and effectiveness by one researcher may be countered by alternative interpretations using other indicators. Sharply contrasted differences in interpretation result, for example, when alternative variables are used which focus on the 'legitimacy of the opportunity structure' (e.g., Form and Rytinna, 1969, Moorhouse and Chamberlain, 1974 – also see Mann, 1970, for a useful overall review of differences in indicators). What is plain, is that systematic preferences exist in the selection and interpretation of variables which relate to the overall theoretical position of researchers, including different conceptions of class and class orientation to be discussed later.

Problems in the selection and interpretation of variables and agreement on findings are formidable ones. But some progress can be claimed both in a clearer recognition of these problems and in the greater diversity of indicators and research foci now in use in survey research. What is also clearly demonstrated in recent research, and contrary to the cherished conceptions of some structural-functional sociologists, is that 'value consensus does not exist to any significant extent' (Mann, 1970), and that values and behaviour are generally far less organized and more situationally fluid than often assumed by earlier researchers.

(5) *Direct action and 'protest potential'*
A further frequent assumption of earlier politics researchers was of widespread satisfaction with conventional channels of political activity. However, an increasing recourse to less orthodox means of political action in recent years has brought a revision of this view,

with a corresponding interest in new indicators of political activity. An example here is Marsh's (1977) Guttman scale of 'Protest Potential' – the willingness to participate in political protest, a scale running from signing petitions, through lawful demonstrations, and extending to boycotts, strikes, occupations, and sit-downs. Rather than simply seen as 'irrational' and threatening to 'stable democracy', as among some orthodox researchers, such increasing protest potential is open to the different interpretation that it provides indication of the kind of heightened critical consciousness and alternative rationality envisaged by theorists such as Habermas. Inglehart (1977), for example, has explored the existence of 'post-industrial' attitudes in these terms. Marsh's research indicates that protest potential is highest among younger middle class Labour supporters, but this protest potential is also found far more generally than earlier assumed. Nor can it automatically be assumed that high levels of systemization of political attitudes are an essential requirement for protest and direct action or 'class consciousness'. While some theorists, for example Mann, see the widespread existence of mainly concrete and pragmatic or 'ambivalent' conceptualizations of politics and class as inhibiting radical action, others, such as Moorhouse and Chamberlain, regard radical action and the development of class consciousness as possible simply on such a 'pragmatic' basis.

(6) *Authoritarianism*
As the only really widely used personality scale, 'authoritarianism' (the well known F-scale – Adorno *et al.*, 1950) is the only personality variable which can merit even initial consideration as a 'key variable' in the present context. The potential political significance of such a variable is clear: its subdimensions include 'authoritarian submission' and 'authoritarian aggression'. A shorter version of the F-scale was used by Campbell *et al.* (1954). However, 'substantiated propositions about the impact of authoritarianism on political behaviour are few' (Milbrath, 1965). Thus, the 'working class authoritarianism' claimed by some researchers (e.g., Lipset, 1960) is dismissed by other researchers as resulting from 'acquiescence set' by working class respondents (Greenstein, 1971) or as a misreading of 'rational' opposition to the system (Miller and Reisman, 1961). Tapping similar dimensions, but less loaded and arguably more pragmatic and potentially useful as a variable are scales such as Marsh's (1977) scale of 'Repression Potential', which 'measures' willingness to see government use force in checking strikes and demonstrations.

Conclusions on political participation variables

For politics 'key variables' in this section then, a widening array of variables and a challenge to the previous interpretation of variables can be reported. However, it remains essential not to underestimate the many interpretative problems remaining. Researchers making use of attitudinal variables should proceed with caution in their selection and interpretation of variables. What research has made clear is a pattern of normative and behavioural complexity: absence of 'consensus', 'ambivalent' and contradictory attitudes, a situational variability of individual political and class orientations, and a potentiality for transformations of consciousness and action, all of these requiring analysis in the context of questions raised by holistic social structural, rather than narrowly psychological, theories.

(c) *Concepts and indicators of class and status*

Whatever the divisions between orthodox, neo-Marxian, and neo-Weberian approaches, there is general agreement on the importance of class and status as a factor in individual politics and in accounting for the stability or potentiality for radical political transformation of societies. This being so, variables have been sought which capture this relation of politics to class and status.

(1) *The use of standard occupational class and status categories*
Certain problems which arise in connection with standard occupational and class and status categories must first be noticed (also see Marsh in this volume). Conceptions such as Lazarsfeld *et al.*'s (1944) 'socio-economic status' are rightly criticized (Mills, 1959) for their failure to relate adequately to theoretical conceptions of class. Standard occupational class scales such as the Hall-Jones scale and, until this was changed in 1971, the Registrar General's 'social classes' have sometimes had the disadvantage of failing to provide for adequate separation of skilled manual and routine non-manual workers, the most significant point of cleavage in the overall pattern of party preference. Goldthorpe *et al.*, for example, used Hall-Jones categories, but modified these to include an intermediate, routine non-manual category. IPA market research categories have also been widely employed, and here separation of routine non-manual and manual occupations is made. Further difficulties exist in connection with the widespread convention of defining class in terms of 'head of household's occupation' rather than in terms of an individual's own

occupation where this is different. On the one hand, head of household's occupation may be seen as the decisive source of the class position. Against this, since a majority of 'heads of household' are male, this practice will mask whatever independent political significance female occupation possesses (also see Marsh and Purcell in this volume).

(2) *Alternatives in class theory*
In addition to problems of this kind, obvious problems arise from the fact that conceptualizations of class and status are bound up with daunting theoretical issues. In particular, four conceptual approaches to class and status can be noted, corresponding for the most part to theoretical positions earlier identified.

> i) *'Class' as non-manual/manual occupation* Typically this is seen as involving *overall* differences in occupational location and life chances.

> ii) *'Marxian class'* Parkin (1979) distinguishes between formulations involving 'minimal' definitions of the proletariat (including only direct producers of surplus value and excluding all those performing managerial functions and sharing in the role of capital – Poulantzas, 1975) and 'maximal' definitions which also include the 'new working class', e.g., new technical workers (Mallet, 1975), and the newly 'proletarianised' (Braverman, 1974), or potentially embracing all intermediate 'contradictory' class locations (Wright, 1978).

> iii) *Neo-Weberian multidimensional analysis* – e.g., analytical distinctions between market, work, and status situations (Lockwood, 1958), or multiple bases of inclusion/exclusion (Parkin, 1979).

> iv) *Consumption 'sectors' cross-cutting occupational class* – e.g., 'private' as against 'collective' consumption sectors (Dunleavy, 1980). To a degree, a valuable analytical purchase on the relations between class and politics can be seen as achieved by all four approaches, and ideally, the formulation of politics 'key variables' will take account of each of these.

(3) *Class and class deviant political orientations: operational indicators and issues*
Whatever reservations there may be about the validity of employment of occupational class for some purposes, the fact that the main

cleavage in party identification occurs between non-manual and manual groups fully justifies this as a first approach for politics variables. The most-used conceptualization of class and class deviant political orientations have been created on this basis, with neo-Weberian, neo-Marxian and other conceptions of class and status also added to standard occupational categories as the need arises.

i) *'Subjective class'* The prominence of this variable as an indicator of class and political orientation in connection with the 'affluent worker' and *embourgeoisement* hypothesis (Abrams, 1960a) is well known. Butler and Stokes elicited 'subjective class' using the following question: 'There's quite a bit of talk these days about different social classes. Most people say that they belong to either the middle class or the working class. Do you ever think of yourself as being in one of these classes?' Respondents reluctant to declare themselves in these terms, were asked: 'Well, if you had to make a choice, would you call yourself middle class or working class?' However, fewer than 50 per cent of respondents usually volunteer a 'subjective class' without further prompting (Crewe *et al.*, 1977), and the value of 'subjective class' as an indicator of class orientation and political consciousness is widely seen as suspect for this and other reasons. While some association between 'middle class' subjective identity and working class Conservatism is found, Runciman (1966) and Goldthorpe *et al.* among others have exposed the equivocal meanings associated with 'middle class' subjective identity, many of these inconsistent with an hypothesis of *embourgeoisement*. As Crewe *et al.* (1977) suggest, a reluctance to express subjective class identity may be more significant as a variable. Such reluctance is associated, for example, with a lack of partisan identification and with limited 'support for labour principles' (e.g., support for trades unions, public ownership, or welfare provision).

ii) *Class orientations — Goldthorpe and Lockwood categories* In the terminology used by Goldthorpe and Lockwood, it is 're-lational' factors (e.g., residential community, work situation, as well as kin network), rather than merely pecuniary factors, which ultimately influence 'normative' and political orientations. Here Goldthorpe and Lockwood's variable 'white collar affiliations' is a useful indicator of a tendency to class deviant political orientation. However, it is these re-

Table 1   Class orientations – Goldthorpe and Lockwood categories

Ideal type	Social context	Class concepts	Likely party identification
Traditional (proletarian)	Occupational and residential community	Two main classes them and us; in terms of power and authority	Traditional Labour
Deferential	Small firm; agriculture; older workers; job involvement; status hierarchy	Three (or more) classes; in terms of lifestyle and social background – prestige model	Working class Conservative
Privatized/ instrumental	Absence of occupational or residential community	Large central and residual classes; in terms of wealth and consumption	Labour support – conditional, but collective instrumentalism and potential militancy

searchers' more elaborate 'ideal types' and operational variables linking class imagery and social structure which have attracted most attention. In contrast to Abrams' or Butler and Stokes's closed questions, Goldthorpe and Lockwood's operational approach to class imagery used open-ended inquiry: 'People often talk about there being different social classes – what do you think?'

With this question 'as the starting point for a general discussion of class of a relatively unstructured kind', replies were coded to provide data in the following areas: a respondent's view of the number and names of classes, his own class position, the major factors determining class position, opportunities for mobility, and the necessity and desirability of the class system. These coded data were then used to determine repondent's class orientations in terms of the categories given in Table 1. In these terms, an overall tendency towards familial 'privatisation' and 'instrumentalism', and away from traditional ('proletarian') working class solidarity, was seen as occurring by Goldthorpe and Lockwood. While militant 'collective instrumentalism' was acknowledged as possible in these circumstances, and support for labour found strong among 'affluent' workers, this support was expected to be more conditional than hitherto.

While Goldthorpe and Lockwood's procedures can be seen as useful in comparison with simple 'subjective class' identity, they are not without problems of their own. So much is indicated from their wider use by researchers, who have found a lack of mutual exclusivity between 'power' and 'prestige' models (Brown and Brannen, 1970), a predominance of 'pecuniary' orientations within 'traditional' locations, e.g., dockworkers (Hill, 1976), and the frequent occurrence of inconsistent or ambivalent orientations (Davis, 1979). A useful overall post-mortem on the *Affluent Worker* study is provided by Bulmer (1975).

iii) *'Deference'* The concept of 'deference' is associated with further hypotheses regarding 'working class Conservatism'. Here again, the operational indicators used have been controversial.

In McKenzie and Silver's (1968) study the biographies of hypothetical prospective prime ministers were presented to respondents: 'preference for a candidate of elite origin' indicating 'deference', and 'preference for candidate of working class origin' a 'secular' orientation. A longer method also used takes into account respondents' evaluations of political parties and attitudes towards traditional symbols – a method found to correlate well with the shorter method, and also allowing for a 'mixed' category. Uncertainties about 'deference' as a variable arise, however: from its compatibility with Labour voting in many cases (only among older working class voters are a majority of 'deferentials' Conservative voters), and from the fact that researchers have found 'proletarian' orientations more frequently than 'deferential' imagery in locations where high levels of deference would be expected in terms of either McKenzie and Silver or Goldthorpe and Lockwood categories (e.g., Newby, 1977). Not only did Newby find individual class imagery often inconsistent within interviews, his conclusion was that 'powerlessness' and 'ambivalence' rather than a normative 'deference' best characterized, for example, the agricultural worker's general situation. Martin and Fryer (1975) are others to raise doubts concerning the behavioural implications of deference (e.g., it does not preclude support for strikes in concrete circumstances), although Goldthorpe and Lockwood's characterization of the deferential 'world view' is seen as 'substantially vindicated' by these researchers.

iv) '*Middle class radicalism*' Researchers interested in exploring 'middle class radicalism' have done so using a variety of class orientation and attitudinal variables. These have included 'subjective class', 'support for Labour principles', and attitudes towards traditional cultural symbols (e.g., Parkin, 1967, Rawllings, 1975), without however any of the combinations of indicators used achieving the relatively standardized usage found in connection with 'working class Conservatism'.

(4) *Further operationalizations of class and politics*

Efforts have also been made to explore political orientations in relation to Marxian and other alternative class categories, such as those suggested by Wright or Dunleavy. For example, Edgell and Duke (1982) have used a composite index of consumption location (combining variables such as housing tenure, and use of private and public transport, social services, and education). The same researchers have also conducted analysis using Wright's neo-Marxian class categories. Here, once again, however, standard usages have not been established.

Conclusions on class and status variables

The general verdict on class and status variables might be that there exists a widening array of theoretical perspectives and operational variables, but that there remains much room for improvement before survey research can be said to reflect fully the theoretical alternatives in class analysis. In the analysis of class orientations, as in general for political attitudes, analysis has not always been well served by over-confident interpretations of simple 'closed' indicators. Against this, the complex mosaic of attitudes and orientations revealed by survey research can be presented as a sign of greater sociological understanding, rather than the relative 'impasse' seen by some commentators. A careful attention to theory – and arguably to a range of theories – is vital in the selection and interpretation of operational variables. The inherent limitations of survey research should also be continually borne in mind, for example, with a recognition of the importance of participant and related forms of ethnographic observation in rounding-out or correcting more standardized survey data on class locations and class struggles. Also to be taken into account in the interpretations of data are factors such as cultural hegemony or 'mobilisation of bias', which should be allowed for by explicitly raising wider questions about the sources of attitudes and ideologies. The importance of adequate theory in directing attention to processes and interests other than those reflected in surface appearances cannot be overestimated. There must also be a recognition that survey data on political or class orientations cannot constitute an *overall* test of complex theory where this theory, as true for much Marxian theory, is couched in far wider terms, including reference to general tendencies continually at work beneath surface relations.

General conclusions

In conclusion, the following summary 'recommendations' can be advanced:

i) *'Party affiliation' variables* can be seen as generally reliable variables, but if used as more general social indicators these variables will ideally be used only along with other politics variables.

ii) Where *'political participation' variables and attitudinal variables* are used, it would appear essential that multiple indicators of particular variables are employed and that the interpretation of variables is guarded and made in the light of alternative theories.

iii) In connection with *political aspects of class and status*, there is first a clear case for seeking to extend analysis beyond conventional conceptions of class. The placing of any great weight of interpretation on simple closed indicators of class orientation is especially to be avoided. Here, as for most politics variables, multiple indicators of variables are preferable, and ideally interpretations will receive grounding in research which extends beyond surveys and includes a consideration of alternative theories.

References

Abrams, M. (1960a), 'The "Socialist Commentary" survey' in Abrams, M. and Rose, R., *Must Labour Lose?*, Harmondsworth, Penguin.
Abrams, M. (1960b), 'Social trends in electoral behaviour', *British Journal of Sociology*, vol. 13:228–42.

Adorno, T. *et al.* (1950), *The Authoritarian Personality*, New York, Harper.

Almond, G. and **Verba, S.** (1963), *The Civic Culture*, Princeton University Press.

Bachrach, P. (1969), *The Theory of Democratic Elitism*, London, University of London Press.

Benney, M., Gray, A. and **Pear, R.** (1956), *How People Vote*, London, Routledge & Kegan Paul.

Berelson, B., Lazarsfeld, P. and **McPhee, W.** (1954), *Voting*, Chicago, University of Chicago Press.

Braverman, H. (1974), *Labour and Monopoly Capital*, New York, Monthly Review Press.

Brown, R. and **Brannen, P.** (1970), 'Social relations and social perspectives among shipbuilding workers', *Sociology*, vol. 4:71–84, 197–221.

Budge, I. (1976) *Agreement and Stability in Democracy*, Chicago, Markham.

Budge, I., Crewe, I and **Farlie, D.** (1979), *Party Identification and Beyond*, London, Wiley.

Budge, I. and **Farlie, D.** (1974) 'Political recruitment and dropout', *British Journal of Political Science*, Vol. 5:63–8.

Bulmer, M. (ed.) (1975), *Working Class Images of Society*, London, Routledge & Kegan Paul.

Butler, D. and **Stokes, D.** (1969) *Political Change in Britain*, London, Macmillan (2nd edn 1974).

Campbell, D., Gurin, G. and **Miller, W.** (1954), *The Voter Decides*, Evanston, Row, Peters & Co.

Campbell, D., Converse, P., Miller F. and **Stokes, D.** (1960), *The American Voter*, New York, Wiley.

Crewe, I. (1974), 'Do Butler and Stokes explain political change in Britain?', *European Journal of Political Research*, vol. 2:47–92.

Crewe, I. (1983), 'The disturbing truth behind Labour's rout', *The Guardian*, 13 and 14 June.

Crewe, I., Alt, J. and **Sarlvik, B.** (1977), 'Partisan Dealignment in Britain', *British Journal of Science*, vol. 6:273–90.

Dahrendorf, R. (1959), *Class and Class Conflict in Industrial Societies*, London, Routlege & Kegan Paul.

Davis, H. (1979), *Beyond Class Images*, London, Croom Helm.

Dunleavy, P. (1980), 'The political implications of sectoral cleavages', *Political Studies*, vol. 28:364–83 and 527–49.

Edgell, S. and **Duke, V.** (1982), 'Reactions to the public expenditure cuts: occupational class and party realignment',

Sociology, vol.16:431–9.

Form, W. and **Rytinna, J.** (1969) 'Ideological beliefs on the distribution of power in the United States', *American Sociological Review*, vol. 34:19–31.

Gallie, D. (1979) 'Social radicalism in the French and British working classes', *British Journal of Sociology*, vol. 30:500–24.

Goldthorpe, J. and **Lockwood, D.** (1963), 'Affluence and the British class structure', *Sociological Review*, vol. 11:133–63.

Goldthorpe, J., Lockwood, D., Bechhofer, F. and **Platt, J.** (1968), *The Affluent Worker, Political Attitudes and Behaviour*, Cambridge, Cambridge University Press.

Goldthorpe, J., Lockwood, D., Bechhofer, F. and **Platt, J.** (1969), *The Affluent Worker in the Class Structure*, Cambridge, Cambridge University Press.

Greenstein, F. (1971), *Personality and Politics*, Chicago, Markham.

Habermas, J. (1976), *Legitimation Crisis*, London, Heinemann.

Hamilton, W. (1971), 'Dimensions of self-designated opinion leadership and their correlates', *Public Opinion Quarterly*, vol.35:266–74.

Hill, S. (1976), *The Dockers*, London, Heinemann.

Inglehart, R. (1977), *The Silent Revolution – Changing Values and Political Styles among Western Mass Publics*, Princeton University Press.

Jessop, B. (1980), 'The Transformation of the state in post-war Britain', in Scase, R., *The State in Western Europe*, London, Croom Helm.

Lazarsfeld, P., Berelson, B. and **Gaudet, H.** (1944), *The People's Choice*, New York, Columbia University Press.

Lipset, S. (1960), *Political Man*, London, Heinemann.

Lockwood, D. (1958), *The Blackcoated Worker*, London, Allen & Unwin.

Mallet, S. (1975), *The New Working Class*, Nottingham, Spokesman Books.

Mann, M. (1970), 'The social cohesion of liberal democracy', *American Sociological Review*, vol.35:423–39.

Marsh, A. (1977), *Protest and Political Consciousness*, Beverly Hills, Sage.

McKenzie, R. and **Silver, A.** (1968), *Angels in Marble: Working Class Conservatism in Urban England*, London, Heinemann.

Martin, R. and **Fryer, R.** (1975) 'The deferential worker', in Bulmer, M. (ed.), *Working Class Images of Society*, London, Routledge & Kegan Paul, pp. 98–115.

222   *David Jary*

Milbrath, L. (1965), *Political Participation*, Chicago, Rand McNally.
Miller, S. and **Reisman, M.** (1961), 'Working class attitudes: a critique of Lipset', *British Journal of Sociology*, vol. 12:263–76.
Mills, C. (1959), *The Sociological Imagination*, London, Oxford University Press.
Moorhouse, F. and **Chamberlain, C.** (1974), 'Lower class attitudes', *Sociology*, vol. 8:387–405.
Mughan, A. (1974), 'Party identification, voting preference and electoral outcomes in Britain 1964–74', *British Journal of Political Science*, vol. 9:115–28.
Newby, H. (1977), *The Deferential Worker*, London, Allen Lane.
Newton, K. (1974), 'Voluntary associations in community politics', *SSRC Newsletter*, July, pp. 5–7.
Parkin, F. (1967), *Middle Class Radicals*, Manchester, Manchester University Press.
Parkin, F. (1979), *Marxism and Class Theory: a Bourgeois Critique*, London, Tavistock.
Parry, N. and **Crossley, J.** (1950), 'Validity of response to survey questions', *Public Opinion Quarterly*, vol. 14:61–80.
Poulantzas, N. (1975), *Classes in Contemporary Capitalism*, London, New Left Books.
Prandy, K., Stewart, A. and **Blackburn, R.** (1974), 'Concept and measures: the example of unionateness', *Sociology*, vol.8:427–46.
Prothro, J. and **Grigg, C.** (1960), 'Fundamental principles of democracy', *Journal of Politics*, vol. 22:107–94.
Rawlings, C. (1975), 'Two types of middle class labour voter', *British Journal of Political Science*, vol. 5:107–12.
Robinson, W., Rusk, J. and **Head, K.** (1968), *Measures of Political Attitude*, University of Michigan.
Runciman, W. (1966), *Relative Deprivation and Social Justice*, London, Routledge & Kegan Paul.
Stacey, M. (ed.) (1969), *Comparability in Social Research*, London, Heinemann.
Stouffer, S. (1955), *Communism, Conformity and Civil Liberties*, New York, Doubleday.
Teer, F. and **Spence, J.** (1973), *Political Opinion Polls*, London, Hutchinson.
Wright, E. (1978), *Class, Crisis and the State*, London, New Left Books.

Voluntary associations 11

C. G. Pickvance

Voluntary association membership is not a 'key variable' on a par with age, gender or occupation. Yet it is frequently included as a second-rank variable in survey research.

In this chapter we shall first consider the theoretical frameworks within which data on voluntary associations can be understood, and second, the practicalities of collecting such data. The theme of the chapter is that data on voluntary association membership has no significance in itself, and that according to the theoretical perspective adopted different types of data about voluntary associations and the nature of participation need to be collected.

1 Theoretical approaches

1.1 *Four perspectives on voluntary associations*

There is a long tradition of empiricist studies of voluntary association participation in American sociology. This has yielded a mountain of data on the extent of participation and its correlates – see Smith and Freedman (1972) and Smith (1975) for reviews. But by the 1970s this had become an exhausted seam and only articles on the participation of racial and ethnic minorities, and women, were being published. As will be seen the theoretical contribution of this work has been limited. This is both cause and effect of the fact that the character of participation was never inquired into in any depth. It was left to the community studies tradition to furnish some evidence about what participation involved. The four theoretical perspectives discussed here are therefore chosen because data on voluntary association participation is relevant to them rather than because they have been used frequently in past studies. (As we shall see later voluntary associations are not the only phenomenon of interest to each perspective.)

(a) *Social stratification and community power*
Studies of voluntary associations within this perspective attempt to answer questions such as

> – to what extent are leadership, membership and social mixing in voluntary associations influenced by the occupational structure?
> – what resources are available to members and leaders of particular voluntary associations and to what ends are they used at the community level?
> – are the members and leaders of one voluntary association also members and leaders of other voluntary associations or local institutions?
> – if such interlocking or overlapping takes place does a group exist which consciously works towards the achievement of certain goals?

This theoretical perspective thus requires the collection of data on the occupations, institutional and associational affiliations, and resources of members and leaders of voluntary associations. By itself such data would provide a static picture. In order to follow changes over time in the possession of resources, the interlocking of leaders and members, and the emergence of groups, the use of observation and documents as well as interviewing is necessary.

The 'social stratification' and 'community power' approaches differ in that the latter has the local community as frame of reference as well as locus of observation. In the case of the 'social stratification' approach, the frame of reference may be either local or national. Where it is national the assumption is that the community concerned is in some sense typical or theoretically crucial. For example, Bottomore's (1954) classic study takes a national frame of reference, and uses the findings that voluntary association leadership, membership and class mixing are all influenced by occupational rank, to suggest the same conclusion for towns throughout the country. In the same way Goldthorpe *et al.* (1969:93–4) use participation in voluntary associations as an indicator of the extent to which the affluent workers of Luton have a middle-class lifestyle. Luton is taken to be a critical case for testing propositions about a nationally-occurring phenomenon because of certain characteristics of its industry and labour force.

Voluntary associations, according to the national 'stratification' perspective, are merely one type of social phenomenon in which social processes thought to occur nationally can be observed. From the 'community power' perspective, the particular configuration of community institutions and associations is of interest for its own sake and generalization requires a typology which differentiates communities according to relevant characteristics.

(b) *Pluralism*
The pluralist perspective is probably the most frequently used of those discussed here. It does not appear to require detailed data on participation and is therefore used as a way of giving theoretical significance to data collected with no theoretical reason in mind.

The relevance of voluntary associations to power is seen differently in the two versions of the pluralist perspective (Olsen, 1972). In the 'mediation' version they are seen as promoting a plural distribution of power by the fact that they enable individuals to come together and participate directly in political activity, thereby 'mediating' between the individual and the political system. In the 'mobilisation' version, it is argued that involvement even in voluntary associations without political aims, by widening people's interests and contacts and providing them with leadership skills, eventually mobilizes them politically. As Olsen points out, the two versions of the thesis are not incompatible, and both processes may take place within the same association.

The central issue within the pluralist perspective is the extent of participation in intermediate associations of all kinds, so voluntary associations are only one relevant form of 'participation'. At first sight, therefore, this approach does not require data of any complexity. However on closer examination it can be seen to make strong assumptions about processes within voluntary associations, and that the simple data collected are insufficient to throw light on these (Cutler, 1973).

First, in many associations it is neither the explicit nor the implicit function to give access to power to the membership. For this reason, Rose expressly limits the mediation function of participation to 'social influence associations' – which, according to his own estimate, represent less than one in six of all associations (1954: 52, 55, 68). Other writers, however, make no such restriction. (Some evidence on members' perceptions of associations as political, and of political activity in them is given in Almond and Verba (1965: 250–1) and Verba and Nie (1972:ch. 11).) The contrary argument that voluntary associations are used by public authorities to exert social control rather than allow access to power is suggested by many studies. For example many associations are extensions of government agencies and others are dependent upon public authorities for financial and other resources, and thus success. Studies of voluntary associations in inner-city and slum areas have particularly stressed their role as means by which external agencies exert control. (See Babchuk and Gordon 1962, Roberts 1973, Taub *et al.* 1977.)

Second, many voluntary associations are not run democratically and their function in socializing members into democratic values and allowing democratic participation by the citizen is, to say the least, arguable. Indeed in many associations there is mass apathy, and very few individuals spend more than a few hours a month in participation. Rose, one of the writers who adheres to this view of the function of voluntary associations (1954: 51), is aware of this awkward fact and attempts to set it aside by arguing that members have 'ultimate control' through their right to vote, or ability to resign (1954: 56).

Finally, participation in voluntary associations is generally seen as an index of the importance of secondary relationships, whereas in fact such participation often involves primary relationships. A study by Bell and Boat (1957) shows that over 80 per cent of voluntary association members had one or more close friends there, and over 50 per cent of members had nine or more close friends in such associations. In the fields of organization theory and industrial sociology the earliest writers, Weber and Roethlisberger and Dixon, recognized the existence of informal relationships within nominally formal organizations, but this is still not generally accepted among writers on voluntary associations.

It would seem that the main reason for the failure to examine these assumptions is the division of labour between practitioners of surveys and of community studies, and the ease with which the former technique can be employed without revealing anything about the nature of the association, or the character of participation within it.

(c) *Community structure*

This perspective has been used particularly since the 1970s with the growth of 'structural' studies of the inter-relation of individuals, organizations and institutions at the community level. (See for example, Benson 1975, Laumann *et al.* 1978, Galaskiewicz 1979.) It is related to the community power perspective but the focus is on patterns of relationship, rather than their power content.

Voluntary associations are seen as related to community structure in two ways. First they are linked with each other and with institutions. Warner and Lunt (1941: 301–55) have indicated the importance of linkages among associations, and distinguish between 'complex' associations which have such links and 'simple' ones which do not. They subdivide 'complex' associations into 'parent', 'satellite' and 'co-ordinate' associations. Seventy-five per cent of all voluntary associations in Yankee City were 'satellite' associations, i.e. had formal ties with a 'parent' association or institution. The existence of such linkages is likely to be important in determining, for example, an association's access to members, resources and information.

Second, voluntary associations give rise to extensive personal ties. Inter-relationships between committee members of voluntary associations have been shown diagrammatically by Stacey (1960) and Stacey *et al.* (1975) and ties between members, by Young and Larson (1965). It has also been argued that such overlapping will be more frequent in smaller communities (Frankenberg, 1966: 237–54). The way in which voluntary associations create ties which are used in other contexts, and draw on ties formed in other contexts is discussed in Cutler (1973), Pickvance (1976) and Galaskiewicz and Shatin (1981).

In these two ways voluntary associations are one source of the ties which structure a community and these ties have new effects. Thus Coleman (1956) has argued that the outcome of community conflicts will be influenced by the distribution of voluntary association ties throughout a community's population, and by the extent to which members of given associations are drawn from the same social category. This argument goes back to Simmel and Gluckman's notion of cross-cutting ties.

The 'community structure' approach, then, focuses on relationships between association members, and between voluntary associations and institutions. At one level this approach can be pursued by simply establishing what organizations exist in a community (McPherson, 1981), and therefore to what extent different categories of the population are 'organised' or linked by cross-cutting ties. However further levels of structure can only be uncovered by a combination of interviewing and observation.

(d) *Work–Leisure*

The final approach to voluntary associations is the 'work–leisure' perspective which asks whether there are systematic relations between leisure activities (including voluntary associations) and work activities. Parker (1976) distinguishes three types of work–leisure relationship, 'extension', 'opposition', and 'neutrality'.

There is a connection between this perspective and the stratification perspective, in that both view aspects of occupation as the primary determinant of participation. The difference between them is that the 'work–leisure' approach focuses on the subjective experience of work, and the skills involved in work, whereas the 'stratification' approach focuses on occupational rewards and status.

The number of studies employing this perspective is rather small. This is partly because it cannot be used as an *ex-post facto* analytical approach, due to the data it requires on work relations.

The work–leisure perspective has been used most explicitly by Hagedorn and Labovitz (1968a, 1968b) who argue that work skills and attitudes are *generalized or extended* to other areas of life. For example, they obtained information on people's relationships with colleagues, superordinates and subordinates, whether such relationships were frequent, whether they were required by the work task, whether they were thought important, etc. This information was taken to indicate leadership ability, willingness to be led, and ability to interact. The 'compensation' or 'opposition' relationship between work and leisure has been illustrated in a number of studies, e.g. Ross and Wheeler (1971: 3–51). In one of them it is argued that skilled manual workers with administrative and leadership abilities, who are unable to use them at work will use them in voluntary associations (Mitchell and Lupton, 1954: 47).

A closely related approach is that of Wilensky (1960, 1961a) who argues that where the individual's experience of work involves discretion in the work task, sustained contacts with clients, and is 'orderly' (in that job changes involve progressive advancement within the same occupation), social participation will be extensive and work integrated with the rest of life. When these conditions are absent, there will be a division between work and leisure, and social participation will be uncertain. In contrast to Wilensky's interest in 'orderly careers' is Stebbins's (1970) discussion of 'subjective careers'. More generally, the 'sociology of occupations' literature seems an important and little tapped source of theoretical insight for studies of voluntary associations within the work–leisure perspective.

Finally it must be pointed out that whereas the work–leisure approach sees participation in work and leisure as being logically independent of each other, individual involvement in both spheres may reflect a prior orientation. This was suggested in a study of 1950s CND supporters whose choice both of occupation (e.g. welfare, creative) and CND participation reflected a predisposition to avoid involvement in capitalist enterprise (Parkin, 1968: 175–192). In such a case the apparent 'extension' from work to leisure is a spurious relation in Lazarsfeld's sense.

The work–leisure approach thus requires data on work relations which is not normally collected and makes particularly clear the need to consider theoretical perspectives before including questions on voluntary associations in a questionnaire.

So far we have seen that voluntary associations can be examined from any of four perspectives, and that the relevant data required about them vary accordingly. But none of these perspectives views voluntary associations as its exclusive domain of interest. In all cases many other types of social activity or grouping are also relevant and data on them is equally important to collect. This can be seen from Table 1. The precise distinction between voluntary associations and the other groupings in this table will be discussed after we have considered typologies.

Table 1   Types of social grouping/activity of focal interest (√) or not (x) for each theoretical perspective

Theoretical Perspective	Type of grouping or activity of focal interest				
	Institutions	Organized commercial leisure activity e.g. cinema, sports	Participation in voluntary associations	Participation in informal groups i.e. other than previous three columns	Private leisure e.g. reading
Social stratification and community power	√	x	√	√	x
Pluralism	x	x	√	√	x
Community structure	√	x	√	√	x
Work–leisure	√	√	√	√	√

1.2 *Theoretical perspectives and typologies*

Theoretical perspectives not only guide the collection of data about voluntary associations, but are also the basis on which associations are grouped into 'types'. Since associations have an infinite number of attributes, the criteria by which certain of these are ignored and others picked out as crucial in the formation of types must reflect the theoretical approach adopted. For example the stratification approach would suggest that the class composition of associations is the crucial criteria for grouping them, rather than their explicit goals, size, frequency of meeting, etc.

Logically then there is a close relation between theoretical approaches and voluntary association typologies. In practice, however, there is no such simple relation since the typologies in use may be relevant to more than one theoretical approach – though as will be suggested there is some clustering of typologies and theories. It should be noted that many analyses make no use of typologies and simply re-use the categories used to gather the data, e.g. political, recreational, social and welfare, as though these were of self-evident theoretical significance. And when typologies of voluntary associations have been used they have usually been constructed *after* completion of data collection with the result that little research has gathered data on all the theoretically significant features of voluntary associations.

The oldest and most widely-used typology of voluntary associations is probably that based on the function of the association. Rose distinguished between *expressive* associations which express or satisfy the interests of their members in relation to themselves (e.g. sports, recreational and hobby clubs) and *social influence* associations which seek to 'achieve some condition or change in some limited segment of the society as a whole' (1954: 52). But he was aware that the manifest and latent functions of the association might diverge. For example, associations with primarily sociable or recreational purposes might engage in political activity. Closely related distinctions have been proposed by subsequent writers: *expressive* and *instrumental* (Gordon and Babchuk, 1959), *solidary* and *purposive* (Clark and Wilson, 1961) and *established* and *adaptive* (Ehrlich, 1970). Studies using these concepts have shown that they correlate with an association's status-conferring capacity and its members' status (Booth, Babchuk and Knox, 1968), with central urban location (Babchuk and Edwards, 1965) and with the role of personal contacts in joining (Booth and Babchuk, 1969).

Gordon and Babchuk (1959) proposed two other typological dimensions in addition to the instrumental-expressive one. These were *accessibility of membership* (more or less open) and *status-conferring capacity* which may be high or low depending on degree of accessibility, social approval of the association's ends and means, and the ethnic and racial composition of the membership. However, to my knowledge these typologies have not been made use of.

The *class composition* of associations has been used to draw up typologies, by Warner and Lunt (1941:301–55) and Goldthorpe *et al.* (1969: 110–11, 198–9). The purpose of these typologies is to estimate the class range of the association and thereby to show its role in reinforcing class stratification, though class range is only an approximate measure of class mixing, as Bottomore (1954) has shown. Goldthorpe *et al.* (1969: 110–11, 198–9) have argued that class mixing is more likely in associations with diffuse functions and which lack a hierarchical structure. They use these two factors together with class range to draw up a typology of associations. Bottomore (1954: 369–70), however, argued that class mixing would be more likely in associations which were small in size (and where sub-groups were less likely to form) and which had prescribed activities (which would serve to unite members).

A fifth typology is that of Warner and Lunt discussed above which classifies associations by their structural linkages with other associations and institutions, i.e. *simple v. complex* (*parent v. satellite v. co-ordinate*). This typology is related to the question of the extent to which an association participates in the 'horizontal' and 'vertical' pattern of relationships (Warren, 1962: 161–6). The possibility that such a typology be related to the association's stability and survival is discussed by Ross (1972), but otherwise it has not proved very fruitful so far. A similar typology is proposed by Sills. National organizations, he suggests, either have no local units (i.e. members belong directly to the national level) or have local units. In the latter case they may be of either the *corporate type* (a national headquarters and local branches) or the *federation type* (a federation of semi-autonomous local affiliates) according to the 'locus of ultimate authority' (1957:10).

A seventh typology is also mentioned by Sills. This separates *majoral* associations (those which serve the interests of major institutions, e.g. education, labour), *minoral* associations (those which serve the interests of significant minorities, e.g. hobby clubs) and *medial* associations (those which mediate between major segments of the population, e.g. welfare organizations (community and underprivileged), veterans' groups (veterans and government)). Recruitment patterns are said to vary according to type (Sills, 1957: 79–80).

Two further typologies developed by Rossi (1955: 55–64) to apply to many types of organization also apply to voluntary associations. He distinguishes between organizations which depend for members (and clients) on the whole area of the city or on a limited area, i.e. are *metropolitan-oriented* or *locally-oriented*, and between those in which interaction is primarily between members, i.e. are *client-oriented* or *member-oriented*. The theoretical importance of these two dimensions is indicated by their influence on an organization's response to residential mobility. Locally-oriented organizations are more sensitive to local mobility than metropolitan-oriented ones (and may become metropolitan-oriented to counteract its effect), and member-oriented organizations, where the departure of one member breaks a much larger number of relationships, are more sensitive to mobility than client-oriented ones. The local/metropolitan dimension is also significant for the level at which an association contributes to social structure.

The nine typologies of voluntary associations discussed here are not exhaustive. (For others, see Wilensky (1961b: 215–16).) But they are the ones which have been most used in the past or hold the greatest promise for the future.

There is no tight relationship between particular typologies and theoretical perspectives, but a few suggestions about likely links can be made. From the point of view of community power and social stratification all the typologies except those concerned with majoral/minoral/medial distinctions, and client/member orientations seem particularly relevant. Those relating to instrumentality, accessibility of membership, class composition, and majoral/medial functions, etc. appear most relevant to the pluralist approach. All of the typologies except the majoral/minoral one seem relevant to the issues within the community structure approach. But none of the typologies appears particularly connected with the work–leisure perspective, probably because little work on voluntary associations has been done from this perspective.

2 Collecting data on voluntary associations

We now examine the practicalities of collecting data on voluntary associations and consider how voluntary associations should be defined and questions about membership and participation worded.

2.1 *Defining voluntary associations*

Six criteria are involved in common-sense and sociological definitions of voluntary associations. The first four of these were implicit in Table 1.

(a) *Institutions* v. *non-institutions*

There would be general agreement that voluntary associations are not institutions in the sense of social structures devised to organize action in the main areas of social life, such as firms, schools, governments. Churches are not considered as voluntary associations on these grounds.

(b) *Commercial* v. *non-commercial*

Voluntary associations are generally considered to be non-commercial in that access is via membership which confers rights over a period of time. Commercial activity on the other hand involves the payment of money on a single occasion and the right to engage in the activity does not carry into the future. The 'non-commercial' criterion might be thought superfluous since the notion of formal membership introduced below overlaps with it to some extent. However the existence of organized commercial leisure activities such as 'cinema clubs' and casinos where access is restricted to 'members only' makes the 'non-commercial' distinction necessary. However it must be admitted that the dividing line between commercial activities and certain sorts of voluntary association is a hazy one.

(c) *Public* v. *private*

This contrast has a number of connotations: outside the household *v.* within the household; outside the immediate family *v.* within the immediate family; with access open to any person *v.* restricted access. In the first two respects voluntary associations are public, at least in name. However in the third sense voluntary associations are public in a more particular sense. Access is open to all in that membership does not debar named individuals, but it is frequently restricted to specific categories of people, e.g. Roman Catholics, divorced persons, people over sixty-five, people who served in the armed forces, etc. (From a legal point of view voluntary associations have something of a private character since racial discrimination in the admission of members is not illegal.)

(d) *Formal* v. *informal*

Voluntary associations are often described as formal associations and clearly the notions of membership and elected leadership, and the fact of having a name and constitution are key elements of the concept. But this does not mean they lack an informal structure. The contrast is with informal groupings such as darts clubs, or groups of pub 'regulars' which *only* have an informal structure. The criterion of formal structure may lead to the exclusion of some new types of organization, e.g. self-help groups (Smith and Pillemer, 1983). It has also been criticized for identifying a form of participation favoured by the middle class and excluding the less formal types of 'participation' favoured by the working class. These are important criticisms and can be met by including questions about participation outside voluntary associations.

In addition to these four criteria which were implicit in Table 1, we shall add two more in order to arrive at an acceptable definition of the voluntary association.

(e) *Statutory* v. *non-statutory*

Voluntary associations are non-statutory bodies, i.e. they are not established by law. Two points, however, must be noted. Voluntary associations may have to conform to certain legal requirements in order to gain certain benefits and the fact that they are non-statutory does not mean that they have no contact with government. As we saw earlier the role of government in instigating and financing voluntary associations is a common one.

(f) *Voluntary* v. *non-voluntary*

Voluntary associations are said to be voluntary in two senses: participation in them is not remunerated as in a paid occupation, and participation in them is freely chosen rather than being required, e.g. by one's job. (A third sense of voluntary, which is found in the social services field, is ignored here since it is identical with 'non-statutory'.)

In my view only the first sense need form part of the definition of a voluntary association: most voluntary associations are voluntary in that the members are 'volunteers'. (This is not altered by the fact that many employ a paid staff too: employee/volunteer relations are a classic source of tension within voluntary associations.) The second sense of voluntary as involving free choice has been stressed by Rose (1967:216) and Smith *et al.* (1972). For them voluntary action is a residual type of action which is free of economic, social or political constraint, and voluntary associations are one sphere in which it can be found. Against this I would argue, with Palisi (1968), that this notion of voluntary action is a metaphysical one which pre-empts the possibility of analysis of the forces affecting voluntary association participation. In fact, as mentioned earlier, the literature is full of such analyses.

A decision to reject the term 'voluntary' in the 'voluntary action' sense has certain practical implications. Trade unions and professional associations should not be excluded from the category 'voluntary association' on the grounds that membership, in some at least, is obligatory in order to obtain certain jobs. Likewise, churches cannot be excluded as voluntary associations because of the (partly) ascriptive character of church membership. However they are excluded here for a different reason, viz., that they are institutions.

The six criteria identified are the ones that appear to be most commonly implied in the voluntary association concept. No single criterion is sufficient to mark off voluntary associations from other groupings (Palisi, 1968), but we suggest that by combining the six criteria we do succeed in demarcating what are referred to as voluntary associations in sociological usage.

> The definition resulting from these six criteria is as follows: A *voluntary association* is a non-statutory, non-commercial organization, which is not an institution, which has a formal structure (e.g. a name, a constitution, a membership and elected leadership) and where membership is unpaid and open to any person within the eligible social category.

This definition implies that a number of types of participation are excluded: in informal groupings (which are relatively more important among the working class); in churches – because they are institutions; and in local councils, and boards of governors of schools and hospitals which are established by statute. Political parties are a somewhat marginal category, since they conform to the definition of a voluntary association in all respects including, arguably, that of not being an institution. It would seem wisest to include them within the category of voluntary association, but to ensure that they are kept as a distinct sub-category.

2.2 *Asking questions on voluntary associations*

We have assumed in this chapter that the reader's interest in voluntary associations was as a 'key variable', or as a social phenomenon which could be related to others, rather than as an object of interest in its own right. However, we do not wish to promote the unreflective inclusion of questions about voluntary associations. If they are to be included it must be because they are of some theoretical relevance. The number of surveys which include such questions but which do not present analyses of responses to them suggests that there is uncertainty about why participation in voluntary associations is important.

Our purpose here is to outline the types of data about voluntary associations which are of sociological relevance, and to make some suggestions about the particular form of questions to be used in survey research.

(a) *The coverage of data on voluntary associations*
Any question about voluntary associations requires that the respondent understands what is being referred to. The scope of the concept is therefore the first question requiring resolution.

It is obviously impractical to present respondents with the definition of the voluntary association we have arrived at. Two alternatives are possible. The first consists of presenting to the respondent a list of *specific* associations known to exist in the locality, and which have been checked, as far as possible, to see that they conform to the definition used. Various techniques have been used to draw up such lists: the most common are the pilot survey, or newspaper search, but bank records and registers of legally-declared associations have also been used.

The second strategy consists of listing the categories of associations on a prompt-card. The categories most frequently referred to in previous studies, and which conform to the definition proposed here are as follows:

Church organizations	Sports
Trade unions	Social
Professional associations	Women's
Work-based social clubs	Ex-service
Business and professional clubs	Fraternal
Political party	Benevolent/Mutual Aid
Other political clubs	Charitable
Music and dramatic	Social Service/Welfare/Self-Help
Other cultural and educational	Youth
Hobbies/recreational	Civic and Community.

This list could be presented on a prompt-card in full, or in abbreviated form by combining the categories. (See Goldthorpe, 1980.) The categories are not intended to be mutually exclusive, but merely to help people to recall the full range of their associational involvement.) From the point of view of the community power and community structure perspectives (and possibly the work–leisure perspective) only those associations which have local branches and/or meetings will usually be relevant.

(b) *Membership and participation*
Having established the range of associations of interest, most researchers will include as a basic minimum questions on membership and participation.

On the face of it the concept of membership of an association is clear-cut: every respondent should know whether they belong or not to associations of given kinds. In practice there are two complexities. First it may be possible to join different levels of an organization. This is particularly likely in the case of what Sills calls 'corporate-type' associations – which may allow national and local membership – as in CND. The researcher needs to be clear whether both are of interest: in community power and community structure studies membership of national associations or levels may be of no interest.

Second, there is a distinction between formal and subjective membership. Formally, a member is someone who has joined and paid a current subscription. However even people who are in arrears with their subscriptions – possibly through no fault of their own – may still state they are members, i.e. in the subjective sense. I would suggest that for sociological purposes it is this subjective sense of membership which is the most important. Formal membership on the other hand is of prime importance for the association, e.g. when it is the basis of rights (to appoint delegates) or duties (to pay sums to higher levels of the association). The frequent conflicts in party and trade union conferences about formal membership levels are evidence of this.

Participation refers to the degree of involvement in an association. It is not necessarily contingent upon membership and may even be encouraged before membership is expected or required. There is therefore a category of people who participate without being members – this includes women who participate in associations their husbands belong to, or vice versa. To capture the participation of this group it seems preferable to ask whether a person is 'connected with' an association and then to ask about their degree of participation, and only later about their subjective and/or formal membership.

The meaning of 'participation' (both for the individual and the association) varies widely among those concerned. (See Sills, 1957: ch. III; Weissman, 1970: chs. 2 and 8.) At one extreme is the person who is 'not active' or 'just pays their subscription'. (In such cases membership will be understood as something formal, and subjectively weak.) At the other extreme is the clutch of committee members who carry out the bulk of the routine work of the association and are more likely to participate in, and be aware of, its higher levels. Resignation threats by this group carry a lot of weight. The President or Patron of a local branch may be a local notable who plays a passive role in regular branch activities but whose 'participation' helps to sustain the association's status in the community, and attract resources to it. The meaning of participation for others may be very varied: some 'participants' in 'social service' voluntary associations may perceive them as an alternative source of services to commercial access; some may participate for extrinsic reasons, e.g. professionals dependent for their livelihood on private clients. (The analysis of extrinsic reasons for participation in voluntary associations is an untapped field of sociological analysis.)

Participation is of interest for different reasons according to the theoretical perspective concerned. It is generally measured by asking how frequently a person attends, the proportion of meetings attended, the time spent per month in connection with the association, whether they belong to the committee or hold an office, etc. From the work–leisure perspective, for example, committee membership and office-holding are important in so far as they permit the exercise of skills acquired at work. For the stratification, community power and community structure perspectives, offices and committee memberships are indicators of potential power positions. For the pluralist perspective, time spent in association activity is itself important in that it indicates an absence of apathy and alienation.

Questions on participation tend to presuppose an ideal-typical voluntary association with occasional meetings. In fact some associations with their own premises, such as golf or tennis clubs, and social clubs, may be open all the time and have perhaps only an Annual General Meeting. Similarly, some charitable organizations operate by individual activity co-ordinated by a local body without regular meetings. And other issue-oriented organizations work through campaigns rather than meetings. In such cases questions relating to meetings are irrelevant and the inclusion of a question about the form of activity should be considered. Also, in the case of committee members, it is important to separate frequency, etc. of committee meetings from those of ordinary meetings.

The above discussion of membership and participation is intended to indicate some of the hazards in asking questions on these subjects and the need to resolve problems according to the theoretical perspective being adopted. The diversity of purposes of research in which voluntary associations are a 'key variable' means that no universally applicable questions can be recommended. However some indicative questions may be suggested which can be modified as necessary.

A simple *question about membership* is

> 'Could you tell me whether you are connected with any clubs, societies, or organizations, or anything like that?' (SHOW PROMPT CARD) Add 'which meet in (say) the Manchester area' or exclude national associations as appropriate.

(The question 'are you a member?' will usually be understood in the subjective sense of membership which is acceptable, but will exclude those who participate without even a subjective sense of membership.)

For each association named, *questions about participation* may be asked. A question about formal status is:

> 'Are you an ordinary member/supporter/etc. or do you belong to the committee or hold a particular position in it?'

Questions which do not ask about precise membership status include

> 'How often do you go to meetings of the association' (if it has meetings) and 'How many times does it meet a year'. 'What proportion of the meetings have you attended in the past year' or 'Would you say you were a very active/fairly active/ or fairly inactive member'.

(For office holders and very active members questions about participation at other levels of the association may be asked.)

(c) *Voluntary associations and personal relationships*
This is a second major area of investigation which goes beyond basic information on membership and participation and starts to provide an insight into the character of the association itself. Two aspects of the subject can be separated: internal and external.

The question of people's relationships with others *within* the association is relevant to all theoretical perspectives, though for different reasons. For example, personal relationships may be examined for evidence of their primary character, of class mixing, of the use of social skills, of cross-cutting ties and hence social solidarity, or of influence and power.

Observation is usually the best method of studying personal relationships, but where an association is large, or the period of fieldwork short, sociometric questions can be posed. Bottomore (1954) found that when he asked members who their close friends were in the association, their choices were not always reciprocated. As well as locating patterns of friendship and acquaintance it may be of interest to inquire how the friendship originated, whether it started inside or outside the association, whether members associate in other contexts, etc. This procedure will enable the identification of cliques of friends, of relatives, of attenders at the same church, of supporters of the same political party, of colleagues, etc.

A second aspect of personal relationships concerns the links of members outside the association. At a formal level this refers to their 'status-sets', i.e. their associational memberships and institutional positions. These links can be mapped by interviewing, and by the use of local directories of organizations, Who's Who directories, etc. But the integration of members into the formal social structure of the community is of equal interest.

This may be pursued by asking the names of individuals in the person's social network, or by obtaining summary information on categories such as friends, relatives, acquaintances and neighbours. The way in which relationships formed in one context are used in other contexts can also be followed up. (See Mitchell, 1974 on network research.)

The ramifications of participation in a voluntary association for the wider social structure is of relevance to all theoretical perspectives except the work–leisure perspective – where only the initial act of participation is of interest.

Typical initial questions on personal relations among members are, for each association:

> 'Do you know any members/supporters of (the association) as friends or acquaintances, rather than just knowing their names? Could you tell me their names?' (A list of names can be shown as a reminder.)

It cannot be assumed that people will answer this question 'correctly'. Their perceptions however, are important, and will indicate their level of information – which in turn reflects their own participation and that of others in the association. Inactive members may be unaware that people they know in other contexts are members. The terms 'friends' and 'acquaintances' should be defined, e.g. 'people whose homes you visit' and 'people whom you would stop to talk to in the street'.

'How did you first meet X?' (e.g. this association, other association, neighbour, etc.)
'Have you ever met him/her outside (the association)?'
If so 'In what connection?'

(d) *Questions relating to other typologies*
The questions on personal relationships just discussed are relevant to a number of typologies, but as was pointed out earlier there are other typologies which have not been applied because the required information has not been sought. There are therefore good reasons for including, where appropriate, questions which will permit the further use of these typologies. For example,

'Is (the association) a branch of a national organization, a local association affiliated to others, or a local association without any affiliations?' (*corporate-type* v. *federation-type* v. *simple*).
'Do the members/supporters come from all over (say) the Manchester area, or do they live in a particular district, and, if so, which?' (*metropolitan-oriented* v. *locally-oriented*).

To establish whether an association is seen as *instrumental* or *expressive*, several approaches are possible. Statements about the association's goals and the purpose of members' participation may be presented to members and their responses summed to place the association on an instrumental/expressive scale (Jacoby and Babchuk, 1963). Alternatively, open-ended questions may be asked, and the answers coded for their instrumental or expressive content, e.g.

'What do you see as the purpose of attending meetings/participating in the activities of (the association)?'

(The answer to this may be quite different from the perceived purpose of the association as a whole in the case of corporate-type associations.)

'What are the social backgrounds of the members of (the association)?'
'Is membership of (the association) restricted by social status/race/etc.?' (*Open* v. *closed access; high, low, mixed class,* etc.)
'Does (the association) provide services to non-members or do activities involve only members?' (*Client-oriented* v. *member-oriented.*)

All of these questions refer to members' perceptions of the associations in which they are involved. For some purposes this is unimportant and the variety of perceptions of a given association may be an object of interest in itself. For others comparisons with objective measures can be made.

In this section we have indicated some of the practicalities of gathering data on voluntary associations. The intention has been to show how questions about voluntary associations can be used to throw light on the issues raised within the various theoretical approaches and typologies discussed earlier. We hope to have shown how prior reflection on why one is interested in voluntary associations can lead to the gathering of appropriate data and thereby help towards the development of a theoretical understanding of voluntary association participation.

References

Almond, G.A. and **Verba, S.** (1965), *The Civic Culture* (Abridged edition), Boston, Little, Brown.
Babchuk, N. and **Edwards, J.N.** (1965), 'Voluntary associations and the integration hypothesis', *Sociology Inquiry*, vol. 35, pp. 149–62.
Babchuk, N. and **Gordon, C.W.** (1962), *The Voluntary Association in the Slum* (University of Nebraska Studies No. 27), Lincoln, University of Nebraska Press.
Bell, W. and **Boat, M.D.** (1957), 'Urban neighbourhoods and informal social relations', *American Journal of Sociology*, vol. 62, pp. 391–8.
Benson, J.K. (1975), 'The interorganizational network as a political economy', *Administrative Science Quarterly*, vol. 20, pp. 229–49.
Booth, A. and **Babchuk, N.** (1969), 'Personal influence networks and voluntary association affiliation', *Sociological Inquiry*, vol. 39, pp. 179–88.
Booth, A., Babchuk, N. and **Knox, A.B.** (1968), 'Social stratification and membership in instrumental-expressive voluntary associations', *Sociological Quarterly*, vol. 9, pp. 427–39.
Bottomore, T.B. (1954), 'Social stratification in voluntary associations', in Glass, D.V. (ed.), *Social Mobility in Britain*, London, Routledge & Kegan Paul.
Clark, P.B. and **Wilson, J.Q.** (1961), 'Incentive systems: a theory

of organizations', *Administrative Science Quarterly*, vol. 6, pp. 129–66.

Coleman, J.S. (1957), *Community Conflict*, Glencoe, Free Press.

Cutler, S.J. (1973), 'Voluntary association membership and the theory of mass society', in Lauman, E.O., *Bonds of Pluralism: The Form and Substance of Urban Social Networks*, New York, Wiley.

Ehrlich, H.J. (1970), 'Critique', in Field, A.J., *Urban Power Structures: Problems in Theory and Research*, Cambridge, Massachusetts, Schenkman.

Frankenberg, R. (1966), *Communities in Britain*, Harmondsworth, Penguin.

Galaskiewicz, J. (1979), 'The structure of community organizational networks', *Social Forces*, vol. 57, pp. 1346–64.

Galaskiewicz, J. and **Shatin, D.** (1981), 'Leadership and networking among neighbourhood human service organizations', *Administrative Science Quarterly*, vol. 26, pp. 434–48.

Goldthorpe, J.H. (1980), *Social Mobility and Class Structure in Modern Britain*, Oxford, Clarendon Press.

Goldthorpe, J.H. *et al.* (1969), *The Affluent Worker in the Class Structure*, Cambridge, Cambridge University Press.

Gordon, C.W. and **Babchuk, N.** (1959), 'A typology of voluntary associations', *American Sociological Review*, vol. 24, pp. 22–9.

Hagedorn, R. and **Labovitz, S.** (1968a), 'Participation in community associations by occupation: a test of three theories', *American Sociological Review*, vol. 33, pp. 272–83.

Hagedorn, R. and **Labovitz, S.** (1968b), 'Occupational characteristics and participation in voluntary associations', *Social Forces*, vol. 47, pp. 16–27.

Jacoby, A.P. and **Babchuk, N.** (1963), 'Instrumental and expressive voluntary associations', *Sociology and Social Research*, vol. 47, pp. 461–71.

Laumann, E.O., Galaskiewicz, J. and **Marsden, P.V.** (1978), 'Community structure as interorganizational linkages', *Annual Review of Sociology*, vol. 4, pp. 455–84.

McPherson, J.M. (1981), 'Voluntary affiliation: a structural approach', in Blau, P.M. and Merton, R.K. (eds), *Continuities in Structural Inquiry*, London, Sage.

Mitchell, G.D. and **Lupton, T.** (1954), 'The Liverpool estate', in *Neighbourhood and Community*, Liverpool, University of Liverpool Press.

Mitchell, J.C. (1974), 'Social networks', *Annual Review of Anthropology*, vol. 3, pp. 279–99.

Olsen, M.E. (1972), 'Social participation and voting turnout: a multivariate analysis', *American Sociological Review*, vol. 37, pp. 317–33.

Palisi, B.J. (1968), 'A critical analysis of the voluntary association concept', *Sociology and Social Research*, vol. 52, pp. 392–405.

Parker, S.R. (1976), *The Sociology of Leisure*, London, Allen & Unwin.

Parkin, F. (1968), *Middle Class Radicalism*, Manchester, Manchester University Press.

Pickvance, C.G. (1976), 'On the study of urban social movements', in Pickvance, C.G. (ed.), *Urban Sociology: Critical Essays*, London, Tavistock.

Roberts, B.R. (1973), *Organising Strangers: Poor Families in Guatemala City*, London, Texas University Press.

Rose, A.M. (1954), 'A theory of the function of voluntary associations in contemporary social structure', in Rose, A.M., *Theory and Methods in the Social Sciences*, Minneapolis, University of Minnesota Press.

Rose, A.M. (1967), *The Power Structure*, New York, Oxford University Press.

Ross, J.C. (1972), 'Toward a reconstruction of voluntary association theory', *British Journal of Sociology*, vol. 23, pp. 20–32.

Ross, J.C. and **Wheeler, R.E.** (1971), *Black Belonging: A Study of the Social Correlates of Work Relations Among Negroes*. Westport, Connecticut, Greenwood.

Rossi, P.H. (1955), *Why Families Move*, Glencoe, Free Press.

Sills, D.L. (1957), *The Volunteers*, Glencoe, Free Press.

Smith, C. and **Freedman, A.** (1972), *Voluntary Associations: Perspectives on the Literature*, Cambridge, Harvard University Press.

Smith, D.H. (1975), 'Voluntary action and voluntary groups', *Annual Review of Sociology*, vol. 1, pp. 247–70.

Smith, D.H. and **Pillemer, K.** (1983), 'Self-help groups as social movement organizations: social structure and social change', *Research in Social Movements, Conflict and Change*, vol. 5, pp. 203–33.

Smith, D.H., Reddy, R.D. and **Baldwin, B.R.** (1972) 'Types of voluntary action: a definitional essay', in Smith, D.H., Reddy, R.D. and Baldwin, B.R. (eds), *Voluntary Action Research: 1972*, Lexington, Massachusetts, Lexington Books.

Stacey, M. (1960), *Tradition and Change*, Oxford, Oxford University Press.

Stacey, M., Batstone, E., Bell, C. and **Murcott, A.** (1975), *Power, Persistence, and Change*, London, Routledge & Kegan Paul.

Stebbins, R.A. (1970), 'Career: the subjective approach', *Sociological Quarterly*, vol. 11, pp. 32–49.
Taub, R.P., Surgeon, G.P., Lindholm, S., Otti, P.B. and **Bridges, A.** (1977), 'Urban voluntary associations, locality based and externally induced', *American Journal of Sociology*, vol. 83, pp. 425–42.
Verba, S. and **Nie, N.H.** (1972), *Participation in America*, New York, Harper and Row.
Warner, R.L. and **Lunt, P.S.** (1941), *The Social Life of a Modern Community*, New Haven, Yale University Press.
Warren, R.L. (1962), *The Community in America*, Chicago, Rand McNally.
Weissman, H.H. (1970), *Community Councils and Community Control*, Pittsburgh, University of Pittsburgh Press.
Wilensky, H.L. (1960), 'Work, careers, and social integration', *International Social Science Journal*, vol. 12, pp. 543–60.
Wilensky, H.L. (1961a), 'Orderly careers and social participation', *American Sociological Review*, vol. 26, pp. 521–39.
Wilensky, H.L. (1961b), 'Life cycle, work situation and participation in formal associations', in Kleemeier, R.W. (ed.), *Ageing and Leisure*, New York, Oxford University Press.
Young, R.C. and **Larson, O.F.** (1965), 'A new approach to community structure', *American Sociological Review*, vol. 30, pp. 926–34.

Do concepts, variables and indicators interrelate? 12

Martin Bulmer and Robert G. Burgess

The essays in this book attempt to redress the underdeveloped state of conceptualization in empirical sociological research. For some aspects of social research are clearly more susceptible to codification and formalization than others. Selection of units of study, methods of collecting (both quantitative and qualitative) data, and means of assessing the reliability of data so produced, have all received much attention. Other aspects of research – the initial delicate stages of problem–formulation and research design, the fraught phase of writing up – either have been neglected or treated in terms of formulæ (for example, the logic of experimental design) whose applicability to at least some types of social research is in doubt.

The realm of concepts falls clearly in the latter category. Analysis of the role of concepts in empirical social research has been to a very considerable extent neglected, both a symptom and a cause of the gulf which continues to separate sociological theory from sociological research. Despite a number of important attempts to bridge the gulf (as different as Znaniecki 1934; Kaplan 1964 and Lazarsfeld 1977), it is fair to say that in the available literature on how to do research, the awkward problems of the formation and justification of concepts are rapidly passed over to get to more tractable fields like sample design or questionnaire construction.

It is not that sociologists neglect the analysis of concepts, but frequently they mean different things by it. The empirical sociologist who, for example, turns hopefully to a recent work entitled *Concept Formation in Social Science* (Outhwaite 1983) will be sorely disappointed. The author at the end of a highly abstract essay in the philosophy of social science, concedes that it will be held against him that

> abstract discussion of problems of concept formation is
> sterile; what social theorists should be doing is constructing

substantive theories whose conceptual merits will come out
in the wash of intertheoretical discussion . . (T)his view,
however tempting it may seem in the present state of sociological theorising, rests on a misunderstanding of the conceptual problems of the social sciences. (Outhwaite, 1983:155)

The heady delights of abstract theorizing and philosophizing are
widely admired and were at one time seen to be *the* area of development in sociology and the social sciences. At the theoretical and
meta-theoretical levels, enormous effort is devoted to the dissection
and explication of terms, the results of which appear in series with
titles such as *Key Concepts in the Social Sciences* (for example, Wilson
1970 and the series it appears in and Sartori 1984). Sociology
graduates are produced who can discourse knowledgeably about the
concept of social class without necessarily having very much idea
about how to measure it empirically.

On the other hand, the better specification and measurement of
variables is the separate concern of those who do empirical research,
the results appearing in volumes such as the present one and its two
predecessors (Stacey 1969; Gittus 1972). At a slightly more abstract
level, one can find powerful statements of the rationale of concept
formation and rigorous empirical measurement integrally bound
together, often using examples drawn from psychology such as
'intelligence'. (For two examples see Lazarsfeld 1966 and Smith and
Medin 1981.) A wide gulf separates the two types of discussion. It is
remarkable how little one type of work informs the other. For too
much discussion in the philosophy of social science assumes *a priori*
that the gulf between theory and empirical data is an unbridgeable
one, tending all too often to stereotype what they consider to be
empirical sociology. Outhwaite, for example, groups most of it in his
category of 'positivism', and then proceeds to demolish the tenability
of that approach with reference to the Vienna School of logical
positivists (Outhwaite 1983:6–10). Most contemporary empirical
sociologists in Britain would, one imagines, be surprised to have their
work assimilated to that of the rarely-read Otto Neurath (1973).

Lack of sensitivity to the problems of bringing theory and data into
connection with each other cannot alter the fact that the explicit use of
concepts is one of the most important characteristics differentiating
sociology from purely idiographic activities such as narrative history
or ethnography. Concepts perform several functions in sociology.
They provide a means of summarizing and classifying the formless
mass of social data. In Myrdal's words, 'Concepts are spaces into
which reality is fitted by analysis' (1961: 273). One aim of conceptual

analysis is commonly to make explicit the character of phenomena subsumed under a concept. Concepts, too, provide a degree of fixity or determinateness in making observations in social science. As L.J. Henderson put it 'A fact is a statement about experience in terms of a conceptual scheme' (quoted in Parsons 1970: 830). Put slightly differently, concepts specify routes which may be followed in analysing phenomena. 'Concepts mark out paths by which we may move most freely in logical space. They identify nodes or junctions in the network of relationships, termini at which we can halt while preserving the maximum range of choice as to where to go next' (Kaplan 1964: 52).

Concepts in themselves are not theories. They are categories for the organization of ideas and observations. In order to form an explanatory theory, concepts must be interrelated. But concepts do act as a means of storing observations of phenomena which may at a future time be used in a theory. Similarly while concepts are distinct from observations, the formation of concepts is a spur to the development of observable indices of the phenomena subsumed under the concept. Concepts, then, mediate between theory and data. They form an essential bridge, but one which is difficult to construct and maintain.

One of the most significant difficulties, which has much exercised philosophers of science, is the *paradox of categorization*. Where do concepts come from in the first place, and what provides the justification for the use of particular concepts?

> If my categories of thought determine what I observe, then what I observe provides no independent control over my thought. On the other hand, if my categories of thought do not determine what I observe, then what I observe must be uncategorized, that is to say, formless and nondescript – hence again incapable of providing any test of my thought. So in neither case is it possible for observation, be it what it may, to provide any independent control over thought. . . . Observation contaminated by thought yields circular tests; observation uncontaminated by thought yields no tests at all (Scheffler 1967:13–14).

It is sometimes argued that attempts to reconstruct the logic or psychology of concept-formation are wasted, by comparison with engaging in conceptual analysis through empirical research. As Lazarsfeld and Barton observed, 'One cannot write a handbook on "how to form fruitful theoretical concepts" in the same way as handbooks are written on sampling or questionnaire construction' (1951). The virtue of a collection such as the present one is that it breaks away from purely abstract or contextless discussion of the process of concept-formation to ground an account in research practice and the analysis of specific theoretical problems, such as how to define and study work or social class.

Systematic reflection about the task of concept formation may also throw light on the paradox of categorization. For concept-formulation in the analysis of sociological data has a dual character. It involves both the levels of theoretical abstraction and empirical observation, however those are defined and conceived. And it exemplifies *par excellence* the Kantian dictum that perception without conception is blind; conception without perception is empty. The development of fruitful concepts in sociology proceeds neither from observation to category, nor from category to observation, but in both directions at once and in interaction. The distinctive character of concepts in empirical social science derives from this dual theoretical and empirical character. The process is one in which concepts are formed and modified both in the light of empirical evidence *and* in the context of theory. Both theory and evidence can exercise compelling influence on what emerges.

In a recent discussion of discrepancies between concepts and their measurement, Norman Bradburn discusses the examples of the terms 'urban' and 'rural' and how they are measured in social science data (1982: 147). Similar types of problem arise as do with other concepts in social science – whether unemployment, or integration, or job satisfaction. All have measurement problems associated with them, but there is a healthy dialectic back and forth between attempts to measure concepts and attempts to clarify the meaning of concepts. Measurement can pinpoint ambiguities in definition to be resolved. Conceptual clarification can lead to better measurement.

If one begins with 'hard' or 'harder' science, it is necessary to be clear that the crude caricatures of 'positivisim' such as that put forward by Outhwaite do not stand up under examination. It is true that some of what Blumer terms definitive concepts (1954) may be treated as observables, as in an operational definition of intelligence as what intelligence tests measure. As Hempel, however, has emphasized, many of the terms with which both natural and social sciences are concerned are not observables but dispositional concepts, referring to a tendency to act in a particular way under certain conditions. A further type of concept, at a higher level of abstraction, is the theoretical construct. Such constructs are introduced jointly, at both theoretical and empirical levels, by setting up a theoretical system formulated in terms of them, and by giving this system an interpretation in terms of observables, which confers empiricial meaning on the theoretical constructs.

Such highly abstract terms have a central theoretical role, but their use depends on not only their theoretical relevance but the fact that empirical observations make sense in terms of these concepts.

> Comprehensive, simple and dependable principles for the explanation . . . of observable phenomena cannot be obtained merely by summarizing and inductively generalizing observational findings. A hypothetico-deductive-observational procedure is called for. . . . Guided by his knowledge of observational data, the scientist has to invent a set of concepts – theoretical constructs, which lack immediate experiential significance, a system of hypotheses couched in terms of them, and an interpretation of the resulting theoretical network; and all this in a manner which will establish explanatory . . . connections between the data of direct observation (Hempel 1952: 36–7).

A sophisticated quantitative researcher such as Lazarsfeld was well aware of these characteristics of the harder sciences, and sought to develop concepts and indicators in a similar manner in social science. This should not be caricatured as the survey researcher running crudely measured fact-sheet variables against every possible dependent variable. Several chapters for example, show that the process of developing a construct or variable as part of a theory is much more complicated than that.

The implication should also be avoided that quantitative researchers are straining to fit all data into neat little numbered boxes (see Bulmer in this volume). These limitations are well expressed by the American statistician William Kruskal:

> (T)here is no ultimate truth about most – perhaps all – classifications. It would be lovely if there were a truth that one might hope to approach asymptotically and treat deviations from as simple measurement errors. Alas, no; there is essential ambiguity most or all of the time, yet an ambiguity that needs to be understood as well as possible if society is sensibly to use statistical results based on ineluctable fuzziness. . . . Classification problems arise in all fields of science and beyond (Kruskal 1981: 511).

The use of the term 'measurement', like the use of the paired terms 'concept' and 'indicator' (cf. Lazarsfeld 1977), may carry rather unfortunate connotations if it suggests that the use of concepts to bridge the gap between theory and data is the preserve of quantitative sociology, especially survey research. This is far from being the case. As most of the contributors to this volume demonstrate, the use of the term 'key variable' does not *ipso facto* commit one to quantitative work and is fully compatible with a qualitative approach. The same is true in considering the relationship between concepts and empirical data. There is a strong tradition of concept-formation and theorizing through detailed analysis of qualitative data.

The best-known of these is the procedure developed by Florian Znaniecki, known as analytic induction. Analytic induction is intended to maintain faithfulness to the empirical data while abstracting and generalizing from a relatively small number of cases. Its aim is to 'preserve plasticity' by avoiding prior categorization. No definition of a class or category of data precedes the selection of data to be studied as the representative of that class. The data analysis begins before any general formulations are proposed (i.e. the procedure is inductive rather than deductive). It abstracts from a given concrete case the features that are essential, and generalizes them.

First (a) discover which characters in a given datum of a certain class are more, and which less, essential. Then (b) abstract these characters and assume that the more essential are the more general than the less essential and must be found in a wider variety of classes. Follow this by (c) testing this hypothesis by investigating classes in which both the former and the latter are found. Finally, (d) establish a classification, i.e. organize all these classes into a scientific system based on the functions the respective characters play in determining them (Znaniecki 1934, ch.6). The procedure was applied in empirical research by Angell (1936) and Lindesmith (1947), and has found favour more recently among qualitative methodologists (cf. Denzin 1970; Hammersley and Atkinson 1983: 202–6; Mitchell 1983). The alternative approach via grounded theory (Glaser and Strauss 1968) has perhaps found somewhat less favour. Both, however, are a means of developing and refining concepts in close conjunction with empirical data, emphasizing the point that variable construction is not the preserve of quantitative research.

But how can the gap that exists between concepts and indicators be bridged? The researcher needs to consider how to translate theories and concepts into research questions and in turn into questions that may be used with respondents. This process is often described in a somewhat mechanical fashion that oversimplifies what occurs in practice. For example, McCall (1969) discusses measurement as a deductive approach to the construct-indicator problem where:

> the researcher begins with a more or less well defined
> theoretical construct and, given the conditions of his chosen
> substantive context, logically deduces a number of empirical
> properties of pertinent unit objects that would be entailed by
> the existence of that construct. These properties serve as
> indicators of the construct. (McCall 1969: 231)

However, when we turn to reports from those engaged in such
operations we find that it is far from logical and straightforward for as
Maclean and Genn (1979) report in the context of a study of illness
and injury:

> Even with a very clearly defined concept, there are problems
> in developing an indicator which will measure that variable
> and not something else (the problem of validity) and do so
> systematically without bias (the problem of reliability).
> (Maclean and Genn 1979: 22)

They suggest that those variables that are often tested rarely reflect
the complexity of the hypotheses that are framed as researchers often
identify those elements of social life that are most easily measurable.

While codified procedures are rarely employed in ethnographic
research the problem of the relationship between concepts and
indicators is still present and is traditionally approached in an
inductive way through the theoretical interpretation of particular
incidents. Indeed, many ethnographers would, like Ditton (1977),
consider that their work is 'theorised description'. Here, the researcher does not begin with a well worked out set of hypotheses to be
tested and measured (cf. Becker *et al.* 1968; Dalton 1964) but instead
works within a general framework to orientate the investigation (cf.
Geer 1964). Such a set of orienting concepts allow the researcher to
collect descriptive accounts which are used as a basis for theoretical
categories. In this situation the researcher has to establish the
relevance of indicators for the theoretical construct. Second consideration has to be given to the weighting of indicators and finally, to the
confirmation of a theoretical proposition. At first glance such procedures may appear to have little to do with the world of measurement,
variables and indicators, for some writers have drawn an artificially
sharp distinction between the procedures involved in qualitative
investigation and those that are associated with quantitative survey
based studies (cf. Bogdan and Biklen 1982). However, the important
point that is rightly stressed by McCall is that many of the best studies

use both approaches to complement each other (cf. Zelditch 1962; Sieber 1973). Most space has been devoted to the ways in which the gap can be bridged between concepts and indicators and, therefore, it is this relationship that will be principally examined, drawing on particular examples of empirical investigation. Among the tasks that confront the social researcher who deals with concepts and indicators is the problem of translating concepts derived from classical writing in sociology into items and indicators that can be measured, the problem of handling central concepts in sociology such as social class, and the problem of defining and measuring attitudes and behaviour in such diverse areas as studies of religion and health.

In social science in general and sociology in particular, much research and writing is guided by theories and concepts that have been taken from the classical writings of Durkheim, Marx and Weber. Concepts such as 'anomie', 'alienation' and 'bureaucracy' can all be found in the writing of classical sociological theorists, but how can they be applied to the study of contemporary society? How can such concepts be translated into items that can be measured? One can find many examples of scepticism about whether particular concepts are empirically researchable. Steven Lukes (1967: 134–7) raises doubts as to whether modern versions of 'alienation' and 'anomic' have any reference to the classical concerns of Marx and Durkheim. Nevertheless, one concept that has received comprehensive treatment in the literature is 'alienation' which has frequently been coupled with the work situation. But how, might we ask, have investigators examined alienation from work?

Marx considered that work should be a voluntary conscious activity which would contribute to the individual's physical and mental powers and which would have its own intrinsic value. It was when employees were denied freedom and personal development that Marx referred to alienation. In particular he defined alienation in two ways. First, the separation of workers from the products of their labour when they cannot influence what is produced and how it is made. Second, the separation of workers from the means of production when producers do not own or control factories and equipment. Among contemporary writers it is Melville Seeman (1959) who has attempted to outline the main dimensions of alienation. In particular, he distinguished five different ways in which the concept has been used to refer to powerlessness (an inability to influence the course of events in one's life space); meaninglessness (an inability to predict events together with one's own and others' behaviour); normlessness (a belief that morally undesirable means are the only way to achieve ends); isolation (the feeling of not being part of a social network) and self-estrangement (a feeling that activities are undertaken for extrinsic reasons rather than intrinsic meaning and personal value).

It was these conceptions of alienation that were used by Blauner (1964) in his comparative study of alienation in different industries. In turn Seeman (1967) drew questions from Blauner's study in order to develop an index of work alienation. In particular, he took fifteen questions from Blauner's study which differentiated between skill industries (printing), machine industries (textiles), assembly line industries (automobiles) and automated workers (chemicals). On the basis of the replies he constructed an index of work alienation to see whether respondents found their work interesting and rewarding. The items that were used in the index were as follows:

1　Is your job too simple to bring out your best abilities, or not?
2　Can you do the work on the job and keep your mind on other things most of the time or not?
3　Which one of the following statements comes closer to describing how you feel about your present job? (Four statements, uncited, from 'interesting nearly all the time' to 'completely dull and monotonous').
4　Does your job make you work too fast most of the time, or not?
5　Does your job really give you a chance to try out ideas of your own, or not?
6　If you had the opportunity to retire right now, would you prefer to do that, or would you prefer to go on working at your present job?
7　On an ordinary workday, do you have the opportunity to make independent decisions when you are carrying out your tasks, or is it rather routine work?
(Seeman 1967: 275)

In turn, there have been other approaches to operationalizing alienation drawing on the work of Marx and the work of Seeman (1959). In particular, Sheppard (1972) has attempted to operationalize the five dimensions of alienation that Seeman identified: powerlessness, meaningless, normlessness, instrumental work orientation as a particular form of self estrangement and self evaluative involvement.

At first glance it may appear that it is relatively straightforward to translate abstract concepts and theories into research questions. In particular, Marsh (in this volume) has illustrated the conceptual and technical problems associated with attempts to operationalize and measure social class. However, further evidence on the difficulties of operationalization is provided from three areas of study: measuring the social class of women, measuring religious attitudes and behaviour and studying illness and injury.

As Arber, Gilbert and Dale (1984) have shown in discussing approaches used to measure women's social class position, distinctions can be made between approaches that measure women's class position in terms of the family's lifestyle and those approaches that examine class in terms of the individual's position in the labour market. However, the basic problem that exists is the way in which researchers can operationalize women's class position. For example, what problems are involved in characterizing women's class position in terms of their husband's employment? How can researchers use other measures to grasp a married woman's class position? What measures can be used to examine the class position of women who are unmarried, separated or divorced? (cf. Goldthorpe 1983; Stanworth 1984).

Similar problems of operationalization can be seen when looking at religious attitudes and behaviour. First, we need to consider whether it is possible to measure religiosity. For example, if religion is equated with church attendance, a downward trend will be revealed. Yet such behaviour may not reflect the role of religion in society. In these circumstances, Krausz (1972) has suggested that the researcher should focus on measurements that concern an individual's identification with or adherence to a religious group. Accordingly, he suggests that different indices need to be adopted for different religious groups as adherence to particular groups may be associated with particular forms of behaviour. For example, Catholics might be all those who are baptized by the Catholic church, while members of the Church of England are those that are confirmed and nonconformists are broadly speaking those who have been received into membership (although this may vary according to denomination or sect). Accordingly, Krausz (1972) advocates that if concepts and categories are to be operationalized, categories need to be devised that will allow for comparability among groups.

However, there are further problems associated with measurement that can be illustrated from Maclean and Genn's project (1979) on illness and injury. In particular, their project set out to establish the social and economic consequences of illness and injury but as they point out there are a number of problems involved here. First, the project involves an area of interest rather than a quantifiable variable.

Second, there is the problem of identifying the central concept and finally establishing a set of criteria to close the gap between a key concept and an indicator. Accordingly, they indicate how question design is so problematic that ideas are often reduced to focusing on those concepts that are most easily measurable.

While many texts indicate that a number of stages are involved in translating concepts into research questions, the reality is very different. It is rare for the process to be a simple linear process for as Maclean and Genn remark of their investigation:

> In a project of this kind we could not expect to define the purposes of the screen first, then design a questionnaire to implement these, and lastly to test it for reliability and validity. In practice, all these stages were closely related and every decision depended on others. We had to make a start by working with provisional and ill-defined ideas, and gradually refine and develop these until final decisions could be taken. (Maclean and Genn 1979: 55)

Accordingly, theoretical and methodological processes have often to be modified in the light of what is practicable in a research programme. Often researchers find that feedback between the empirical operations and the initial theoretical ideas becomes essential with the result that concepts and indicators are used to 'build bridges' between different parts of the research process.

One central characteristic of concepts in sociology emphasized in the contributions to this book is their embeddedness in theory. Concepts are not simply rule-of-thumb definitions for which one develops appropriate indicators and then ventures out into the field. Such a view may be adequate for fact-finding survey research by market research firms, but is inadequate for sociology. Concepts are part of a theoretical web which represents a more abstract attempt to comprehend the phenomena under investigation. The concepts sociologists use are embedded in theory. What this means needs considering carefully, for it is liable to misunderstanding.

The first error of interpretation to avoid is that this is somehow a unique characteristic of sociology. This is not the case. Many concepts in natural science, such as 'election' or 'gene', display this characteristic in extreme form. Such concepts derive their meaning not only from their role as a theoretical term in a theory, but also from observational evidence in experiments. Analogies of the zip fastener or 'semantical zipper' (Braithwaite 1953; Hanson 1969) are used to suggest that the scientist works from conclusions back to premises (up the zip). Propositions in electrical theory are propositions about observations of measuring instruments. The meaning of the terms derives from their use in that context. These meanings are then transferred back up through the steps of the theory (the zip) until at the top one reaches the higher level term 'electron'. The term's meaning is established in the context of the system of which it forms a part, so much so in some cases that it may be best to avoid explicit definition at all. This underlines the point made earlier. Concepts are not just developed out of observations, nor are they imposed *a priori*. Their use is justified in terms of their context in a particular theory and particular observations which the theory seeks to explain.

To refer to a 'particular theory' runs, in sociology, the danger of raising the *canard* of relativism. The theory embeddedness of concepts is too easily interpreted as judging the use of concepts in terms of acceptance or rejection of the overall theory. For example, Marxist critics of sociological concepts of 'class' have claimed that in order to analyse class relations properly, it is necessary to have a prior understanding of the labour theory of value and the processes of capital accumulation (cf. Nichols 1979:160). On the other hand, critics have suggested that this sort of assertion simply means that its proponents have first decided who they want to include in the working class, and then constructed their 'theory' around this. What relativists cannot accept is the interdependence of, and interplay between, theory and data in concept formation. Outhwaite, for example, criticizes Max Weber for the methodological premise that theories, wherever they come from, must 'bump up against' reality and be judged by it (1983: 88). Yet this is precisely the way in which many concepts are refined and made more effective in sociological research.

What relativists, with their 'all-or-nothing' approach, also fail to recognize is that different concepts may be embedded to differing extents in theory. Sociological concepts are capable of being ranged along an empirical-theoretical continuum. At one end are direct observations, such as marking a ballot paper, or the demographic events of birth and death. Next come indirect observations, using a term in ways which involve subtle and complex perception of action. As Kaplan puts it, 'Do we see genes when we look into a pair of blue eyes?' (1964: 55). The construct of 'prayer' involves a number of assumptions about posture, location and religious belief if it is to be observed empirically. Some terms cannot be observed directly, but are theoretical constructs. Examples are the terms 'government', 'taboo' and 'money'. They are, however, in principle, statable in

terms of particular empirical observations. At the other end of the
continuum, theoretical terms cannot be defined even in principle in
terms of observables. Concepts such as 'marginal utility' or 'the
Protestant ethic' derive their meaning from the part they play in the
theory in which they are embedded.

Thus concepts may stand in varying relations to theory. What is of
particular interest in this connection is the demonstration in several
chapters of the theoretical implications of apparently straightforward
'face-sheet' variables. For example, although age may be treated
straightforwardly as one variable to run against one or more dependent variables, the interpretation of any resulting associations is
considerably more problematical. To what extent, for example, are
age effects a result of differential socialization? There is clear evidence
that voting behaviour is influenced in this way (cf. Butler and Stokes
1974, chapter 3). 'Generation' or 'cohort' effects are of particular
importance in the study of social mobility and in the statistical
analysis of life history data such as occupational histories (cf. Kertzer
1983). Increasing interest in historical sociology suggests the need to
relate analyses to the life experience of cohorts which are identified.
'Face-sheet' analysis is the start of what may be an intricate and
lengthy theoretical analysis.

Undoubtedly one reason for the resort to shallow relativism is the
unsuitability of many of the concepts which sociologists use. 'Power'
is a prime example (cf. Lukes 1974), leading to claims that 'the
naively conceived project of "measuring" political power in local
communities turns out to involve crucial conceptual, theoretical and
perhaps moral choices' (Outhwaite 1983: 19). In this volume the
difficulties of defining 'race' and 'ethnicity' are the most extreme case.
Perhaps what is needed is a dual awareness both of the theory-
ladenness of concepts and the obstacles to precise definition and
definitive measurement. The obstacles to the construction of robust
indicators affect much more quantitative subjects than sociology and
were alluded to earlier. From the standpoint of theory, perfection is
not likely to be attainable either.

> There is a certain kind of behavioural scientist who, at the
> least threat of an exposed ambiguity, scurries for cover like a
> hermit crab into the nearest abandoned logical shell. But
> there is no ground for panic. That a cognitive situation is not
> as well structured as we would like does not imply that no
> inquiry made in that situation is really scientific. On the
> contrary, it is the dogmatism outside science that proliferates
> closed systems of meaning; the scientist is in no hurry for

closure. Tolerance of ambiguity is as important for creativity in science as it is anywhere else. (Kaplan 1964: 70–1)

Ambiguity and a degree of indeterminateness is an inevitable feature of many concepts in social science, a limitation which we need to learn to live with.

Sociology, in common with many other disciplines, reflects social and intellectual change. Indeed, within this book some of the contributors have neatly illustrated the ways in which concepts and indicators have changed over time. For example, Bulmer has highlighted the different ways in which the concepts race and ethnicity have been interpreted over a thirty year time span in a variety of empirical studies, while Morgan has discussed the way in which the concepts sex and gender have moved from a situation where they were rarely questioned or used by social scientists to a position where they are of crucial significance in recent studies. It is examples such as these that serve to remind us that sociology is not practised in a social, historical and political vacuum. Indeed, there is much evidence to suggest that sociology is *not* timeless and is not isolated from the political and historical context in which researchers are located. We have only to turn to some of the sub-fields of sociology to see the way in which this is clearly revealed.

In reviewing the sociology of health and illness, Stacey with Homans (1978) has shown how developments within the sub-discipline have not merely reflected developments in sociology itself, for Margaret Stacey writes:

> While the sociology of health and illness may now be emancipating itself from the dominance of the medical profession, it tends, in common with other branches of sociology, to be parasitic on developments that are taking place in society at large. Sociologists did not predict that health and illness would be critically important areas for study and decision making. Rather, they responded to tensions felt in society and then proceeded to analyse and interpret them. Sociologists can be seen also to be responding to the requests of those with authority, prestige and resources. (Stacey with Homans 1978: 284–5)

Accordingly, as Stacey indicates, practice rather than theory has been central to the development of this sub discipline. However, we might consider *how* such developments have influenced research and writing in this field of study. For example, Dingwall *et al.* (1977) have drawn our attention to the way in which such shifts in the sub-discipline have been acccompanied by a shift in the models and concepts that are used as a basic framework in empirical studies. In particular, there has been a shift away from a medical model based on biological events to a perspective where a variety of models and concepts is used to examine health, illness and treatment. Such developments have been documented by Stacey (1982) and are reflected in the discussion of this field by Macintyre (in this volume).

However, it is not merely practice that influences sociological thinking but also theory. In reviewing studies of crime and deviancy Cohen (1980) shows how theoretical developments have occurred over a decade. In particular, he discusses the shifts from the functionalism of American writing to various forms of neo-Marxism. In turn, he also discusses how labelling theory has had to meet the challenge of Marxism. Such changes have not merely been confined to the field of deviancy as Banks (1982) and Davies (1983) have been able to chart a series of similar shifts in the study of education where interactionism and interactionist studies have had to meet the challenge of neo-Marxism. Indeed, the chapter by Burgess (in this volume) highlights how such changing theoretical fashions influenced the concepts and units of study in a variety of investigations about education.

In the fields of deviancy and education writers have also taken account of the feminist challenge and made the studies of girls and women much more central, for little over a decade ago Rowbotham could state:

> It is as if everything that relates only to us [women] comes out in footnotes to the main text, as worthy of the odd reference. We come on the agenda somewhere between 'Youth' and 'Any Other Business'. We encounter ourselves in men's cultures as 'by the way' and peripheral. According to all the reflections we are not really there. (Rowbotham 1973: 35)

Sociologists have subsequently been forced to reconceptualize areas of study and to include both men and women in their studies, samples and analyses.

A further area of study in which some reconceptualization has been demanded is the area of 'work'. Here, as Purcell (in this volume) indicates, sociologists have had to attach a range of different meanings to the word work and have had to take account of changing conditions of employment, the formal and informal economy, the impact of computers, the micro-chip and information technology (cf.

Bell 1982). Accordingly, sociologists and other social scientists have had to consider different ways in which to conceptualize and measure the world of work (cf. Cook *et al.* 1981).

However, there is a danger in seeing that concepts and variables are in a state of flux, for much work is cumulative and builds in an incremental fashion. For example Cook *et al.* (1981) have shown how the study of job satisfaction has developed over forty-five years and the ways in which a set of general evaluative questions have been established without citing specific features of a job. In such studies, a number of general categories are established around the central theme of job satisfaction which is phrased in terms of attraction, interest and boredom. For example, the sets of items that were devised by Brayfield and Rothe (1951) and by Quinn and Staines (1979) are separated by almost thirty years, but the categories and concepts used are very similar. Sociologists have therefore devised a series of measures about job satisfaction which are non-specific but which take account of change over time; a situation that facilitates comparison and the cumulation of data.

On the basis of this discussion, four conclusions may be briefly highlighted. The first and most important is that concepts are not divisible from indicators nor the reverse. The interrelationship between theory and data – so necessary for fruitful sociological work to be done – is focused around clear and careful specification of concepts and (when and where appropriate) their measurement. Second, specification of concepts, as the contributors to this volume show, is far from being a mechanical task. It requires the exercise of the sociological imagination. If concepts are not adequately specified, then their use in empirical research is likely to be reduced. Third, the comparability of concepts, variables and indicators needs to be a continuing concern. If the contemporary diversity of sociology and social research makes the emergence of a unified conceptual scheme unlikely, it is nevertheless essential to be aware of how one's work relates to that of others. Researchers need to consider how the concepts and indicators that they use relate to those used in local and national studies both now and in the past, in an attempt to find some common ground and with a view to enabling comparisons to be made. Fourth, concepts are not developed in a vacuum but in a social context. The context does not justify or explain (still less explain away) the concept but it helps to make sense of it and the way(s) in which it is used. Our belief in the importance of social context is such that we confidently expect that ten years from now a successor volume to the present one will be needed to bring the story up to date.

References

Angell, R.C. (1936) *The Family Encounters the Depression*, New York, Scribners.

Arber, S., Gilbert, G.N. and **Dale, A.** (1984) 'Measuring social class for women'. Paper presented at BSA Annual Conference on Work, Employment and Unemployment, University of Bradford.

Banks, O. (1982) 'The sociology of education 1952–1982', *British Journal of Educational Studies*, vol. 30, no. 1, pp. 18–31.

Becker, H. *et al.* (1968) *Making the Grade*, New York, Wiley.

Bell, C. (1982) 'Work, non-work and unemployment – a discussion' in R.G. Burgess (ed.) *Exploring Society*, London, British Sociological Association, pp. 13–28 (2nd edn, Longman, 1986).

Blauner, R. (1964) *Alienation and Freedom*, Chicago, University of Chicago Press.

Blumer, H. (1954) 'What is wrong with social theory?', *American Sociological Review*, vol. 19, no. 1, pp. 3–10.

Bogdan, R. and **Biklen, S.K.** (1982) *Qualitative Research for Education: An Introduction to Theory and Methods*, Boston, Allyn & Bacon.

Bradburn, N.M. (1982) 'Discrepancies between concepts and their measurements: the urban-rural example' in W. Kruskal (ed.), *The Social Sciences: their nature and uses*, Chicago, University of Chicago Press, pp. 137–48.

Braithwaite, R.B. (1953) *Scientific Explanation*, Cambridge, Cambridge University Press.

Brayfield, A.H. and **Rothe, H.F.** (1951) 'An index of job satisfaction', *Journal of Applied Psychology*, vol. 35, pp. 307–11.

Butler, D. and **Stokes, D.** (1974) *Political Change in Britain* (2nd edn), London, Macmillan.

Cohen, S. (1980) 'Symbols of trouble: introduction to the new edition' in S. Cohen, *Folk Devils and Moral Panics* (2nd edn), London, Martin Robertson, pp. i-xxxiv.

Cook, J.D., Hepworth, S.J., Wall, T.D. and **Warr, P.B.** (1981) *The Experience of Work*, London, Academic Press.

Dalton, M. (1964) 'Preconceptions and methods in men who manage' in P. Hammond (ed.), *Sociologists at Work*, New York, Basic Books, pp. 50–95.

Davies, B. (1983) 'The Sociology of Education' in P. Hirst (ed.), *Educational Theory and its Foundation Disciplines*, London, Routledge & Kegan Paul, pp. 100–45.

Denzin, N. (1970) *The Research Act*, London, Butterworths.
Dingwall, R., Heath, C., Reid, M. and **Stacey, M.** (eds) (1977) *Health Care and Health Knowledge*, London, Croom Helm.
Ditton, J. (1977) *Part-Time Crime: An Ethnography of Fiddling and Pilferage*, London, Macmillan.
Geer, B. (1964) 'First days in the field' in P. Hammond (ed.) *Sociologists at Work*, New York, Basic Books, pp. 322–44.
Gittus, E. (ed.) (1972) *Key Variables in Social Research*, London, Heinemann.
Glaser, B.G. and **Strauss, A.L.** (1968) *The Discovery of Grounded Theory*, London, Weidenfeld & Nicolson.
Goldthorpe, J.H. (1983) 'Women and class analysis: in defence of the conventional view', *Sociology*, vol. 17, no. 4, pp. 465–88.
Hammersley, M. and **Atkinson, P.** (1983) *Ethnography: principles in practice*, London, Tavistock.
Hanson, N.R. (1969) *Perception and Discovery: an introduction to scientific inquiry*, San Francisco, Chandler.
Hempel, C.G. (1952) *Fundamentals of Concept-Formation in Empirical Science*, Chicago, University of Chicago Press.
Kaplan, A. (1964) *The Conduct of Inquiry*, San Francisco, Chandler.
Kertzer, D.I. (1983) 'Generation as a sociological problem', *Annual Review of Sociology*, vol. 9, pp. 125–49.
Krausz, E. (1972) 'Religion as a key variable' in E. Gittus (ed.) *Key Variables in Social Research*, London, Heinemann, pp. 1–33.
Kruskal, W. (1981) 'Statistics in society: problems unsolved and unformulated', *Journal of the American Statistical Association*, vol. 76, pp. 505–15.
Lazarsfeld, P.F. (1966) 'Concept-formation and measurement in the behavioral sciences: some historical observations', in G.J. Direnzo (ed.), *Concepts, Theory and Explanation in the Behavioral Sciences*, New York, Random House.
Lazarsfeld, P.F. (1977) 'Evidence and inference in social research' in M. Bulmer (ed.), *Sociological Research Methods*, London, Macmillan, pp. 78–90.
Lazarsfeld, P.F. and **Barton, A.H.** (1951) 'Some principles of classification in social research', in D. Lerner and H. Lasswell (eds), *The Policy Sciences*, Palo Alto, Ca., Stanford University Press.
Lindesmith, A. (1947) *Opiate Addiction*, Bloomington, Ind., Principia Press.
Lukes, S. (1967) 'Alienation and anomie', in P. Laslett and W.G.

Runciman (eds), *Politics, Philosophy and Society*, Third Series, Oxford, Blackwell, pp. 134–56.

Lukes, S. (1974) *Power: a radical view*, London, Macmillan.

McCall, G.J. (1969) 'The problem of indicators in participant observation research' in G.J. McCall and J.L. Simmons (eds), *Issues in Participant Observation: A Text and Reader*, New York, Addison Wesley, pp. 230–7.

Maclean, M. and **Genn, H.** (1979) *Methodological Issues in Social Surveys*, London, Macmillan.

Mitchell, J.C. (1983) 'Case and situation analysis', *Sociological Review*, vol. 31, pp. 187–211.

Myrdal, G. (1961) 'Value-loaded concepts', in H. Hegeland (ed.), *Money, Growth and Methodology*, Stockholm, Gleerup, pp. 273–88.

Neurath, O. (1973) *Empiricism and Sociology*, Dordrecht, Reidel.

Nichols, T. (1979) 'Social class; official, sociological and marxist', in J. Irvine *et al.* (eds), *Demystifying Social Statistics*, London, Pluto, pp. 152–71.

Outhwaite, W. (1983) *Concept Formation in Social Science*, London, Routledge & Kegan Paul.

Parsons, T. (1970) 'On building social system theory: a personal history,' *Daedalus*, vol. 99, quotation at p.830.

Quinn, R.P. and **Staines, G.L.** (1979) *The 1977 Quality of Employment Survey*, Ann Arbor, Michigan, Institute for Social Research, University of Michigan.

Rowbotham, S. (1973) *Woman's Consciousness, Man's World*, Harmondsworth, Penguin.

Sartori, G. (ed.) (1984) *Social Science Concepts: a systematic analysis*, London, Sage.

Scheffler, I. (1967) *Science and Subjectivity*, Indianapolis, Bobbs-Merrill.

Seeman, M. (1959) 'On the meaning of alienation', *American Sociological Review*, vol. 24, pp. 783–91.

Seeman, M. (1967) 'On the personal consequences of alienation in work', *American Sociological Review*, vol. 32, pp. 273–85.

Sheppard, J.M. (1972) 'Alienation as a process: work as a case in point', *The Sociological Quarterly*, vol. 13, pp. 161–73.

Sieber, S.D. (1973) 'The integration of fieldwork and survey methods', *American Journal of Sociology*, vol. 78, pp. 1335–59.

Smith, E.E. and **Medin, D.L.** (1981) *Categories and Concepts*, Cambridge, Mass., Harvard University Press.

Stacey, M. (ed.) (1969) *Comparability in Social Research*, London, Heinemann.

Stacey, M. (1982) 'The sociology of health, illness and healing' in R.G. Burgess (ed.), *Exploring Society*, London, British Sociological Association, pp. 49–67 (2nd edn, Longman, 1986).

Stacey, M. with **Homans, H.** (1978) 'The sociology of health and illness: its present state, future prospects and potential for health research', *Sociology*, vol. 12, no. 2, pp. 281–307.

Stanworth, M. (1984) 'Women and class analysis: a reply to Goldthorpe', *Sociology*, vol. 18, no. 2, pp. 159–70.

Wilson, B. (ed.) (1970) *Rationality*, Oxford, Blackwell.

Zelditch, M. (1962) 'Some methodological problems of field studies', *American Journal of Sociology*, vol. 67, pp. 566–76.

Znaniecki, F. (1934) *The Method of Sociology*, New York, Farrer & Rinehart.

Name index

Abrams, M., 210, 215, 216, 219
Acker, J., 39, 49
Acker, S., 101, 117
Ackernecht, E.W., 78, 94
Adorno, T., 212, 220
Agnello, T., 19–20, 27
Airth, A.D., 90, 94
Alderson, M.R., 87, 89, 90, 94
Allen, S., 12, 27, 56, 60, 66, 72, 158, 172
Almond, G., 201, 210, 220, 225, 242
Alt, J., 201, 220
Anderson, M., 76, 94
Andrew, A., 102, 117
Angell, R.C., 251, 262
Arber, S., 136, 140, 145, 148, 255, 262
Archer, M.S., 100, 101, 117
A.R.M.S., 78, 94
Asker, N.F., 190, 196
Atkinson, P., 5, 11, 42, 50, 251, 263

Babchuk, N., 226, 230, 231, 241, 242, 243
Bachrach, P., 204, 220
Bacon, A.W., 180, 187, 194
Bailey, P., 190, 194
Bakke, E.W., 167, 172
Bakwin, H., 94
Baldwin, B.R., 244
Ball, S.J., 108, 111, 117, 120
Banks, M.H., 94
Banks, O., 100, 118, 260, 262
Banton, M., 57, 72
Barton, A.H., 248, 263
Batstone, E., 244

Bechhofer, F., 49, 162, 172, 221
Becker, H., 22, 27, 252, 262
Bell, C., 244, 261
Bell, W., 226
Bellaby, P., 101, 118
Bengtson, V., 16, 25, 27
Benn, C., 109, 118
Benney, M., 201, 220
Benson, J.K., 226, 242
Bentley, S., 60, 72
Berelsor, B., 201, 203, 209, 220, 221
Bergner, M., 91, 94
Bermingham, J.P., 134, 135, 147
Bernard, J., 45, 49
Bernbaum, G., 100, 118
Bernstein, B., 100, 114, 118
Bertaux, D., 22, 27
Beveridge, W., 166, 172
Biklen, S.K., 6, 10, 252, 262
Birch, F., 183, 194
Birdwhistell, R.L., 34, 35, 49
Birley, J.L.T., 92, 95
Birren, J., 21, 27
Blackburn, R.M., 104, 118, 131, 169, 172, 222
Blackstone, T., 115, 118
Bland, R., 146, 147
Blaney, R., 81, 83, 86, 98
Blauner, R., 153, 154, 172, 254, 262
Blaxter, M., 86, 89, 93, 94, 95
Blishen, B., 130, 147
Blumer, H., 249, 262
Blyth, W., 142, 147
Boat, M.D., 226
Bobbitt, R.A., 91, 94
Bogdan R., 6, 10, 40, 49, 252, 262

Bone, M., 92, 95
Booth, A., 230, 242
Booth, C., 125, 147
Bornat, J., 60, 72
Boston, G., 126, 148
Bottomore, T.B., 224, 231, 240, 242
Bradburn, N.B., 92, 94
Bradburn, N.M., 249, 262
Braithwaite, R.B., 256, 262
Brake, M, 38, 49
Brannen, J., 42, 45, 49
Brannen, P., 194, 217, 220
Braverman, H., 214, 220
Brayfield, A.H., 261, 262
Bridges, A., 245
Brightbill, C.K., 181, 194
Brim, O.G., Jnr., 36, 49
British Broadcasting Corporation, 183, 194
British Sociological Association, 4
British Travel Association, 183, 194
Britten, N., 140, 148
Broadman, K., 91, 95
Brohm, J.M., 185, 194
Broom, L., 132, 148
Brown, C., 62, 69, 72
Brown, G.W., 92, 95
Brown, R.K., 161, 162, 172, 182, 194, 217, 220
Bruegel, I., 163, 172
Bryant, J., 76, 95
Bucher, C.A., 180, 194
Bucher, R.D., 180, 194
Budge, I., 203, 208, 210, 220
Bulmer, M., 4, 7–9, 10, 24, 54–75, 93, 217, 220, 246–65
Burawoy, M., 185, 194
Burch, W.R., 180, 195
Burgess, R.G., 1–11, 22, 99–122, 246–65
Burns, T., 190, 194
Butler, D., 149, 201, 203, 206, 207, 208, 210, 214, 216, 220, 258, 262
Butler, N., 21, 22, 27, 28
Butterfield, W.J.H., 81, 83, 86, 98
Byford, D., 111, 112, 121
Byrne, E., 101, 118

Caillois, R., 192, 194
Campbell, A., 92, 95
Campbell, D., 201, 207, 212, 220

Caplovitz, D., 92, 95
Carley, M., 87, 95
Carlson, R.E., 180, 194
Carr-Hill, R.A., 89, 93, 95
Carstairs, G.M., 84, 95
Central Statistical Office, 148, 157, 172
Chamberlain, C., 202, 211, 212, 222
Chambers, D., 186, 196
Chanan, G., 108, 118
Chase, D.R., 184, 194
Cheek, N.H., 180, 195
Child, E., 192, 195
Child, J., 192, 195
Children's Rights Workshop, 37, 49
Chiplin, B., 170, 172
Clammer, J., 71, 73
Clark, P.B., 230, 242
Clarke, M., 79, 95
Clegg, C.W., 94
Cleveland, M.A., 91, 96
Cloyd, J.W., 38, 49
Cockburn, C., 165, 172
Cohen, A., 56, 73
Cohen, S., 260, 262
Coleman, J.S., 227, 243
Collard, J., 42, 45, 49
Converse, P., 220
Converse, P.E., 92, 95
Cook, J.D., 261, 262
Cooper, B., 111, 118
Cormack, R.J., 102, 114, 118
Corrigan, P., 188, 191, 195
Cousins, J., 194
Coward, R., 47, 49
Cowgill, D., 25, 27
Coxon, A.P.M., 129, 132, 148
Craft, A., 115, 119
Craft, M., 115, 119
Craig, J., 142, 151
Crewe, I., 201, 203, 208, 214, 215, 220
Critcher, C., 190, 195
Crocker, L.H., 80, 97
Cross, M., 64, 70, 73
Crossley, J., 207, 222
Culyer, A.J., 83–4, 87, 88, 89, 90, 95
Cunningham, H., 190, 195
Cunnison, S., 37, 49
Curran, J., 193, 195
Cutler, S.J., 225, 227, 243

Dahrendorf, R., 138, 171, 172, 205, 220
Dale, A., 136, 140, 145, 148, 255, 262
Dalison, B., 92, 95
Dalton, M., 252, 262
Daniel, W.W., 58–9, 62, 67, 73
Davidson, N., 87, 93, 98
Davie, R., 21, 22, 27, 28
Davies, B., 116, 119, 260, 262
Davis, H., 205, 217, 220
Deacon, A., 167, 173
Deem, R., 101, 119, 184, 188, 195
Delamont, S., 101, 108, 118, 119
Delphy, C., 156, 173
Denzin, N., 22, 27, 251, 263
Department of Education and Science, 27, 103, 104, 111, 119
Department of Employment, 153, 173
Dingwall, R., 77, 95, 259, 263
Ditton, J., 252, 263
Dixey, R., 184, 195
Dohrenwend, B.P., 92, 95
Dohrenwend, B.S., 92, 95
Douglas, J.D., 38, 43, 49
Douglas, J.W.B., 21, 22, 23, 24, 27, 28, 105, 107, 113, 114, 119
Dowie, R., 87, 89, 90, 94
Doyal, L., 95
Duffield, B., 183, 195
Duggan, G., 198
Duke, V., 37, 46, 50, 218, 220
Dumazedier, J., 178, 179, 187, 195
Duncan, O.D., 130, 131, 148, 150
Duncan-Jones, P., 148
Dunleavy, P., 214, 220
Dunning, E., 181, 195
Durkheim, E., 45, 49, 100, 154, 253

Easlea, B., 37, 49
Easterday, L., 43, 49
Edgell, S., 37, 46, 50, 218, 220
Edwards, H., 185, 195
Edwards, J.N., 230, 242
Edwards, S.M., 38, 50
Ehrlich, H.J., 230, 243
Eichler, M., 33, 34, 35, 36, 37, 40, 50
Eisenberg, P., 167, 173
Eisenstadt, S.N., 154, 173
El-Badry, M.A., 77, 95
Elder, G., 16, 25, 28

Elias, D.P.B., 140, 148
Elliot, D., 126, 133, 145, 148
Ellis, M., 181, 195
Ennis, P.H., 180, 195
Epson, J.E., 80, 89, 96
Equal Opportunities Commission, 39, 43, 50, 163, 170, 173
Erdman, A.J., 91, 95
Erikson, R., 136, 148

Fabrega, H., 84, 96
Fara, S.F., 179, 196
Faraday, A., 22, 23, 28
Farlie, D., 220
Featherstone, M., 25, 28
Feldberg, R.L., 41, 50
Ferguson, M., 37, 50
Field, D., 77, 94, 96
Filstead, W.J., 6, 11
Finch, J., 8, 12–30, 32, 40, 43, 50, 76, 93, 156, 157, 173, 178
Floud, J., 100, 114, 119
Fogarty, M., 17, 28
Fogelman, K., 105, 107, 111, 114, 119
Foner, A., 12, 16, 19, 23, 25, 28, 29
Ford, A.B., 91, 92, 96
Ford, G., 96
Form, W., 211, 221
Foucault, M., 38, 50
Fox, A.J., 140, 141, 148
Fox, J., 133, 149
Frake, C.O., 84, 96
Francis, D.P., 4, 11
Frankenberg, R., 227, 243
Freedman, A., 223, 244
Freud, S., 154
Friedman, H., 165, 173
Frieze, I.H., 40, 41, 50
Frith, S., 192, 195
Fröbel, F., 169, 173
Fromm, E., 182, 195
Fryer, D., 168
Fryer, R.H., 217, 221
Fuller, M., 115, 119
Furlong, M., 16, 25, 27

Galaskiewicz, J., 226, 227, 243
Gallie, D., 201, 221
Gamarnikow, E., 46, 48, 50
Garfinkel, H., 40, 50
Garland, H., 82, 96

Garnsey, E., 50, 140, 148
Gaudet, H., 221
Gebhardt, P., 189, 195
Gee, F.A., 125, 145, 149
Geer, B., 252, 263
General Household Survey, *see*
  OPCS
Genn, H., 252, 255, 256, 264
Gershuny, J., 155, 173, 191, 196
Gibson, B.S., 91, 94
Giddens, A., 179, 196
Gilbert, G.N., 136, 140, 145, 148,
  255, 262
Gist, N.P., 179, 196
Gittus, E., 2, 4, 11, 32, 50, 247, 263
Glaser, B.G., 251, 263
Glass, D., 114, 119
Glass, R., 57–8, 67, 73
Glenn, E.N., 41, 50
Glyptus, S., 186, 196
Godbey, G., 184, 193, 194, 196
Goffman, E., 37, 50
Goldblatt, P.O., 140, 141, 148
Goldstein, H., 22, 27
Goldthorpe, J.H., 50, 127, 128, 132,
  133, 135, 136, 140, 145, 146, 148,
  149, 202, 205, 213, 215, 216, 217,
  221, 224, 231, 236, 243, 255, 263
Goodlad, J.S.R., 186, 196
Goodrich, C., 170, 173
Goodson, I.F., 108, 111, 119, 120
Gordon, C.W., 226, 231, 242, 243
Gossett, T.F., 73
Graham, H., 33, 43, 50
Graunt, J., 87
Gray, A., 201, 220
Gray, J., 102, 112, 114, 120
Gray, P., 125, 145, 149
Green, A., 101, 110, 121
Green, H., 135, 149
Greenstein, F., 212, 221
Gregory, S., 188, 196
Grigg, C., 210, 222
Gross, E., 179, 191, 196
Groves, D., 13, 28, 157, 173
Guppy, L.N., 129, 149
Gurin, G., 220

Habermas, J., 203, 204, 212, 221
Hagedorn, R., 228, 243
Hakim, C., 9, 11, 105, 120, 157, 159,
  160, 163, 165, 169, 173, 174
Halfpenny, P., 6, 11
Hall, J., 127, 130, 149
Halsey, A.H., 100, 104, 108, 114,
  115, 119, 120
Hamilton, W., 210, 221
Hammersley, M., 5, 11, 42, 50, 108,
  120, 122, 251, 263
Hanmer, J., 39, 51
Hanson, N.R., 263
Harding, J., 112, 120
Hargreaves, D.H., 108, 109, 110,
  111, 120
Hargreaves, J., 185, 196
Harker, D., 192, 196
Harper, W., 180, 196
Harris, T., 92
Hartley, J.F., 167, 168, 174
Hartnett, A., 99, 120
Haskey, J., 140, 146, 149
Hatt, P.K., 128, 145, 150
Hawes, W.R., 157, 159, 174
Haywood, L.J., 192, 196
Head, K., 222
Heath, A.F., 104, 108, 114, 155, 120,
  140, 148
Heath, C., 263
Heinrichs, J., 169, 173
Hempel, C.G., 249, 250, 256, 263
Henry, S., 155, 174
Hepworth, M., 25, 28
Hepworth, S.J., 262
Herzlich, C., 84–5, 96
Hester, S., 110, 120
Hill, M., 167, 174
Hill, S., 217, 221
Himmelweit, H., 114, 120
Hobhouse, L., 154
Hodge, R.W., 129, 149
Hoinville, G., 14, 28
Holland, W.W., 79, 96
Holmes, L., 25
Holt, R., 181, 196
Homans, H., 259, 265
Hope, K., 127, 128, 132, 133, 136,
  145, 149
House of Commons Home Affairs
  Committee, 62, 64–5, 70, 71, 73
Howe, G.M., 76, 96
Huizinga, J., 181, 196
Humphreys, L., 38, 51

Hunt, A., 156, 174
Hunt, S.M., 91, 96
Hyman, R., 160, 174

Ibrahim, H., 190, 196
Illich, I., 48, 51
Inglehart, R., 212, 221
Inkeles, A., 129, 149
International Labour Office, 149

Jackson, B.A., 91, 96
Jackson, P.R., 94
Jacobs, P., 168, 174
Jacoby, A.P., 241, 243
Jaffe, M.W., 91, 96
Jahoda, M., 167, 168, 174
Jary, D., 9, 19, 189, 196, 200–22
Jeffery, P., 60, 67, 73
Jenkins, C., 178, 196
Jessop, B., 205, 221
Johnson, C.E., 70, 73
Johnson, M., 12, 25, 29
Johnson, Mark, 64, 70, 73
Joint Industry Working Party, 134,
   135, 149
Jones, C.L., 129, 148
Jones, D.C., 127, 130, 132, 149
Jowell, R., 14, 28

Kahan, M., 146, 149
Kaluzynska, E., 156, 174
Kanter, R.M., 46, 51
Kaplan, A., 246, 248, 257, 258, 263
Kaplan, M., 178, 179, 180, 185, 196
Karabel, J., 100, 120
Katz, S., 91, 96
Kaufman, R., 15, 17, 28
Keddie, N., 110, 120
Kelley, J., 137, 138, 150
Kellmer-Pringle, M., 21, 27
Kelly, A., 111, 120
Kelly, J., 180, 196
Kemp, N.J., 94
Kertzer, D.I., 258, 263
Kessler, S.J., 33, 34, 40, 51
Knox, A.B., 230, 242
Kohn, R., 90, 96
Koos, E.L., 83, 86, 96
Krausz, E., 255, 263
Kraye, O., 169, 173
Kressel, S., 91, 94

Kruskal, W., 72, 73, 250, 263
Kuhn, L.L., 38, 52

Labovitz, S., 228, 243
Lacey, C., 108, 109, 120
Lancaster-Jones, F., 148
Lane, D., 130, 149
Lane, R.E., 191, 197
Larson, O.F., 227, 245
Laslett, P., 76, 96
Laufer, R., 16, 25, 27
Laumann, E.O., 226, 243
Lawrence, D., 59, 73
Layton, D., 111, 121
Lazarsfeld, P., 5, 11, 167, 173, 174,
   201, 202, 213, 220, 221, 229, 246,
   247, 148, 250, 263
Lee, P.C., 34, 35, 36, 41, 45, 51
Leete, R., 133, 149
Lemert, E.M., 80, 96
Leonard, D., 25, 28
Lewes, F.M.M., 184, 197
Lewis, C.G., 62, 75
Lewis, G., 84, 97
Liebow, E., 45, 51
Linder, S.B., 192, 197
Lindesmith, A., 251, 263
Lindholm, S., 245
Linton, R., 12, 28
Lipset, S., 203, 212, 221
Lipsky, R., 192, 197
Little, K., 57, 73
Llewellyn, C., 50, 141, 149, 156
Locker, D., 80, 97
Lockwood, D., 135, 150, 202, 205,
   214, 215, 216, 217, 221
London Business School Centre for
   Economic Forecasting, 153, 174
Long, J., 183, 195
Lorge, I., 91, 95
Lowe, J., 12, 29
Lukes, S., 253, 258, 263, 264
Lunn, J.A., 135, 150
Lunt, P.S., 227, 231, 245
Lupton, T., 32, 51, 228, 243

McCall, G.J., 251, 252, 264
MacCannell, D., 197
Mc Cormack, T., 180, 197
McDonnell, P., 148
McEwen, J., 91, 96

McGoldrick, A., 187, 197
McIntosh, S., 188, 197
Macintyre, S., 6, 7–8, 9, 76–98, 260
McKee, L., 43, 51
MacKenna, W., 33, 34, 40, 51
McKenzie, R., 201, 217, 221
Maclean, M., 252, 255, 256, 264
McNabb, R., 165, 175
McPhee, W., 220
McPherson, A.F., 102, 114, 120
McPherson, J.M., 227, 243
Maddox, E.J., 82, 97
Main, B., 112, 121
Mallet, S., 214, 221
Mann, M., 4, 11, 169, 172, 211, 212, 221
Mannell, R.C., 180, 197
Mannheim, K., 12, 28
Manning, P., 79, 96
Marsden, D., 167, 174
Marsden, P.V., 243
Marsh, A., 212, 221
Marsh, C., 8, 9, 113, 123–52, 162, 213, 214, 254
Marshall, T.H., 1, 11
Marsland, D., 26, 28, 188, 197
Martin, F.M., 114, 119
Martin, J., 14, 28
Martin, M.K., 35, 51
Martin, R., 217, 221
Martin, W., 189, 197
Marx, K., 100, 137, 138, 139, 154, 253, 254
Mason, K., 23, 28
Mason, S., 189, 197
Mason, W., 23, 28
Massey, D., 161, 169, 170, 174
Matthews, S.W., 33, 34, 35, 41, 42, 51
Mead, M., 36, 51
Mechanic, D., 80, 86, 97
Medin, D.L., 247, 264
Meegan, R., 161, 169, 170, 174
Meisel, J., 185, 197
Mellor, F., 110, 120
Meredeen, S., 165, 173
Metcalf, D., 166, 175
Middlemass, K., 166, 175
Middleton, R., 12, 28
Milbrath, L., 209, 212, 221
Miles, D.L., 91, 97

Miles, I., 94, 97
Miller, F., 220
Miller, S., 212, 222
Miller, W., 220
Mills, C.W., 26, 28, 165, 175, 203, 213, 222
Millum, T., 37, 51
Miner, H., 94, 97
Ministry of Education, 114, 121
Mintz, S.W., 45, 51
Mitchell, G.D., 228, 243
Mitchell, J.C., 240, 243, 264
Mitchell, R.E., 7, 11
Monk, D., 134, 150
Monks, T.G., 109, 121
Moore, J., 12, 17, 29
Moore, R., 56, 58, 74
Moorhouse, H.F., 155, 175, 202, 211, 212, 222
Morgan, D.H.J., 5, 8, 24, 31–53, 93, 259
Morgan, M., 139, 150
Morrice, J.R., 91, 94
Morris, J.N., 79, 80, 89, 97
Morris, T.C., 142, 150
Morrison, H., 161, 175
Mortimore, P., 111, 112, 121
Moser, C.A., 66, 67, 73
Moskowitz, R.W., 91, 96
Mughan, A., 207, 208, 222
Muller, M., 76, 97
Murcott, A., 175, 244
Murgatroyd, L., 39, 51, 140, 146, 150
Murphy, J.E., 179, 197
Murphy, M.J., 141, 150
Musgrove, F., 12, 28
Myrdal, G., 247, 264

National Dwelling and Housing Survey Report, 61, 74
Nava, M., 26, 29
Neitz, M.J., 34, 51
Neugarten, B., 12, 17, 29
Neurath, O., 247, 264
Newby, H., 202, 217, 222
Newell, D.J., 90, 94
Newland, K., 88, 97
Newlands, K., 156, 175
Newman, B., 192, 197
Newman, O., 184, 197

Newson, E., 22, 29
Newson, J., 22, 29
Newton, K., 209, 222
Nichols, T., 257, 264
Nie, N.H., 225, 245
Nissell, M., 17, 29
Noble, M., 198
Norris, G.M., 169, 175
North, C.C., 128, 145, 150

Oakley, A., 33, 34, 39, 43, 47, 48, 51, 92, 97, 140, 150, 155, 175
Oakley, R., 39, 51, 140, 150
O'Brien, M., 43, 51
Oglesby, C., 181, 197
Olsen, M.E., 225, 244
O'Muircheartaigh, C., 4, 11
OPCS, 13–14, 29, 61, 66, 67, 69, 74, 81–2, 97, 106, 107, 112, 121, 124, 125, 126, 131, 132, 150, 175, 183
Osborn, A.F., 142, 150
Osborne, R.D., 102, 114, 118
Ottaway, A.K.C., 121
Otti, P.B., 245
Outhwaithe, W., 246, 247, 249, 257, 258, 264

Paddick, R., 182, 197
Pahl, R.E., 154, 155, 167, 171, 173, 175
Palisi, B.J., 234, 244
Pan American Health Organization, 76, 97
Park, R.E., 55, 74
Parker, S., 6, 9, 178–99, 228, 244
Parkin, F., 214, 218, 222, 229, 244
Parry, N., 207, 222
Parry, N.C.A., 191, 193, 198
Parsons, T., 12, 29, 79, 91, 97, 248, 264
Paterson, E., 86, 94
Patterson, S., 56, 58, 66, 74
Payne, G., 39, 51, 52
Pear, R., 201, 220
Pearse, I.H., 80, 97
Pennell, I., 95
Perrone, L., 39, 53, 138, 152
Peston, M., 167, 169, 176
Petersen, W., 54, 70, 72, 74
Petty, W., 87
Philips, C., 111, 121

Philips, J., 190, 198
Phillips, A., 165, 176
Pickvance, C., 6, 7, 9, 209, 223–45
Pilgrim Trust, 167, 176
Pillemer, K., 234
Piper, J., 179, 198
Platt, J., 52, 221
Plummer, K., 22, 23, 28, 29
Pollard, W.E., 91, 94
Pollert, A., 46, 52, 165, 176
Pollins, H., 73
Ponse, B., 38, 52
Poole, W.K., 23, 28
Portocarero, L., 136, 148
Poulantzas, N., 214, 222
Prais, S.J., 162, 176
Prandy, K., 104, 118, 131, 210, 222
Price, C., 74
Price, M., 154, 176
Price, R., 160, 174
Protho, J., 210, 222
Pryce, K., 62, 74
Purcell, J., 170, 176
Purcell, K., 9, 32, 37, 39, 46, 52, 153–77, 178, 214, 260

Quinn, R.P., 261, 264

Raffe, D., 102, 112, 114, 120, 121
Rampton Committee, 115, 121
Randall, V., 37, 52
Rasmussen, P.K., 38, 52
Ratcliffe, P., 62, 69, 74
Rawllings, C., 218, 222
Reddy, R.D., 244
Reid, I., 34, 52, 103, 113, 121
Reid, M., 263
Reisman, M., 212, 222
Reiss, A.J., 128, 129, 150
Reiss, I.L., 45, 52
Research Services Linited, 150
Resler, H., 163, 176
Rex, J., 56, 58, 62, 69, 74
Reynolds, D., 110, 121
Reynolds, W.J., 91, 97
Richardson, R., 166, 175
Richmond, A.H., 56, 59, 65, 67, 69, 74
Ridge, J.M., 104, 108, 114, 115, 120, 121
Riley, M.W., 12, 19, 20, 21, 23, 25, 29

Riordan, J., 190, 198
Ritchie, J., 62, 72
Roberts, B.R., 226, 244
Roberts, H., 52, 113, 121
Roberts, J., 182, 198
Roberts, J.M., 192, 198
Roberts, K., 178, 180, 186, 187, 188, 198
Robinson, R.V., 137, 138, 150
Robinson, W., 211, 222
Rodgers, W.L., 92, 95
Rodgers, M., 190, 192, 198
Rogers, R., 198
Rose, A.M., 225, 230, 234, 244
Rose, E.J.B., 68, 74
Rosenfield, R.A., 39, 52
Ross, J., 22, 28, 105, 107, 119
Ross, J.C., 228, 231, 244
Rossi, P.H., 129, 149, 232, 244
Rothe, H.F., 261, 262
Routh, G., 164, 176
Rowbotham, S., 260, 264
Runciman, W.G., 134, 151, 214, 222
Runnymede Trust and Radical Statistics Group, 68, 74
Rushing, W.A., 91, 97
Rusk, J., 222
Rutter, M., 108, 109, 110, 121
Ryan, M., 184, 198
Ryder, N.B., 23, 30
Rytinna, J., 211, 221

Salter, B., 102, 121
Samphier, M., 194
Sanday, P.R., 36, 52
Sarlvik, B., 201, 220
Sartori, G., 247, 264
Saunders, S., 39, 51
Scarman, L.G., 171, 176
Scheffler, I., 248, 264
Schermerhorn, R.A., 54, 75
Schofield, M., 38, 52
Seabrook, J., 167, 168, 176, 187, 198
Sedgewick, P., 91, 97
Seeley, J., 184, 198
Seeman, M., 253, 254, 264
Sharp, R., 101, 110, 121
Shatin, D., 227, 243
Shaw, M., 94, 97
Sheppard, J.M., 254, 264
Sherman, B., 178, 196

Showler, B., 166, 176
Shrewsbury, J.F., 76, 97
Shryock, H.S., 65, 75
Sieber, S.D., 253, 264
Siegel, J.S., 65, 75
Siegel, P.M., 129, 149, 151
Sillitoe, K.K., 61, 75, 183, 198
Sills, D.L., 231, 232, 237, 244
Silver, A., 201, 217, 221
Silver, D.B., 84, 96
Silver, H., 113, 121
Silverman, D., 6, 11
Simon, B., 109, 118
Simpkins, A.F., 187, 198
Simpson, H., 22, 28, 105, 107, 119
Sinfield, A., 165, 168, 169, 170, 176
Singer, R.N., 181, 198
Sisson, K., 170, 176
Sloane, P.J., 170
Smith, C., 223, 244
Smith, C.S., 198
Smith, D.H., 223, 234, 244
Smith, D.J., 59, 62, 67, 69, 75
Smith, E.E., 247, 264
Smith, H.W., 1–2, 11
Smith, M.A., 184, 187, 198
Smith, T.W., 56, 70, 71, 72, 75
Snyder, E.E., 181, 198
Sokoloff, N.J., 176
Sontag, S., 93, 97
Sorrentino, C., 169, 176
Spence, J., 206, 207, 222
Spilerman, S., 15, 17, 28
Spreitzer, E., 181, 198
Stacey, M., 2, 4, 11, 13, 30, 31, 32, 52, 154, 176, 198, 200, 222, 227, 244, 247, 259, 260, 263, 264, 265
Stafford, E.M., 94
Staines, G.L., 187, 198, 261, 264
Stanley, L., 43, 52
Stanworth, M., 255, 265
Stebbins, R.A., 228, 245
Stenhouse, L., 43, 52
Stern, J., 176
Stevenson, T.H.C., 133, 151
Stewart, A., 104, 118, 131, 222
Stewart, R.S., 26, 34, 35, 41, 45
Stokes, D., 149, 201, 203, 206, 207, 208, 210, 214, 216, 220, 258, 262
Stoll, C.S., 52
Stougger, S., 210, 222

Strauss, A.L., 251, 263
Subcommittee on Comparability of
   Occupation Measurement, 127,
   151
Sullivan, O., 141, 150
Surgeon, G.P., 245
Sutton-Smith, S.B., 192, 198
Swann Committee, 115, 122
Szalai, A., 190, 199
Szasz, T.S., 92, 98

Talbot, M., 188, 199
Tapper, T., 102, 121
Taub, R.P., 226, 245
Taylor, B., 165, 176
Teer, F., 206, 207, 222
Thompson, J.H., 62, 75
Thorne, C., 45, 47, 53
Tomlinson, J., 167, 169, 176
Tomlinson, S., 56, 62, 69, 74, 115,
   122
Touraine, A., 179, 181, 199
Townsend, P., 87, 93, 98, 167, 176
Treiman, D., 129, 132, 149, 151
Tuckett, D., 79, 80, 86, 98
Tunstall, J., 193, 195
Turner, G., 108, 122

United States Department of
   Commerce, 151

Van Moorst, H., 186, 199
Veal, A.J., 183, 199
Verba, S., 201, 210, 220, 225, 242,
   245
Voorhies, B., 35, 51

Wadsworth, M.E.J., 81, 83, 86, 98
Wakeford, J., 43, 53
Walby, S., 39, 53
Waldron, I., 77, 98
Wall, T.D., 94, 262
Wallace, C., 155, 171, 175
Waller, J., 79, 96
Walvin, J., 190, 199
Warner, R.L., 227, 231, 245
Warr, P.B., 262
Warren, C., 53
Warren, R.L., 231, 245

Warwick, D.P., 57, 73
Watson, J.L., 67, 75
Wax, R.H., 42, 53
Webb, M., 39, 53
Webber, R.J., 142, 151
Weber, M., 100, 154, 253, 257
Weinberg, A., 117, 122
Weissman, H.H., 237, 245
West, D., 23, 30
Westergaard, J., 163, 176
Westwood, S., 168, 176
Wheeler, R.E., 228, 244
White, T., 90, 96
Wilensky, H.L., 228, 232, 245
Wilkin, M., 104, 122
Williams, R., 181, 191, 199
Williams, R.G.A., 79, 85–6, 98
Willis, P., 113, 122, 167, 176
Willmott, P., 129, 152, 183, 191, 199
Wilson, B., 247, 265
Wilson, J., 186, 199
Wilson, J.Q., 230, 242
Wing, J.K., 92, 95
Winsborough, H., 23, 28
Wise, S., 43, 52
Wolf, E.R., 45, 51
Wolff, H.G., 91, 95
Wolff, J., 199
Wood, D., 147, 152
Wood, M.E., 24, 30
Woods, P., 101, 108, 110, 120, 122
World Health Organization, 88, 98
Wormald, E., 34, 37, 52, 53
Wright, E., 205, 214, 222
Wright, E.O., 39, 53, 124, 137, 138,
   147, 152
Wright, T.P., 57, 75
Wrigley, E.A., 76, 98
Wuthnow, R., 12, 30

Yallom, M., 45, 47
Young, M., 129, 152, 183, 191, 199
Young, M.F.D., 100, 101, 111, 122
Young, R.C., 227, 245

Zeisel, H., 21, 30, 167, 174
Zelditch, M., 253, 265
Zetterberg, H.L., 3–4, 10, 11
Znaniecki, F., 246, 151, 265

Subject index

age, 12–30; age cohort, 17, 21–4; age
   groups, 16–19
alienation, 253–5
analytic induction, 251
authoritarianism, 212
authority, 137–9
autonomy, 137–9

Butler and Stokes model, 203

census, 68, 105, 126, 159
classification of occupations, 162
classificatory variables, 3–4
classrooms, 108–10
community power, 224–5
community structure, 226–7
comparability, 1, 8, 189–90, 261
concepts, 1–3, 10, 56–65, 179–82,
   246–65; conceptualization, 57–68,
   90–1
conceptual equivalence, 7
constituency surveys, 201
control variable, 124
cross-national studies, 201
culture, 181–2
curriculum, 111–12

data collection and analysis, 183–4,
   232–42
death rate, 89
de-constructing gender, 44–8
deference, 217
definitions, 83–4, 233–5; by lay
   persons, 84–6
dependent variable, 26–7, 123–4
descriptive documentation, 13–16

disability, 90–1
disease, 77–8

education, 99–122, 188–9, 260
educational system, 99–101
employment, 153–77
ethnicity, 54–75, 259
examinations, 111–12

face sheet variables, 3–4, 31, 200
focused studies, 202

gender, 31–53, 114–15, 140–1, 156–
   7, 259
General Household Survey, 83, 91,
   105–7, 112–13, 146, 157, 182, 183

Haringey Test Census, 61–2
health, 76–98, 259–60; health
   indicators, 88–9

illness, 76–98, 259–60
independent variable, 20, 124
indicators, 1, 5, 9–10, 56–7, 68–71,
   86–93, 179–82, 200, 212, 213–19,
   246–65
informal economy, 155–6
interviewing, 42–3

labour force, 159–60
Labour Force Survey, 146, 158, 160
leisure, 178–99, 227–9
life expectancy, 89
life histories, 23–4
lifestyle, 132–5
longitudinal studies, 21–4, 107

market situation, 135–6
measurement, 5, 9–10, 56–65, 71–2,
　86–93, 250–2, 253
morbidity, 91–2
mortality statistics, 89–90

nationwide electoral surveys, 201

occupational classification, 124–7,
　213–14
occupations, 112–13, 123–52

panel studies, 21–4
party affiliation variables, 205, 208–
　9
party identification, 207–8
play, 181
pluralism, 225–6
political attitudes, 209
political participation, 209–10, 213
prestige, 127–30, 217
public and private worlds, 154–5

qualitative research, 6, 22–4, 57–65,
　105–8, 246
quantitative research, 6, 57–65, 68–
　9, 105–8, 246
question formulation, 8–9, 62–5,
　105–7, 184–9, 235–42, 254

race, 54–75, 115, 259–60
recalled vote, 206–7
recommendations, 24–6, 47–8, 71–2,
　93, 116–17, 142–4, 169–71, 193–4,
　219

recreation, 180–1
research process, 5–6, 42–3, 256

schools, 108–10
sex, 31–5
sexual division of labour, 39, 163–5
sexuality, 38–9
signs and symptoms, 93
social class, 114–15, 123–52, 213–19
social mobility, 114, 127–30, 140–1
social status, 131–2, 213–19
social stratification, 113–15, 224–5
socio-economic groups, 133–4
sources, of data, 105–8, 157–8
sport, 181, 185

terminal education age, 104
theory, 2, 19–20, 191–3, 201–5,
　223–32, 247–8
time, 8, 102–5; free time, 182

unemployment, 153–77, 187
unit of study, 102

variables, 1, 3–5, 246–65
voluntary associations, 223–45
voting intention, 205–6

work, 153–77, 188–9, 227–9; paid
　and unpaid, 156–7
workforce, 160–3
workshop behaviour, 41–2